Reshaping
TOMORROW

Is South Asia Ready
for the Big Leap?

edited by EJAZ GHANI

THE WORLD BANK

OXFORD

UNIVERSITY PRESS

Oxford University Press is a department of the University of Oxford.
It furthers the University's objective of excellence in research, scholarship,
and education by publishing worldwide. Oxford is a registered trademark of
Oxford University Press in the UK and in certain other countries

Published in India
by Oxford University Press
YMCA Library Building, 1 Jai Singh Road, New Delhi 110 001, India

© World Bank 2011

The moral rights of the author have been asserted

First Edition published in 2011

ISBN-13: 978-0-19-807502-8
ISBN-10: 0-19-807502-2

Typeset in Adobe Garamond Pro 10.5/12.7
by BeSpoke Integrated Solutions, Puducherry, India 605 008
Printed in India by Artxel, New Delhi 110 020

The findings, interpretations, and conclusions expressed herein are those of the
author(s) and do not necessarily reflect the views of the Executive Director of
the International Bank for Reconstruction and Development/The World Bank or
the governments they represent. The World Bank does not guarantee the accuracy
of the data included in this work. The boundaries, colours, denominations,
and other information shown on any map in this work do not imply any
judgment on the part of The World Bank concerning the legal status of
any territory or the endorsement of acceptance of such boundaries.

Contents

Tables and Figures

Preface

What will South Asia look like in 2025? The optimistic outlook is that India, which accounts for 80 per cent of the regional economic output, is headed towards double-digit growth rates. South Asia too will grow rapidly, primarily due to India. The pessimistic outlook is that, given huge transformational challenges facing the region, growth should not be taken for granted. Which of these two outlooks is likely to prevail? This is what this book is all about. It is about the future, and not the past, and how to make smart choices about the future.

There is strong empirical justification in favour of the optimistic outlook. Growth will be propelled higher by young demographics, improved governance, rising middle class, and the next wave of globalization. There is democracy, for the first time since independence, in all countries in the region. Young demographics will result in nearly 20 million more people joining the labour force, every year, for the next two decades. Almost a billion people will join the ranks of the middle class. India's middle class is well-educated, enterprising, innovative, and more demanding of better services, products, and governance. The region will benefit from the new wave of globalization in services, and increased international migration and human mobility. Indeed the drivers of growth seem to have already moved from the rich world to the poor world. The room for catch-up is huge, given the big gap in average income between South Asia and the rich countries.

However, the empirical arguments for the pessimistic outlook are equally strong. The link between demographics and growth is not automatic. Indeed, a demographic dividend, in the absence of right policies to enable people to be healthy, well educated, and well trained in the skills demanded, could morph into a demographic disaster. Neither does globalization automatically engender growth. Countries need the physical infrastructure—ports, roads, electricity, water, and communications—and peace and security to help ensure wider access to markets and exposure to opportunities. Increased market integration needs to be complemented with appropriate structural reforms to enable land, labour, and capital to be reallocated from low productivity traditional sectors into high productivity modern sectors. A structural transformation at such a mammoth scale will not be easy.

The truth will probably lie somewhere in between. The optimistic outlook that South Asia will achieve double-digit growth rates may be too optimistic. The pessimistic outlook that growth will be derailed by corruption, dilapidated infrastructure, large informal sector traps, and dismal social conditions may be too pessimistic.

What can be done? South Asia needs a bridge to the future. Policymakers should better manage the three key drivers of transformation—growth, inclusiveness, and risk. South Asia has the largest concentration of poor people on earth. So the pace of growth needs to be accelerated to create jobs and reduce poverty. Rapid growth cannot be achieved without more entrepreneurs. India and other South Asian countries have too few entrepreneurs for their stage of development. While South Asia has a disproportionately high rate of self-employment and many small firms, this has not as readily translated into as many young entrepreneurial firms that create jobs and increase productivity as could be hoped. Yet there is no question that entrepreneurship works in the region. Formal-sector job growth has been strongest in regions and industries that have exhibited high rates of entrepreneurship and dynamic economies. Reducing conflict is a prerequisite to political stability, which, in turn, is the prerequisite for implementing pro-growth policies. Even in a best-case scenario, the presence of low-level conflict constrains the policies that governments can implement to promote growth.

Growth without inclusiveness will be difficult to sustain in the future. After decades of being primarily a region of farmers, South Asia is rapidly urbanizing, as millions leave their stagnant villages, and move to the cities. However, urban infrastructure is decaying, and unable to serve the existing population, let alone be prepared for increased rural–urban migration. Modernization has been partial, with a large part of the economy operating in rural and informal sectors, and only a small segment of the population thriving in the globally integrated modern sectors. Growth that results in partial modernization will continue to undermine the ability to move people out of poverty, and to share the fruits of growth more widely.

Growth is not an end in itself. Policymakers should not think of growth separately from inclusion and vulnerability. Increased income disparities should not be viewed as the price to pay for high growth. Neither should gender inclusion, education, and health be considered as second stage reforms. A development response that aims to promote growth first, and then deal with human misery is not sustainable. However, policies to promote social development should be designed in a manner that the growth process itself is not hampered. The region needs policies to raise growth wherever it happens. It also needs policies to redistribute the gains of growth more efficiently and effectively.

Time is of the essence. South Asia is fast reaching the tipping point. There is only a short window of opportunity. Policymakers need to redouble their efforts to promote *rapid, inclusive, and stable growth*.

August 2011   Ejaz Ghani

1

Reshaping Tomorrow
An Overview

Ejaz Ghani*

What will South Asia look like in 2025? The optimistic view is that India, which accounts for 80 per cent of the regional economic output, and is the largest country in the region, is headed towards double-digit growth rates. South Asia too will grow rapidly, primarily due to India. The pessimistic view is that growth should not be taken for granted, as the region faces big transformational challenges ahead.

Which of these two outlooks will prevail? What can be done today to reshape tomorrow? This is what this collection of essays is about. We shift the focus from the past to the future. We do not discuss what is wrong with the current system. Instead, we explore what is coming, and on getting that right.

Is there any empirical evidence to support the optimistic outlook? Yes, there is strong justification in favour of the optimistic outlook. India is already among the fastest growing countries in the world. Part I of this book examines the main reason for optimism. The growth lens focuses

* I am grateful for comments fromPranab Bardhan, Homi Kharas, Kalpana Kochhar, Howard Pack, Raghuram Rajan , and Andrew Steer. I would also like to thank Swaminathan Aiyar, Sadiq Ahmed, Ulrich Bartsch, David Bloom, Deepak Bhattasali, Monish Dutt, Lakshmi Iyer, Vijay Joshi, Saman Kalegama, Vijay Kelkar, Kalpana Kochhar, Rakesh Mohan, Raj Nallari, Stephen O'Connell, Ernesto May, Eswar Prasad, Arvind Virmani, and James Walsh for their comments/suggestions, and several colleagues who participated in the review meeting. However, they are not responsible for any remaining errors. M. Shafiq formatted the tables. The views expressed here are those of the author, and not necessarily of the World Bank.

on the future of demographics, changes in globalization, migration, and the rise of the middle class, and the roles these will play in growth. Favourable trends in demographics, globalization, human mobility, and middle class will further propel growth.

Young demographics will swell up the labour force, one of the two key inputs for growth. Nearly 20 million more South Asians (twice the population of Sweden) will join the labour force, every year, for the next two decades. Almost a billion people will join the ranks of the middle class. The middle class has historically been associated with increased education, entrepreneurship, governance, and growth.

Globalization will continue to increase the flow of goods, services, capital and people. The world has already experienced the benefits (and risks) of goods and financial globalization (Rodrik 2011). It is now the turn of globalization of services and people. The globalization of services has already exploded (Ghani 2010). The differences in demographic trends between the rich and poor countries will generate increased international labour mobility (Pritchett 2006). South Asia is well positioned to benefit from the the globalization of service and people.

There is democracy, for the first time since independence, in all countries in the region. India has attracted global attention for stable democracy. Governance has improved in other countries too, and from several different perspectives (Ghani and Ahmed 2009). First, market-creating institutions have replaced central planning. The abolition of the Licence Raj—industrial licensing, import licensing, and foreign exchange quotas—has created more room for entrepreneurs to expand more freely (Aiyar 2011). Second, market-stabilizing institutions (fiscal and monetary policies) are more robust now. Third, conflict management institutions have improved, although slowly, as the region has avoided extreme outcomes, such as famines (Sen 1983), or the disintegration of states (as seen in the Soviet Union, former Yugoslavia, and Sudan). Indeed, the key elements of a liberal democracy—right to information, free press, independent judiciary, and an active role of the civil society—have taken roots in most countries in the region.

There is huge room for the region to catch up with developed economies, and this will accelerate growth. This catch-up may take place more quickly than expected. It may be achieved in decades rather than centuries (Chamon and Kremer 2008). However, there is an alternative view, which is pessimistic.

The pessimistic view is that growth is neither automatic nor sui generis. The pessimistic outlook has an equally strong empirical justification.

There are no more than a dozen countries that have managed to sustain an average growth rate of 7 per cent a year for 25 years. A number of developing countries have experienced rapid growth and reached middle-income status, but very few have gone beyond. Recent economic history has shown that only Japan, South Korea, and Singapore have successfully transitioned from middle income to high income.

South Asia will face unprecedented transformational hurdles. Growth could be derailed by governance failures, poor human development, dilapidated infrastructure, lack of entrepreneurship, lopsided urbanization, large informal sectors, huge gender disparities, and rising level of violence and conflict (see Dasgupta et al. 2010).

Part II explores the reasons behind the pessimism. The focus is on the three pillars of transformation:

- Growth
- Inclusiveness
- Vulnerability/risk.

Growth takes place through structural transformation, as resources move from low productivity to high productivity sectors, and from traditional to modern sectors. Despite rapid growth, the problem of dualism is still widely prevalent in the region, with the majority of the population still trapped in traditional sectors. After decades of being primarily a region of farmers, India is rapidly urbanizing, as millions try to leave their stagnant villages, and move to the cities. But urban infrastructure is dilapidated, and unable to serve the existing population, let alone be prepared for increased rural–urban migration, or create jobs for a young labour force.

Growth has achieved only partial modernization. Growth has not been inclusive. South Asia remains home to the largest concentration of people living in conditions of debilitating poverty, human misery, gender disparities, and conflict. More than a billion people lived on less than $2 a day in 2005. Nearly 250 million children are undernourished and suffer from hidden hunger. Child mortality and malnutrition levels are amongst the highest in the world. More than one-third of adult women are anaemic. One woman dies every five minutes from preventable, pregnancy-related causes. The share of female employment in total employment is among the lowest in the world. More than 1 million people have been displaced by internal conflict. Although economic growth has reduced the poverty rate, the poverty rate has not fallen fast enough to reduce the total number of poor people.

South Asia may be headed towards an even more lopsided urbanization in the future, with a large part of the economy operating in rural and informal sectors, and a small segment of the population thriving in the globally integrated dynamic modern service sectors. Growth that results only in partial modernization will undermine the ability to move people out of poverty, and share the fruits of growth more widely.

South Asia will face many more risks in the future. Climate change and changes in globalization will pose new vulnerabilities to individuals and families, while urbanization and migration will continue to weaken the traditional sources of resilience against risks. A lot is at stake. There is potential to lift more people out of poverty in South Asia, than in any other part of the world. Sound choices made today will reshape tomorrow.

So what should the policymakers do? There is no silver bullet. There is a great deal of diversity within countries, and across countries, within the region (Ahluwalia and Williamson 2003, Devarajan 2006, Ahmed and Ghani 2007). Bhutan, India, the Maldives, and Sri Lanka have reached middle-income status. The problems they will face will be different from the challenges faced by low-income countries—Afghanistan, Bangladesh, Nepal, and Pakistan—although parts of India are no different from low-income countries. Pluralism in development will have great value (Zoellick 2010). The challenge is to find out what works best, in what context, and in what setting.

REASONS FOR OPTIMISM

South Asia is well positioned to become the fastest growing region in the world, as growth will benefit from young demographics, new waves of globalization, increased labour mobility, and rise of the middle class. We now turn to them.

The Demographic Dividend

In 2020, South Asia will have the youngest population in the world. The median age in India will be 28 years, compared to 37 in China and the USA, 49 in Japan, and 45 in Western Europe. The change in the age structure of the population will generate the demographic dividend, which, in turn, will create the potential for faster economic growth.

Demographic divided impacts growth through five different channels. The first is through the swelling of the labour force, as the baby boomers reach working age. The second is society's ability to divert resources from spending on children, to investing in physical capital, job training, and technological progress. The third is the rise in women's workforce activity that naturally accompanies a decline in fertility. The fourth is that the working age also happens to be the prime period for savings, which is central to the accumulation of physical and human capital and technological innovation. The fifth is the further boost to savings that occurs as the incentive to save for longer periods of retirement increases with greater longevity. The role of demographic dividend in growth is examined in Chapter 2 by Bloom et al.

Figure 1.1 plots the relationship between the demographic dividend (the change in the ratio of working-age, 15–64 years, to non-working-age people) on the horizontal axis, and the annual growth rates in real gross domestic product (GDP) per capita for 150 countries on the vertical axis. Each dot represents a country. Although, one cannot infer a causal relationship, the figure shows a striking association between the demographic dividend and growth.

Growth increases with the increase in the ratio of working-age to non-working-age people. In the case of China, the rise in GDP per capita closely mirrors the rise in demographic dividend. A large part of East Asia's spectacular economic growth derives from a working-age population bulge. East Asia has had a much higher ratio of working-age to non-working-age people compared with other parts of Asia at the time of economic take-off (ADB 1997). In Japan, the demographic dividend had matured much earlier. It has yet to materialize for South Asia.

South Asia has shown a rising pattern of economic growth which appears to correspond to the increasing ratio of working-age to

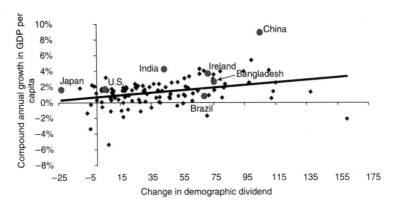

FIGURE 1.1 The Demographic Dividend and Growth in GDP
per Capita, 1980–2009

Source: Author.

non-working-age people. In Afghanistan, Nepal, and Pakistan, there has not yet been a major increase in the working-age share, so no dividend was possible. Bangladesh is somewhat ahead of India in the transition. Sri Lanka has already experienced its demographic dividend and now faces an aging population.

Looking ahead, with the exception of Sri Lanka, all countries in South Asia will experience a significantly faster increase in their working-age share between 2005 and 2050, than they did between 1960 and 2005. They stand to reap the benefits of a demographic dividend.

Table 1.1 shows the rise in size of the labour force. It will increase in all South Asian countries except for Sri Lanka. This increase will be further augmented by greater participation of women in the labour force due to smaller family size. The effect of this rise will be that economies will be more able to produce the goods and services needed.

But demographic dividend should not be taken for granted. The transition can pose new challenges, which will be most acutely felt in the health sector (World Bank 2010). Health problems—heart disease, diabetes, cancer, and respiratory diseases—could undermine the potential demographic dividend, as those in the working age are disabled and as household expenditures rise to cope with more chronic and expensive illnesses. Disability due to non-communicable diseases has forced a large number of South Asian workers to exit the labour force at much earlier ages than in OECD (Organisation for Economic Co-operation and Development) countries. Tackling health problems in South Asia early on with better prevention and treatment would significantly spare poor people the crushing burden of poor health, lost earnings, deepening poverty, and the risk of disability and premature death,

TABLE 1.1   Projected Rise in the Size of Labour Force as a Share of Total Population (per cent)

	2005	2050
Afghanistan	34	43
Bangladesh	46	53
Bhutan	43	52
India	39	47
Maldives	40	50
Nepal	39	48
Pakistan	36	45
Sri Lanka	42	40

Source: Bloom et al., Chapter 2 in this volume.

which are becoming all too common in the changing demographics of the region.

The Rise of the Middle Class

South Asia has long been known as a region of poverty with a smattering of billionaires. That will change dramatically in the next 15 years. By 2025, when the total population will approximate 2 billion, South Asia will become a predominantly middle-class region. Chapter 3 by Homi Kharas examines the co-evolution of growth and the middle class in South Asia.

The middle class—defined as households with daily expenditures between $10 and $100 per person in purchasing power parity terms—will dramatically swell. Indeed, a large bulge of the population that is emerging out of absolute poverty is poised to enter the middle class. By 2025, South Asia could be a predominantly middle-class region with 55 per cent of the population in this category. This change would be almost entirely due to India, the largest and most rapidly growing country in the region. In fact, because its population growth is faster than China's, India's middle class could be the largest in the world (in terms of numbers of people) by 2025.

Table 1.2 shows that South Asia's middle class is just starting to become noticeable in global terms. The 72 million people in this category comprise 3.8 per cent of the global middle class. From 72 million, South Asia could have over 1 billion middle-class consumers by 2025, representing one-quarter of the global total. Sri Lanka, too, even with

TABLE 1.2   South Asia's Middle Class, 2010

	Number of People (million)	Global Share	Share of Country Population
Bangladesh	1.8	0.1%	1.1%
India	59.5	3.2%	4.9%
Nepal	0.3	0.0%	0.9%
Pakistan	7.1	0.4%	4.1%
Sri Lanka	3.6	0.2%	18.5%
South Asia	72.2	3.8%	4.5%
Memo: China	169.3	9.0%	12.5%
USA	232.0	12.3%	73.7%
World	1,889.1	100%	28.2%

Source: Kharas, Chapter 3 in this volume.

relatively modest growth, would have a big expansion in its middle class, which would amount to 30.3 per cent of its population.

So a massive shift towards a middle-class society is in the making. Others have made similar claims, but with different quantification methods. In the final analysis, the precise numbers are less relevant than the trends—and those seem to be strong at present.

Growth, education, home ownership, formal-sector jobs, and better economic security are the cause and consequence of an expanding middle class. A more prosperous South Asia, with democratic governance and a demand for liberal economic policies, could be taking shape.

Accelerated Globalization

History tells us that the pace of growth and growth patterns do relate to globalization. This is examined by Weishi Grace Gu and Eswar Prasad in Chapter 4. They analyse the prospects of the region to integrate further with the global economy, and the implications of the integration for growth. The overall assessment is that South Asia will continue to increase its trade and financial linkages with the global economy, and benefit from the inexorable trend of globalization.

Can growth be sustained if the global recovery from one of the worst crises since the Great Depression remains uneven and fragile? The United States and much of Europe remain mired in the aftermath of the financial crisis that erupted in the fall of 2008 with high unemployment, slow economic growth, financial deleveraging of households, and continuing bank-sector problems. Will slow growth in rich economies impose limits on the pace of export-led growth in poor countries?

India and other South Asian countries are relatively less vulnerable to the global slowdown for three reasons, although they are not immune to it, and global uncertainties do cast a cloud. First, South Asia has followed a more balanced growth strategy. Unlike East Asia, it has relied on *twin engines of growth*—export and domestic consumption. The share of household consumption in the GDP in South Asian countries is much higher than in China. The resilience of the region rests on the huge and rapidly expanding size of the domestic market. Second, South Asia has followed a different globalization strategy (Ghani and Anand 2009). The two different channels of globalization—trade integration and financial integration —have evolved differently in South Asia, compared to other regions.

South Asia's foreign trade has grown over the last decade, which has contributed to rapid growth, similar to the experience in East Asia.

But its trade characteristics are different. While China is considered the global centre for manufacturing, India has acquired a global reputation as a hub for service export. India's growth has been spearheaded by growth in the exports of modern services. The pace at which the share of modern services exports has grown in India has exceeded the growth rate in goods exports from China (Figure 1.2).

The next wave of globalization may very well come from services. Technology has enabled services to be digitized and transported long distance at low cost without compromising on quality. More and more services such as audit, tax returns, and health services, which can be traded with the help of internet, are being digitized. Moreover, the cost differential in the production of services across the world is enormous. In the past, the only means to narrowing such cost differentials was migration, but migration has been heavily regulated and global international migration has remained steady at about 3 per cent for decades. Now that service providers can, by making use of the internet (outsourcing), sell services without crossing national borders, the scope for exploiting cost differentials is much greater. What is more, it is very hard for governments to regulate modern impersonal services transported through the internet, so prospects for rapid expansion in services exports

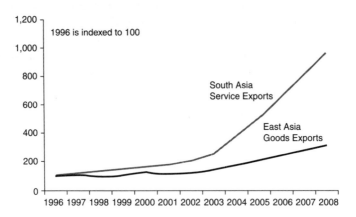

FIGURE 1.2   South Asia's Growth in Service Exports and East Asia's
Growth in Goods Exports

Source: Ghani (2010).

Note: Growth in share of exports in world exports is calculated by taking the respective region's exports as a share of world exports of goods and services. Exports are in current US$ terms. South Asia includes Bangladesh, India, the Maldives, Nepal, Pakistan, and Sri Lanka.

are good. South Asia is well positioned to benefit from globalization of services.

The second model of globalization, financial integration, and foreign capital inflows—remittances, international syndicated bank lending, private capital investments, and bond issues—is also different for South Asia. Capital inflows have surged, as more capital flows into faster-growing emerging markets. However, South Asia is unique in attracting capital flows that are less volatile. The region, particularly Bangladesh and Nepal, have relied more on remittance inflows than portfolio flows and bank loans. Remittance inflows are more stable and persistent than portfolio flows (Figure 1. 3). They also have a few drawbacks, as exchange rate appreciation, associated with remittance inflows, can potentially contribute to Dutch disease and restrict the size of tradable sectors.

Third, it is not growth in the rich countries but the room for catch-up that will most likely determine the pace of growth for developing countries (Rodrik 2011). For most developing countries, this 'convergence gap' is wider now than it has been at any time since the 1970s. So the growth potential is correspondingly larger.

South Asia withstood the global crisis better than other regions because it seems to be on a reasonably balanced growth path. It is increasing trade and financial linkages with the rest of the world, a process that looks set to continue and that has significant benefits for its economies. The advantage of the balanced approach is that it makes it easier for the policymakers to manage both benefits and risks associated

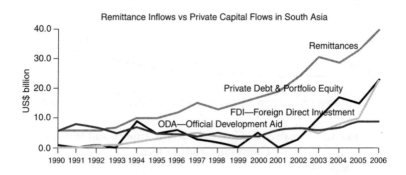

FIGURE 1.3   Remittance Inflows versus Private Capital Inflows in South Asia

Source: Ghani (2010).

with global integration. Benefits include access to capital, technology transfer, knowledge, and risk sharing. The risks are that countries will be exposed to the problems and volatilities of developed economies.

Increased Human Mobility

Current demographic trends suggest an aging population in rich countries and a young population in poor countries. Western Europe will be facing labour shortages as early as 2025. The world has benefited immensely from the liberalization of trade and capital flows. Trade is now substantially free, finance and capital too are substantially free, but labour mobility remains restricted. It is now the turn for liberalizing labour and migration policies. Policymakers need to harness the economic benefits of increased human mobility. This is examined in Chapter 5 by Çağlar Özden and Christopher Robert Parsons.

Figure 1.4 presents the actual dependency ratios in OECD and South Asian countries since 1950 as well as projected ones for 2050. In the case of the OECD, the dependency ratio is expected to rise sharply starting in 2010 while the downward trend in South Asia will continue until 2040. The figure also includes a middle line which represents an average dependency ratio, a theoretical outcome that would be obtained with complete freedom of movement of labour between the two regions. In this case, the dependency ratio does not exhibit the extreme volatility which serves to highlight the potential demographic benefits of increased mobility.

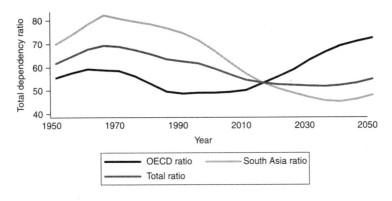

FIGURE 1.4   Historical and Projected Dependency Ratios in the OECD and South Asia, 1950–2050

Source: Özden and Parsons, Chapter 5 in this volume.

The divergent trends of shrinking labour forces in rich countries and growing labour supplies in South Asia (and Sub-Saharan Africa) will create global imbalances. These imbalances can be substantially reduced if labour policies can be liberalized—if both rich and poor countries undertake profound and far-reaching changes in working arrangements, migration, business practices, and government policies. It may now be the turn of labour mobility, just like the liberalization of trade and financial integration policies, to benefit the world.

Increased levels of immigration have already become an economic necessity in many OECD countries and will become so in the rest quite soon. However, strong and growing public opposition to higher migration flows may make it difficult for OECD governments to pass legislation or reach agreements that facilitate the movement of workers from South Asia countries. Governments in rich countries need to search for mechanisms that respond to their labour market pressures without triggering strong public and political opposition, especially in the shadow of the current economic crisis.

One solution is to allow *temporary* movement of workers. This would help rich countries meet their labour needs, while addressing public fears that usually centre upon permanent movement of migrants. Governments in host and source countries can use a range of incentive measures and policies to increase likelihood of migrants' return. Such measures should involve various stakeholders including regulatory agencies and employers in rich countries and recruitment agencies and governments in South Asian countries. The objective of such measures is to facilitate the movement of people through planned, safe, and lawful channels that make temporariness feasible and desirable for all parties involved—sending and receiving countries as well as the migrants themselves.

REASONS FOR PESSIMISM

Can the region avoid idiosyncratic growth patterns, accelerate spatial transformation, unleash entrepreneurship, promote more efficient urbanization, reduce informality traps, harness volatile capital flows, and manage internal conflicts and disparities? What should be the focus of the next phase of reform?

Managing Lopsided Spatial Transformation

Growth at low levels of income is generally accompanied by a rapid shift in the workforce out of rural and traditional sectors (agriculture) and into modern ones (manufacturing and services). This is the iron law of development and this was the experience with the East Asian miracle. However, this does not seem to be happening in South Asia, or not to the same extent as in East Asia. Chapter 6 by Arvind Panagariya explores this.

Figure 1.5 compares the shares of service value added in GDP for a group of countries. The share of the services sector in South Asia is much bigger than in East Asia, given the stage of development. South Asia seems to have made the leap straight from agriculture into services, skipping manufacturing. Its share of employment in the manufacturing sector is, in fact, abysmally low and stagnant.

What explains the slow pace of spatial transformation? Is slow growth behind the slow pace of spatial transformation? Not really, given that South Asia is also amongst the fastest growing regions in the world. Rapid growth has produced billionaires. But, the broad character of the region remains agrarian and rural. This has more to do with the peculiarities of growth patterns—services-led growth which is more skill intensive compared to manufacturing-led growth which is less skill intensive, and the fragmented nature of transformation—than the pace of growth.

Slow growth in manufacturing despite rapid GDP growth should by itself not be a worry, provided it is not in the way of growth in employment opportunities for unskilled and low-skilled workers at decent wages in industry and services so that these sectors still manage to rapidly pull the underemployed workers in agriculture into gainful employment.

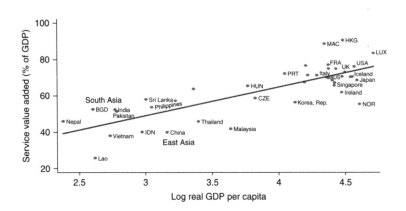

FIGURE 1.5   Service and Manufacturing Sectors in South Asia, 2005

Source: Ghani (2010).

This can happen through a variety of channels in a rapidly growing economy. First, in fast-growing economies, growth in industry and services is almost always faster than that in agriculture. The former may thus pull some workers out of the latter even if manufacturing is growing at approximately the same rate as the GDP as a whole so that its share in the latter is unchanged over time. Second, the composition of output within manufacturing may shift towards unskilled or low-skilled labour-intensive products. This would help raise the overall labour intensity of manufacturing and generate rising numbers of well-paid jobs even when manufacturing grows more slowly than services. Third, even with unchanged composition of output, technology may progressively shift towards increased numbers of unskilled or low-skilled workers. Finally, non-manufacturing sectors, mainly modern services, that drive rapid growth, may themselves increasingly absorb unskilled and low-skilled workers.

It can be debated whether South Asia in the coming decades will be able to mimic the East Asian experience, which was disproportionately based on rapid city-based manufacturing growth in labour-intensive industries. This generated adequate demand for labour thereby relieving rural areas of excess labour and enabling growth in both rural and urban productivity. With the changes in technology that have taken place over the past decade or two, it is an open question whether labour-intensive industry will be able to survive and grow in the manner that the East Asian countries experienced (Pack 2009). Moreover, with the possible slowing down of demand growth in developed countries, new entrants in the field may not be able to benefit from the demand pull that was exercised by the US and Europe over the past couple of decades. This could, however, be substituted by similar demand growth within Asia.

South Asian countries are labour-abundant and must, accordingly, reorient themselves towards specialization in labour-intensive industries. The end to investment licensing, removal of restrictions on investments by big business houses outside the so-called 'core' sectors, elimination of small-scale industries reservation, and import liberalization that were expected to stimulate labour-intensive industries have so far failed. The likely reason is that there still remain binding restrictions on the expansion of labour-intensive sectors that must be addressed. Policymakers need to implement a second phase of reform that could further propel growth and create more jobs.

Without policy correction, the region is heading towards a highly lopsided structure such that while the output share of agriculture will decline to a minuscule level, its employment share will remain disproportionately large. Concomitantly, an extremely large part of the economy would remain traditional and rural while the rest would turn urban and modern, fully linked to the global economy. In other words, the current dualistic nature of the economy will persist with differences further sharpened rather than narrowed. This can be better managed. The rural–urban divide can be narrowed through fluid labour markets, market access, and better business climate and entrepreneurship.

Unleashing Entrepreneurship

Why is entrepreneurship important? It is a central factor in job creation. It helps allocate resources efficiently, supports innovation, and promotes trade. To achieve strong growth and job creation, South Asia will need to improve the business environment and harness entrepreneurship. South Asia has the second worst business environment in the world, and this is possibly linked to low levels of entrepreneurship. Chapter 7 by Ghani et al. provides an analysis of how entrepreneurship relates to growth and job creation.

Figure 1.6 plots new firms per thousand workers on the vertical axis and GDP per capita on the horizontal axis for a group of countries. Each dot is a country. The upward sloping line suggests that increased entrepreneurship is associated with higher incomes. Unfortunately, South

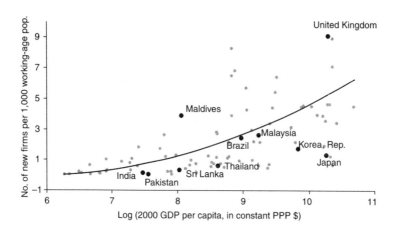

FIGURE 1.6   Entrepreneurship and Growth

Source: Ghani et al., Chapter 7 in this volume.

Asian countries, except the Maldives, are well below the line, suggesting that they have fewer entrepreneurs than their stage of development warrants.

Defining entrepreneurship is hard and controversial, even in rich countries. One metric of entrepreneurship is the ratio of young establishments to employment in the formal sector, somewhat mirroring the cross-country measure of entrepreneurship in Figure 1.6. Counts of young establishments in the formal sector are low in South Asia relative to advanced economies. Small establishments are somewhat more common, but have a smaller employment share than young establishments. Self-employment is virtually non-existent in the formal manufacturing sector in India. The informal sector has much higher rates of small establishments and self-employment, but young establishments are underrepresented.

Figure 1.7 shows the relationship between entrepreneurship and job creation in India using state-level data. The vertical axis is the log employment growth from 1989 to 2005, while the horizontal axis is the log count of young firms per 1,000 workers in 1989. There is a strong upward slope to the trend line, similar to that found across cities in the United States, and it is clear that the relationship does not overly depend upon any one region. There is evidence that entrepreneurship rates are strong and systematic predictors of employment growth in India. The elasticities between initial entrepreneurship levels and subsequent growth

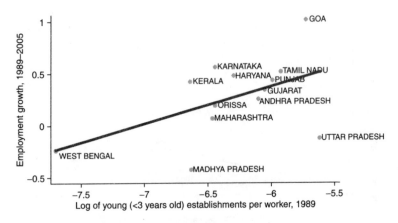

FIGURE 1.7   Entrepreneurs and Employment Growth in Indian Manufacturing

Source: Ghani et al., Chapter 7 in this volume.

across region–industry observations for India are comparable to those observed in the US across cities.

While South Asia has a disproportionately high rate of self-employment and many small firms, this has not as readily translated into as many young entrepreneurial firms as could be hoped. Yet there is no question that entrepreneurship works in the region. Formal-sector job growth has been strongest in regions and industries that have exhibited high rates of entrepreneurship and dynamic economies.

Looking ahead, if South Asia continues to undertake policy steps to help entrepreneurs—lower entry costs, reduce regulatory burdens, and further develop financial access—it has the potential to unleash entrepreneurship and job growth that will strongly expand the formal manufacturing sector. The entrepreneurial potential of the region is very large. Most of these policy steps are not unique to South Asia but are encouraged worldwide. These simple steps will help South Asia realize its growth potential. South Asia has experienced record growth over the past decade. If entrepreneurship in South Asia moves from its position in Figure 1.6 to the trend line or above, given the link between entry, young firms, and job growth, how fast would the region then be growing?

Harnessing Capital Flows

The disjuncture between interest rates in advanced economies and emerging markets has created severe discomfort for monetary policymakers in emerging markets. With the extended zero interest rate policy in the US and Japan, and near zero in the Eurozone, central banks in emerging markets will face a potential problem in the medium term—how to manage the capital account actively, so that capital flows are utilized efficiently and do not suffer from boom–bust possibilities. This issue is examined in Chapter 8 by Barry Eichengreen.

Low rates are appropriate for the slow growth, economic slack, and financial weakness currently characterizing the advanced economies. Higher rates are appropriate for the strong growth, incipient inflation, and potential overheating conditions prevailing in South Asia. But the two policies together provide an incentive for the carry trade—for capital to flow from where the cost of borrowing is low to where the return on investment is high. These financial inflows feed the boom conditions that motivated the adoption of high interest rates by emerging-market central banks in the first place. They frustrate efforts to put in place policies of restraint.

Monetary policymakers have no easy solution to this problem. They may be tempted to raise rates further to counter the inflationary effects of the additional spending induced by capital inflows. But doing so only increases the interest differential providing the incentive for the carry trade, attracting additional inflows. It creates a tendency for the exchange rate to appreciate, which is uncomfortable for domestic producers. Alternatively, central banks may be tempted to cut rates to make the carry trade less attractive and discourage inflows. But by doing so, they only encourage additional borrowing and spending, aggravating overheating risks. It is not surprising that central banks often seem frozen, like deer in the headlights, in the face of this problem.

Capital inflows create very immediate problems in the region and, as such, require a very immediate response. But while addressing immediate problems, it is important for policymakers not to neglect longer-term strategies. In the long run, the best defence against dislocations due to capital flows surges is larger and more inclusive financial markets.

Larger corporate debt markets will mean that foreign capital flows into and out of those markets will do less to move prices and distort firms' funding costs. Larger equity markets will mean that foreign inflows and outflows will similarly do less to move prices and wrong-foot domestic institutions. Developing domestic financial markets and corporate bond markets in particular is a long hard slog. In India it requires institutional and regulatory reform to strengthen transparency, contract enforcement, and market liquidity. In the smaller countries of South Asia—which lack the scale to build bond markets at the national level, but can find it if they are willing to work together with their neighbours—it also requires market integration and regulatory harmonization. Although both domestic market development and regional financial integration will take time, they are no less important for the fact.

Policymakers also need to take into consideration the importance of financial inclusion and regulating the financial system as a whole. In case a big firm fails, it should already have in place a 'living will' that spells out a dissolution plan for authorities—specifically how the firm is connected to other institutions and how those institutions may react to its dissolution.

Promoting Efficient Urbanization

Urbanization is a defining phenomenon of this century. The world was 3 per cent urban in 1800, 14 per cent in 1900, 50 per cent in 2007, and is probably headed in the next few decades towards around 80 per cent, which has been the stabilization point for developed countries. Over 90 per cent of global urban growth is now occurring in the developing world and nearly 2 billion new urban residents are anticipated in the next 20 years. Chapter 9 by Rakesh Mohan examines how urbanization can be harnessed to promote growth and development.

Cities provide the critical requirements for entrepreneurs: skilled workers, financing, access to customers, and knowledge (Glaeser 2011). The connection between per worker productivity and city area population—a measure of agglomeration economies—is particularly strong in cities with higher levels of skill and virtually non-existent in less-skilled metropolitan areas. Urban densities are important for creating synergy as proximity spreads knowledge, which either makes workers more skilled or entrepreneurs more productive.

Will South Asia's future urbanization be different from the urbanization experience of the last half century? In thinking about urban growth in South Asia we need to understand the emerging contours of economic development as they are likely to impact the future pattern of urbanization in the region. The first key difference between past and future urbanization will be that with increasing globalization and ever higher levels of income that the region as a whole can now expect, the residents of South Asian cities will now be much more demanding relative to their predecessors in terms of the quality of urban services that they deem to be their right and the urban amenities that are now seen as normal. Hence it is likely that urban investment will be different in terms of its composition and intensity.

Urbanization in South Asia will define the change over the next 20–30 years. Total urban population in the region will double from an estimated 500 million in 2010 to over a billion in 2040 (Table 1.3). Current projections suggest that urbanization level over the region will be around 50 per cent by 2040, with doubling of the absolute level of urban population over the period.

Second, with increasing globalization, each South Asian city will have to be more competitive on a global scale than has been the case in the past. In the larger countries there will be inevitable tension between the claims of coastal urban areas that possess natural comparative advantage and the vast hinterland that will need greater infrastructure investment for attaining competitiveness. Hence policymakers probably need to give greater attention to the ingredients of competitiveness, the corresponding public investment that will be appropriate in this regard, and the modes of financing that will need to be mobilized.

Third, policymakers will need to pay as much attention to the 'soft' aspects of urbanization as to the bricks-and-mortar type of physical

TABLE 1.3   Urban Population in South Asia

Country	1950		2010		2040		Last 60 years	Next 30 years
	Urban Population (million)	Per cent of Total Population (%)	Urban Population (million)	Per cent of Total Population (%)	Urban Population (million)	Per cent of Total Population (%)	Additional Urban Population (million)	Additional Urban Population (million)
India	62	17.3	367	30.1	764	47.8	305	397
Pakistan	7	17.5	64	37	153	56.9	57	89
Bangladesh	2	4.3	47	28.1	116	48.7	45	69
Nepal	0.2	2.7	5	18.2	18	38.2	5	13
Sri Lanka	1	15.3	2.9	15.1	5.4	27.2	2	2.5
Total	72	15.8	486	30.3	1,056	48.6	414	571

Source: Rakesh Mohan, Chapter 9 in this volume.

investment. Indeed the latter will have to be guided by the expected pattern of economic development in the presence of globalization and the consequent needs for both human resource and physical development.

The financing of urban infrastructure investment that will be needed over the next 20–30 years will need much more focused attention. The task is essentially threefold. First, local governments have to be made creditworthy. Second, urban infrastructure projects must be made commercially viable. If these two requirements are met in the context of a developed capital market, the financial resources that are needed will get generated automatically. However, bond markets in South Asian countries are not yet well developed and will take quite some time to be large enough to meet such resource needs. Third, the building of institutional mechanisms that can efficiently intermediate financial resources for urban investment needs while financial and capital markets are developed needs critical attention. In both the US and Germany, capital market development needed different levels of government and regulatory intervention. Such markets will need to be created for the financing of cities in Asia.

Moreover, policymakers will need to strengthen city management. This will need action at all levels: federal, state, and local. City management needs to be professionalized; city governments need to be made creditworthy; and urban infrastructure projects need to be made commercially viable. Strengthening city management will enable connection with capital markets, both national and international. The objective would be to move from a top–down to bottom–up market-based approach and develop new institutional forms and mechanisms.

Overcoming Informality Traps

Despite rapid growth, the informal sector remains overwhelmingly large and persistent in South Asia compared to the global average (Figure1. 8). More than 80 per cent of non-agricultural jobs in South Asia are in the informal sector. Around nine out of 10 employees in India do not have formal jobs. Women tend to dominate the informal sector. For developing countries as a group, more than half of all jobs—over 900 million workers—can be considered informal. What is even more worrying is that informal employment does not seem to disappear with development (OECD 2009). This is the focus of Chapter 10 by Ravi Kanbur.

Informal jobs are heterogeneous and come in many shapes and forms. Assessments of the evolution of informality at the national level cannot be

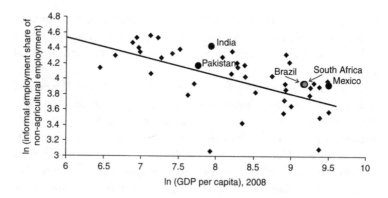

<figure>FIGURE 1.8   High Concentration of Informal Jobs in South Asia</figure>

Source: Author.

divorced from a general discussion of the transition of an economy from an agricultural base towards manufacturing and services. Even within non-agriculture there is a spread between self-employed entrepreneurs, own-account workers, unpaid family workers, and causal labour.

Then there is heterogeneity across sectors. In India, 33 per cent of all male informal workers are engaged in trade, 23 per cent in manufacturing, 16 per cent in construction, 21 per cent in other services (mainly transport and storage), and 7 per cent in other sectors. In Pakistan, the sector that engages the largest percentage of all informal workers is trade (34 per cent) followed by manufacturing and personal services (both around 20 per cent). This heterogeneity should warn us against a uniform policy towards the informal sector.

Why is informality bad? The share of informal workers is strongly correlated with poverty rates (Figure 1.9). Moreover, certain groups, such as children or women tend to be overrepresented in this category of jobs.

The informal sector is often a result of fragmented spatial transformation which creates a large pool of labour that is neither in agriculture nor in manufacturing but waiting for a chance to enter the formal sector. This labour engages in a number of low-productivity and low-income activities, the low income being balanced by the prospects of a high-income job.

The links between working informally and being poor are not always simple. On the one hand, not all jobs in the informal economy yield paltry incomes. Many in the informal economy, especially the self-employed, in fact earn more than unskilled or low-skilled workers

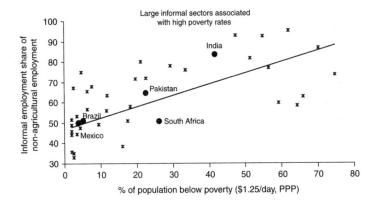

FIGURE 1.9   Strong Association between Informality and Poverty

Source: Author.

in the formal economy. There is much innovation and many dynamic growth-oriented segments in the informal economy, some of which require considerable knowledge and skills. One of these is the fast-growing information and communications technology (ICT) sector in the large cities of India.

Informal employment can be a consequence of insufficient job creation in the formal sector. At the macro level, in a dual-economy framework the size of the informal sector is seen as an indicator of the level of per capita income and development since growth in the modern sector relies upon and then depletes labour in the traditional sector. At the same time, at the micro level, dynamism and growth potential is seen to be negatively affected by the smallness of size of enterprises in the informal sector. There is also the issue of the extent to which regulations and laws affecting the labour market protect those in the informal sector and the extent to which they instead stand in the way of transmitting the beneficial effects of economic growth to the poor in the informal sector and helping them escape from the informal sector to the 'better jobs' in the formal sector.

There is no magic bullet to address the concerns that arise with informality and a range of interventions need to be examined and implemented. Higher growth, but growth whose sectoral pattern is more labour absorbing, is the first and most general policy conclusion. With the given level and structure of growth, extending the coverage of state protection to workers currently uncovered is the second recommendation. At the same time, reviewing current interventions to improve their flexibility and application is also needed. Direct measures to increase the productivity and incomes of enterprises in the informal sector—which include targeted measures of training and enterprise support as well as general measures of bringing legal and other state infrastructure support to these enterprises—are another recommendation. Finally, better enforcement of regulations that do exist and assessing enforcement possibilities before regulations are passed are also recommendations that emerge from the literature.

Informality has not disappeared in South Asia and is unlikely to do so in the coming two decades. Policymakers need to recognize that it is a complex phenomenon and that it is an integral part of the economy and society. Addressing informality to reduce poverty and spur development requires a better understanding of the phenomenon, the readiness to eschew simplistic uniform solutions, and the willingness to adopt a wide range of country-specific tailor-made policies and interventions. Policymakers need to increase good quality jobs not only in the formal but also the informal sector. Moreover informal workers need to be better protected and trained. This may not be easy in future as growth may not be sufficient to eradicate informal employment.

Managing Conflict

While conflicts in Afghanistan and Pakistan have attracted global attention, parts of India, Sri Lanka, and Nepal have also experienced long-running conflicts. The result is human misery, destruction of infrastructure and social cohesion, and death. The knock-on effects are huge. What is conflict? Where is it concentrated? What should policymakers do? These issues are discussed in Chapter 11 by Lakshmi Iyer.

South Asia has experienced very high levels of internal conflict over the past decade. In 2009, direct casualties from armed conflict surpassed 58,000 worldwide; over a third of these were in South Asia. Most countries in South Asia are currently immersed in, or are just emerging from, conflicts of varying nature and scope, ranging from the recently ended civil wars in Sri Lanka and Nepal and escalating insurgency in Afghanistan and Pakistan to low-level localized insurgency in India. South Asian countries, on average, have experienced armed conflict for half of the time since 2000 (Figure 1.10). This is the highest incidence of conflict among all the major regions in the world.

Is conflict a cause or a result of underdevelopment? Conflict is both a cause and an effect. There is strong association between conflict incidence and poverty. Economically lagging regions in South Asia have experienced

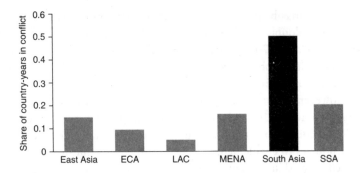

FIGURE 1.10   Proportion of Country-years in Armed Conflict, 2000–8

Source: Iyer, Chapter 11 in this volume.

Notes: Armed conflict here refers to internal armed conflicts, with a minimum of 25 battle-related deaths per year, between the government of a state and one or more internal opposition group(s). ECA: Europe and Central Asia, LAC: Latin America and the Caribbean, MENA: Middle-East and North Africa, SSA: Sub-Saharan Africa.

far greater incidence of internal conflict over the past decade, compared to economically leading regions (Ghani and Iyer 2009). This is very similar to the findings from the cross-country literature and suggests that economic growth is likely to yield benefits in terms of political stability as well, thereby making further economic growth possible.

How persistent is conflict? In terms of fatalities due to conflict, we see a greater degree of persistence in South Asia, that is, places which had some fatalities in 1998 continue to have higher fatalities over the next few years. This suggests that pre-existing conflicts are becoming more intense in terms of fatalities over time. These patterns remain very similar if we examine variation only across the states of India, though the data is noisy.

Managing conflict is a key public policy issue to ensure the future stability and growth of South Asia. A holistic approach, combining military, political, economic, and regional initiatives, is needed to manage conflict over the next decade. Given that conflict is significantly higher in economically lagging regions, economic growth and poverty reduction should be key policy priorities in such areas. Countries can use innovative mechanisms to overcome these policy challenges.

CONCLUSION

So what will South Asia look like in 2025? Will the optimistic outlook prevail or the pessimistic one? The truth probably lies somewhere in between. It may be too optimistic to argue that South Asian countries can achieve double-digit growth rates, or that 70 per cent of India will be middle class by 2025. It may be too pessimistic to argue that growth will be derailed by poor infrastructure, slow pace of human development, lopsided urbanization, rising conflict, and governance failures.

However, growth cannot be taken for granted. The link between demographics and growth is not automatic. Indeed, a demographic dividend could morph into a demographic disaster, in the absence of right policies to enable people to be healthy, well educated, and well trained in the skills demanded by the labour market. The demographic dividend is a time-bound opportunity. It provides policymakers an incentive to redouble their efforts to promote the skills of the working-age cohort so that it has the ability to contribute productively to the economy.

Neither does globalization automatically engender growth. Countries need the infrastructure—ports, transport, and communications—to help ensure wider access and exposure to international markets. Increased market integration needs to be complemented with appropriate structural reforms to take advantage of globalization, that is, to enable resources to be allocated from the low-productivity and non-tradable sectors into high-productivity and tradable ones. This is not just about the shift away from agriculture and into industry and services. It is about the transformation required to move into higher-quality goods and services. Globalization has lifted millions out of poverty, but some aspects of globalization, particularly financial globalization, has increased macroeconomic instability and income inequality.

How will one win the future? It will depend on how the policymakers manage the three drivers of transformation—growth, inclusiveness, and risk. Rapid growth is necessary for more and better jobs and for poverty reduction. However, high levels of inequality, which preclude large segments of society from participating at their full potential, will undermine growth and political stability. If the instability escalates to serious conflict, further negative repercussions for both growth and poverty can arise, potentially reversing years of development. Effective, efficient, and equitable social protection programmes will be needed to directly reduce poverty and inequality, and build resilience by helping individuals and families to smooth their consumption and handle shocks.

Growth should not be an end in itself. Policymakers should not think of growth separately from inclusion. Increased income disparities should not be viewed as the price to pay for high growth. Neither should education, health, and gender parities be considered as second-stage reforms. A development response that aims to promote growth first, and then deal with human misery is not sustainable.

Improved governance will play a key role in successfully implementing the three drivers of transformation. Governance has undergone two subtle shifts that may have larger lessons for the politics of democratic accountability. The first is that while identity politics is still powerful in the region, its importance is diminishing. The second is that rates of incumbency—the likelihood of a sitting legislator or state government being re-elected—are coming down. This is finally leading to governance that is more focused on development than other issues. This change is likely to accelerate in the future.

South Asia needs a bridge to the future that ensures *rapid, sustainable, and inclusive growth*. It needs policies to raise growth wherever it happens. It also needs policies to redistribute the gains of growth more efficiently and effectively.

REFERENCES

Ahluwalia, Isher Judge and John Williamson. 2003. *The South Asian Experience with Growth*. New Delhi: Oxford University Press.

Ahmed, Sadiq and Ejaz Ghani. 2007. *South Asia—Growth and Regional Integration*. New Delhi: World Bank and Macmillan.

Aiyar, Swaminathan. 2011. 'Corruption: Worse, but, with Welcome Exceptions', *The Economic Times*, 10 February.

Asian Development Bank (ADB). 1997. *Emerging Asia: Changes and Challenges*. Manila: ADB.

Bloom, David E. and Jeffrey G. Williamson. 1998. 'Demographic Transitions and Economic Miracles in Emerging Asia', *World Bank Economic Review*, 12 (3): 419–55.

Chamon, M. and M. Kremer. 2008. 'Economic Transformation, Population Growth and the Long-run World Income Distribution', *Journal of International Economics*, 79 (1).

Dasgupta, Dipak, Ejaz Ghani, and Ernesto May. 2010. 'Economic Policy Challenges for South Asia', in Otaviano Canuto and M. Giugale (eds), *The Day after Tomorrow*. Washington, DC: World Bank.

Devarajan, Shantayanan. 2006. *Can Poverty be Eliminated in a Generation in South Asia?*, World Bank.

Devarajan, Shantayanan and Ravi Kanbur. 2005. 'A Framework for Scaling Up Poverty Reduction, with Illustrations from South Asia', August. Revised version published in D. Narayan and E. Glinskaya (eds). 2007. *Ending Poverty in South Asia: Ideas that Work*. Washington, DC: World Bank.

Ghani, Ejaz (ed.). 2010. *The Service Revolution in South Asia*. New Delhi: Oxford University Press.

Ghani, Ejaz and Sadiq Ahmed (eds). 2009. *Accelerating Growth and Job Creation in South Asia*. New Delhi: Oxford University Press.

Ghani, Ejaz and Rahul Anand. 2009. 'How Will Changes in Globalization Impact South Asia?', Policy Research Working Paper 5079, World Bank.

Ghani, Ejaz and Lakshmi Iyer. 2009. 'Conflict and Development—Lessons from South Asia', VoxEU.

Glaeser, Edward L. 2011. *Triumph of the City: How Our Greatest Invention Makes Us Richer, Smarter, Greener, Healthier and Happier*. Macmillan.

Kanbur, Ravi. 2009. 'Macro Crises and Targeting Transfers to the Poor', April, paper prepared for the Growth Commission. Revised version published in *Journal of Globalization and Development*, 2010.

Kanbur, Ravi and Michael Spence (eds). 2010. *Equity and Growth in a Globalizing World*. Washington, DC: World Bank.

Kelkar, Vijay and A. Shah. 2010. 'Indian Social Democracy: The Resource Perspective', Working Paper, OECD.

Organisation for Economic Co-operation and Development (OECD). 2009. *Is Informal Normal? Towards More and Better Jobs in Developing Countries.* Paris: OECD.

Pack, Howard. 2009. 'Should South Asia Emulate East Asian Tigers?', in Ejaz Ghani and Sadiq Ahmed (eds), *Accelerating Growth and Job Creation in South Asia*. New Delhi: Oxford University Press.

Panagariya, Arvind. 2011. 'Thinking Clearly about Governance', *The Economic Times*, 26 January.

Prichett, L. 2006. *Let Their People Come: Breaking the Gridlock on Global Labor Mobility*. Washington, DC: Center for Global Development.

Rodrik, Dani. 2011. *The Globalization Paradox: Democracy and the Future of the World Economy*. New York and London: W.W. Norton.

Sen, A.K. 1983. 'Development: Which Way Now?', *The Economic Journal*, 93 (372): 745–62.

Spence, Michael. 2010. 'The Risk Tsunami', Project Syndicate.

World Bank. 2010. *Capitalizing on the Demographic Transition: Tackling Noncommunicable Diseases in South Asia*. Washington, DC: World Bank.

———. 2011. 'Building Resilience and Opportunity, Consultations on the World Bank's Social Protection & Labor Strategy, 2012–2022', Concept Note.

Zoellick, Robert, B. 2010. 'Democratizing Development Economics', Lecture Delivered to Georgetown University, 29 September.

I

Reasons for Optimism

2

Demographic Change and Economic Growth

David E. Bloom, David Canning, and Larry Rosenberg[*]

LINKS BETWEEN DEMOGRAPHIC CHANGE AND ECONOMIC GROWTH

Identifying factors that influence the pace of national economic growth is a time-worn practice of economists. Strangely, demographic change has often been absent from consideration. But new thinking and evidence have highlighted the powerful contribution that demographic change can make to economic growth, and this line of inquiry has some salient implications for understanding past growth in South Asia and assessing and shaping its future prospects.

South Asia has achieved major improvements in population health in the past six decades. These are indicated by the more than two-thirds decline in infant mortality rate (IMR—the number of infants who die before their first birthday in a given year, divided by the number of live births that year) and, since the early 1980s, the nearly 50 per cent decline in child mortality rate.[1] Such improvements in child survival contributed

[*] Support for this work was provided by the Program on the Global Demography of Aging at Harvard University, funded by Award Number P30AGO24409 from the National Institute of Aging. The content is solely the responsibility of the authors and does not necessarily represent the official views of the National Institute on Aging or the National Institutes of Health. Support was also provided by the William and Flora Hewlett Foundation and the World Bank.

[1] The region's IMR declined from 168 per 1,000 live births in the early 1950s to 53 in 2010. The child (under 5) mortality rate fell from 145 per 1,000 in the early 1980s (the first period for which the UN has data) to 77 in 2010.

to a baby boom because many babies who once would have died survived. The baby boom subsequently abated as couples realized they did not need to have as many births to realize their fertility targets and desired fertility itself diminished. This fertility transition was greatly abetted by the expansion of girls' education, urbanization, the development of financial markets, and the advent of family planning programmes. For the region as a whole, fertility has fallen by more than half since 1950.[2] This set of events—an improvement in child survival followed by a fertility decline—has meant that cohorts born preceding the decline in fertility are relatively large in size. As the large-sized cohorts matured, they came to constitute a working-age group that is, in historical terms, also relatively large. The whole process—a switch from high mortality and fertility rates to low ones—is known as the demographic transition. The countries in South Asia are at different stages of this transition, but all of them have seen a fall in their IMRs and have at least started experiencing a decline in their fertility rates. They have relatively large cohorts of young people who have substantially entered, or will soon enter, the prime ages for work and saving.

Changes in the age structure of the population create potential for faster economic growth, a phenomenon referred to as the demographic dividend. This dividend is a composite of five distinct forces. The first is swelling of the labour force as the baby boomers reach working age. The second is society's ability to divert resources from spending on children to investing in physical capital, job training, and technological progress. The third is the rise in women's workforce activity that naturally accompanies a decline in fertility. The fourth has to do with the fact that the working age also happens to cover the prime years for savings, which are key to the accumulation of physical and human capital and technological innovation. And the fifth is the further boost to savings that occurs as the incentive to save for longer periods of retirement increases with greater longevity.

The demographic dividend is not an automatic result of the demographic changes outlined here. Rather, enjoyment of the dividend is crucially determined by the policy environment. For example, good governance, carefully constructed trade policy, and sound macroeconomic management enhance the prospects of capturing the economic benefits of a favourable age structure. By contrast, undue tampering with competitive forces in labour and capital markets and the failure to provide public goods diminish a country's prospects of benefiting from demographic change.

---

[2] The total fertility rate (TFR—the number of children an average woman would bear during her reproductive years assuming she conforms to the age-specific fertility rates prevalent in a particular year) fell from 6.1 children per woman in the early 1950s to 2.8 in 2010.

In addition, public policy and investment can catalyse or accelerate the demographic transition itself. Investments in general health (for example, childhood immunization programmes and the provision of safe water and sanitation), education (especially for girls), and reproductive health (for example, family planning) are all key.

Heterogeneity within a country may suggest the need to customize policy interventions to local circumstances. For example, based on 2001 data (the most recent state-level data available), life expectancy differences across Indian states were as wide as that currently between Hungary and Senegal, and fertility differences were comparable to that currently between Japan and Kenya. Although some policies (for example, in the areas of macroeconomic management and international trade) are inherently the domain of national decision makers, others, including some aspects of labour policy and decisions that affect fertility and mortality rates, are subject to local influence.

The second section of this chapter examines the demographics of South Asia as a region, with attention to significant aspects of demographic change in particular countries. It also compares demographic indicators in the region with those in several other large developing countries: Brazil, China, and Indonesia. Finally, it looks at the region's economic growth rates and draws connections between these rates and demographic change. The third section examines the size of the potential demographic dividend in the large countries in South Asia and compares this potential to that in countries outside the region. The fourth section expands on the point that the demographic dividend does not arise automatically in response to demographic transition. Rather, policy choices can make a huge difference in whether the potential inherent in demographic change translates into higher rates of economic growth. The fifth section looks at several factors that can get in the way of realization of the demographic dividend, including one (population ageing) that is unlikely to matter as much as is widely thought. The last section concludes by extracting the key messages relevant for South Asia.

DEMOGRAPHICS OF SOUTH ASIA AND CONNECTIONS TO ECONOMIC GROWTH

South Asia and the countries it comprises have been undergoing rapid demographic change during the last few decades.[3] The region saw a rapid fall in IMR (from about 160 per 1,000 live births in the 1950s to about

---

[3] Following the World Bank's definition, this chapter takes South Asia to comprise Afghanistan, Bangladesh, Bhutan, India, the Maldives, Nepal, Pakistan, and Sri Lanka. All demographic data are from United Nations (2009).

60 in 2010. All countries in the region saw significant declines, though Afghanistan's IMR, at about 150, remains much higher than that for the region as a whole. Sri Lanka, even in 1950, had a much lower IMR than any other country in the region, and at 15 it still has the lowest IMR.

In response to falling IMR and other factors, the region's TFR fell from nearly 6 children per woman in the 1960s to about 2.8 in 2010. With the exception of Afghanistan, all countries in the region experienced this decline. Sri Lanka was the first country to begin a rapid decline and in 2010 was just above the long-run replacement level of 2.1 children per woman. The Maldives had the most rapid decline, going from nearly 7 children per woman in 1980 to 2.2 by 2005 and 2 in 2010—one of the fastest in any country in the world.

Since 1950, life expectancy at birth (the average age at death for everyone born in a given year calculated on the assumption that age-specific mortality rates prevailing in that year remain stable over time) increased from under 40 in the early 1950s to 65 in 2010. This indicates that the people of South Asia are much healthier than they were a half-century ago. Only Afghanistan significantly lags behind the other countries in the region; its life expectancy of 45 years was surpassed by the region as a whole in the late 1960s.

The working-age share of the population (which is also reflected in the ratio of working-age to non-working-age population) is a crucial indicator of a region's or a country's potential for reaping a demographic dividend.[4] The mortality and fertility changes discussed so far have combined to create a common pattern in developing countries throughout the world: a falling ratio after World War II, followed by a rise that is still under way. Using the UN's medium-fertility scenario—that is, the scenario the UN considers to be most likely—Figure 2.1 compares South Asia's historical and projected trend in this ratio to that in Brazil, China, and Indonesia (which serve as comparators because they are large, prominent developing countries outside South Asia). The ratio for South Asia is well below that of these comparator countries. It lags behind that of Brazil and Indonesia by nearly 15 years and that of China by about 25 years and will never reach as high a point as the comparator countries are projected to.

---

[4] This chapter follows the most common definition of 'working age', that is, ages 15 to 64 years. The true range of ages at which people work varies by country and over time, as does the share of population of a given age that is working. The results presented herein are not sensitive to a more precise and country-specific definition of the labour force.

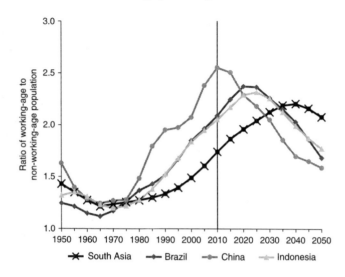

FIGURE 2.1   South Asia's Demographic Change Compared to that of Brazil, China, and Indonesia

Source: United Nations (2009).

(The significance of this pattern is discussed in the latter portion of this section, where the correspondence between demographic patterns and economic patterns will be evident). Very roughly, the countries in the region are all following a somewhat similar pattern. The exceptions are Afghanistan, in which this ratio started increasing only in 2005; Bhutan, where the ratio increased after World War II, before subsequently falling (and then increasing again); and Sri Lanka, where the ratio steadily increased and peaked in 2005. Consistent with its dramatic TFR decline, the Maldives underwent the fastest increase in this ratio.

Because projections in demographic data are based on tracking the ageing of individuals who have already been born to a significant extent, the UN projections regarding the ratio of working-age to non-working age population are reasonably reliable. The UN does create several fertility scenarios (for example, using low-, medium-, and high-fertility assumptions), but obviously the differences in these assumptions do not affect the likelihood of those who are already living being alive and of a particular age at any point in the future. Using the UN's medium-fertility scenario, the ratio for South Asia is expected to peak in 2040. The countries in the region will mostly peak around then, with the exception of Afghanistan, which is projected to still be rising; the Maldives, which

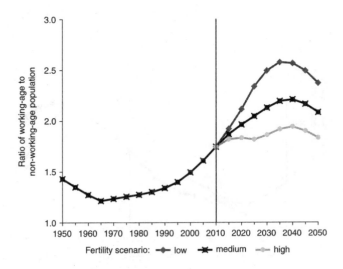

FIGURE 2.2   Ratio of Working-age to Non-working-age Population
Source: United Nations (2009).

will have been high since 2015; and Sri Lanka, which, as noted earlier, has already peaked.

The picture becomes more interesting if the UN's low- and high-fertility scenarios are taken into consideration. Figure 2.2 shows the projected trajectory of the ratio of working-age to non-working-age population under all three UN fertility scenarios. If South Asia follows the low-fertility scenario, the ratio will rise to nearly 2.6 in 2035—the same ratio at which China is currently peaking. If, on the other hand, the region follows the high-fertility scenario, the maximum reached by the ratio will be just over 1.9 in 2040. As will be evident in the discussion later in this chapter, it is likely that this relatively low maximum would impede economic growth in South Asia.

Another aspect of the changing age structure that is potentially economically consequential has to do with the share of the population in the older age group. As fertility rates have fallen and life expectancy has increased, the share and number of the region's elderly have increased, with the share of population aged 60 and older increasing from 5.5 per cent in the 1960s to 7.2 per cent in 2010. UN projections show this figure increasing to nearly 19 per cent (431 million people) by 2050 and the share of those aged 80 and above quadrupling from 0.6 per cent in 2010 to 2.4 per cent (56 million people) by 2050.

It is also interesting to compare demographic change in South Asia to corresponding changes in Brazil, China, and Indonesia. Noteworthy among these comparisons are the following:[5]

1. India's TFR decline began at roughly the same time as Brazil's and China's, but it has been much slower. It is still more than one-half child per woman higher than Brazil's.
2. Declining IMR in India parallels that of Brazil, but the latter has long had about 25 fewer infant deaths per 1,000 live births. Currently, India's IMR is more than twice that of Brazil or China.
3. Changes in life expectancy tell a similar story: India's development parallels Brazil's (especially since about 1980), but the current figure in India (64 years) was reached by Brazil in 1985. Both Brazil and China currently have life expectancies nearly 10 years higher than India's.
4. In the most important summary indicator for assessing progress through the demographic transition the story is the same. The ratio of working-age to non-working-age people in India is the same as it was in Brazil in the late 1990s and China in 1985.
5. Overall, India (and much of South Asia) is far behind Brazil, China, and some other developing countries and even further behind the United States in various aspects of the demographic transition.

The countries in South Asia have proceeded through the demographic transition at varying paces. In particular, fertility decline, a major component of the transition, has occurred throughout the region, but its time of initiation and pace have differed from one country to another. Figures 2.3 and 2.4 show the historical and projected patterns of fertility rates for South Asian countries and the region as a whole. Although the general pattern is the same for most of the countries, Afghanistan, the Maldives, and Sri Lanka stand out for their differences. Each of them offers a potentially instructive situation. Afghanistan, as noted, is by far the least advanced in its demographic transition. With a current TFR of 6.4 (down from 8 in 1995), and still-high IMR, it has barely begun the transition that is well along in the rest of South Asia. Because of

[5] Because India's overall demographic data are similar to those of South Asia as a whole, and because its passage through the demographic transition places it between Bangladesh and Pakistan, the other two large countries in the region, comparisons made with India apply to much of South Asia. Overall, Bangladesh is somewhat ahead of India in the demographic transition and Pakistan well behind.

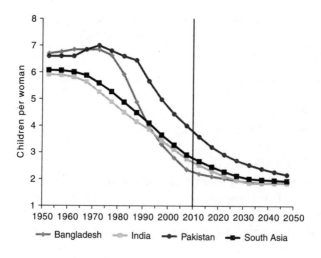

FIGURE 2.3   Varying Rates of Fertility Decline across South Asia's
Large Countries

Source: United Nations (2009).

Afghanistan, the spread in TFR across the region, from the highest to
the lowest, has increased since 1950. In the Maldives, as noted, TFR fell
precipitously, beginning in the early 1990s. By 2000, its working-age to
non-working-age ratio had started increasing with corresponding rapidity,
and it now has the highest ratio in the region. Sri Lanka, with its very
rapid fertility decline, has had a steady increase in its ratio of working-age
to non-working-age population, reaching a peak (2.2), as noted, in 2005.
In 1990, its ratio was 1.67, a figure that South Asia reached only a few
years ago. South Asia will not reach Sri Lanka's 2005 ratio until 2035.
For each of these countries, we could potentially examine the connections
between demographic change and economic growth. In practice, however,
a combination of either a dearth of reliable economic data, rapid swings
in economic growth rates, or severe, longstanding conflicts renders such
an analysis not as useful as it is for other countries.

Not only are there large differences in demographic patterns across
countries; within countries too there are similar differences. India is a
good example. In 2001, the working-age to non-working-age ratio in
Tamil Nadu was 2.1, as compared to 1.2 in Bihar. TFR varied across the
Indian states by a factor of more than 3. Life expectancy in Kerala stood
at 73 years, while in Madhya Pradesh it was 59. These large differences
in different Indian states' passage through the demographic transition are

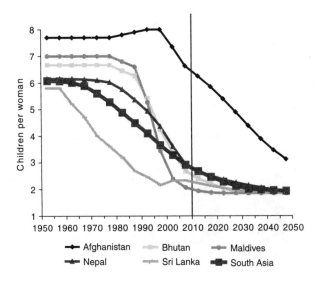

FIGURE 2.4   Variations in Fertility Decline across the Region's
Small Countries

Source: United Nations (2009).

one factor that can help account for the widely varied levels of economic development seen across India. Unfortunately, the least economically developed states of India, which are the ones that will see the largest increase in their working-age population, are the ones least prepared to take advantage of the demographic change that they will undergo. This observation parallels the one in *The Poor Half Billion in South Asia* (Ghani 2010a) that a complex set of conditions contributes to the continuation of patterns that have led to some parts of South Asia chronically lagging behind others in economic development.

Turning now to economic growth: South Asia has experienced a varying, but generally increasing, annual average growth rate in per capita gross domestic product (GDP), beginning at 1.9 per cent in 1960–70, falling to 0.6 per cent in the next decade, rising to 3.2 per cent for each of the next two decades, and climbing to 5.3 per cent since 2000. However, beginning in the 1970s, these rates are well below the corresponding figures for China (see Figure 2.5).

Figure 2. 6 shows how South Asia's relatively slow rate of economic growth has resulted in its GDP per capita falling progressively behind that of Brazil, China, and Indonesia.

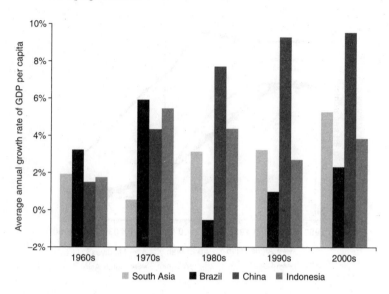

FIGURE 2.5   South Asia's Rising Economic Growth Rate Lagging behind China's

Source: World Bank (2010).

Notes: 1. This figure is based on exchange-rate GDP data, which are available for earlier years than are PPP GDP data. However, the comparisons look the same for PPP data. 2. Figure for '2000s' is from 2000 through 2008.

Figure 2.7 shows a similar pattern when GDP per capita data are based on purchasing power parity (PPP).

The countries in the region have followed a somewhat more varied pattern, with Bangladesh and India matching the regional pattern most closely. Sri Lanka avoided the 1970s South Asian dip in economic growth rate, but now lags behind the region as a whole, with a rate of 4 per cent since 2000. Pakistan grew faster than the region through1985, but has since seen slow growth (averaging 2.4 per cent since 2000). Nepal has languished during the entire period since 1960. Historical data for Afghanistan, Bhutan, and the Maldives are spotty, but the latter two economies have done reasonably well since 2000 (with per capita income growth rates of 6.1 and 5.4 per cent, respectively).

The correspondence between increasing GDP per capita and the increasing ratio of working-age to non-working-age people is striking. In the case of China in particular, the increase in GDP per capita closely mirrors the increase in this ratio. For South Asia too the general rising

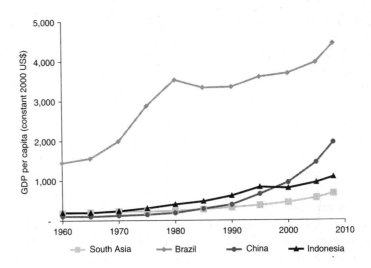

FIGURE 2.6   **Relatively Slow Growth of GDP per Capita in South Asia**

Source: World Bank (2010).

Note: This figure is based on exchange-rate GDP data, which are available for earlier years than are PPP GDP data.

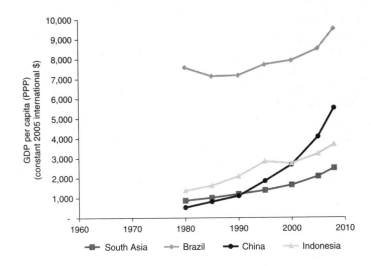

FIGURE 2.7   **Relatively Slow GDP per Capita (PPP) Growth in South Asia**

Source: World Bank (2010).

Note: This figure is based on PPP-adjusted GDP data, which are available from the World Bank database starting only in 1980.

pattern of economic growth in the region since the 1960s corresponds, albeit roughly, to the increasing ratio of working-age to non-working-age people. If the correspondence between demographic opportunity and economic realization of that opportunity continues to hold, the projected increase in the ratio of working-age to non-working-age individuals suggests that South Asia will have a bright economic future.

Indeed, South Asia is projected to add an average of 18 million people to its working-age population every year for the next two decades—and the result will be a very high ratio of working-age to non-working-age individuals, which will peak in 2040 at 2.2:1. As discussed, this ratio augurs well for future economic growth. In addition, smaller families may cause female labour force participation rates to rise from their currently low levels. A Goldman Sachs report (2010) observes that the size of India's labour force would grow by 110 million by 2020 if women's labour force participation by then increases to 38 per cent. All this growth in the size of the labour force can impel economic growth if working-age people are productively employed.

However, existing skill levels (for example, in India) are thought to be far from adequate for what future economies will require. Thus the availability of appropriately skilled people may not be sufficient to impel economic growth. If governments are to capitalize on the high share of working-age people in the population, they will have to ensure that those people are healthy, well educated, and well trained in the skills demanded by the labour market. Pursuing such an agenda fits very well with what many governments seek to do, even in the absence of a potential demographic dividend. However, the dividend, which is a time-bound opportunity, may give policymakers incentive to redouble their efforts to promote the skills of the working-age cohort so that it has the ability to contribute productively to the economy.

SIZE OF POTENTIAL DEMOGRAPHIC DIVIDEND

A country has the opportunity to reap a demographic dividend when the ratio of its working-age to non-working-age population increases appreciably. In East Asia, very large increases in this ratio took place at the time when economic growth surged in that region. (This correspondence in the case of China can be seen by comparing Figures 2.1 and 2.5). Continuing increases have been accompanied by sustained growth. Estimates suggest that one-third of that region's economic growth during the 'East Asian Miracle' period can be accounted for by the effects of demographic change (Bloom and Williamson 1998). Ireland offers another example, where the 1979 legalization of contraception enabled a precipitous decline in fertility. The result, an increased share of working-age people in the population, was a key element underlying Ireland's subsequent rapid economic growth (Bloom and Canning 2003). However, it is important to emphasize once again that these effects do not come about automatically. A set of enabling policies and circumstances must be in place if a country or region is to receive an economic boost from a change in the age structure of its population.

As noted earlier, South Asia and all the countries it comprises of are now undergoing increases in their working-age to non-working-age ratios. The higher the ratio and the faster the pace of its increase, the greater the demographic impetus for more rapid economic growth.

A detailed examination of demographic trends and projections of South Asia's three largest countries (Bangladesh, India, and Pakistan) conveys a sense of where these countries lie in the demographic transition and of the potential magnitude of the demographic dividend.

Figure 2.8 shows these countries' trends in IMR, including UN projections through 2050. All three have seen substantial declines since 1950, but Bangladesh, which was worst placed at that time, experienced the most rapid decline and its IMR is now below that of India and

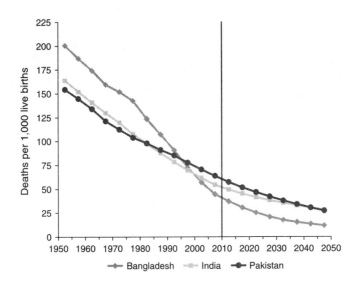

FIGURE 2.8   Declining IMR: India, Bangladesh, and Pakistan

Source: Based on data from United Nations (2009).

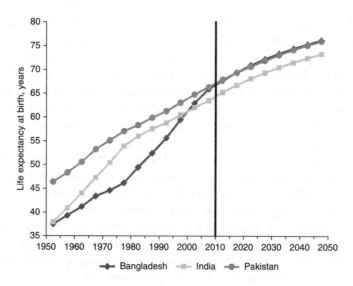

FIGURE 2.9   Steady Rise in Life Expectancy

Source: United Nations (2009).

Pakistan. Declines in IMR and child mortality rate are the first stage of a demographic transition.

A related indicator of declining mortality is rising life expectancy (see Figure 2.9). The increase in life expectancy seen in all three countries reflects increases in survival probabilities at all stages of the life cycle. The most dramatic increase has been in Bangladesh, with an increase of more than 30 years since the middle of the last century. But even in Pakistan, which has seen the slowest increase in South Asia's three largest countries, life expectancy grew rapidly, gaining 20 years during the same period. And Figure 2.9 shows, the UN projects a substantial continuing increase—nearly an additional 10 years before 2050.

In response to falling infant and child mortality, as well as an array of other factors, all three countries have undergone a very substantial decline in TFR (see Figure 2.10). In all three cases, fertility decline began after infant mortality had started falling. The speed of decline was the greatest in Bangladesh, where fertility fell from 6.6 children per woman in the late 1970s to 2.3 in 2010. The UN assumes that fertility will reach replacement level (approximately 2.1 children per woman) by 2020 in Bangladesh and by 2025 in India, and that it is on course to reach that level shortly after 2050 in Pakistan. It is important to note that the UN's

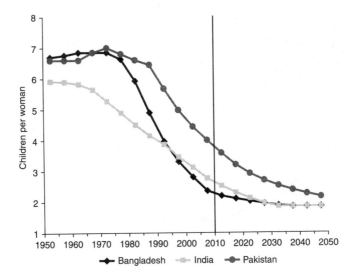

FIGURE 2.10   Falling TFRs: Bangladesh, India, and Pakistan

Source: Based on data from United Nations (2009).

projections of population age structure, discussed later in this chapter, are based in part on its assumptions about future fertility rates.

The lag between the onset of infant mortality decline and subsequent fall in total fertility is important because children born during this period constitute the leading edge of the baby boom. All South Asian countries had started seeing a decline in infant mortality by 1950, but only Sri Lanka, saw a nearly immediate substantial fall in fertility. The other countries experienced various delays. India was next, but most countries saw steep declines only in the 1980s or 1990s (and Afghanistan only in the 2000s).

In Bangladesh, India, and Pakistan, the first relatively large cohorts of young people (the baby boomers) have reached working age. Figure 2.11 shows the trend to date and UN projections for the ratio of working-age (15–64) people to non-working-age (below 15 and 65+) people, usually referred to as dependents. In 1980, this ratio was so low in Bangladesh and Pakistan that there were barely more working-age people than dependents. The ratio has increased rapidly in all the three countries, particularly in Bangladesh, where there are now almost 1.9 working-age people for each dependent. Pakistan's increase has been the slowest, but even there the ratio has nearly reached 1.5.

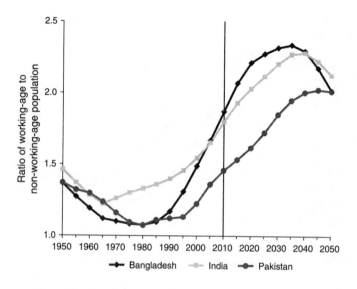

FIGURE 2.11   **Large Changes in Working-age to Non-working-age Ratio**
Source: United Nations (2009).

Generally speaking, the countries in South Asia have yet to enjoy a demographic dividend. In some cases (especially Afghanistan, Nepal, and Pakistan), there has not yet been a major increase in working-age share, so no dividend is possible. In other cases (Bangladesh and India), the demographic dividend has not been enjoyed to an appreciable extent, perhaps because it has been choked off by a non-enabling policy environment. Sri Lanka, which has seen major growth in its working-age share and had relatively open economic policies during some portion of the previous half century, did receive a modest dividend.

Looking ahead, the UN's demographic projections are more favourable for potentiating a demographic dividend. With the exception of Sri Lanka, all the countries in South Asia will experience a significantly faster increase in their working-age share between 2005 and 2050 than they did between 1960 and 2005. Assuming a favourable set of economic policies in the coming years, they stand to reap a demographic dividend—an increase in GDP per capita—of roughly one percentage point per year, compounded annually during the coming decades. This calculation is based on data from United Nations (2009) and a cross-country regression analysis of the contribution of demographic change to economic growth that takes into account an array of variables including economic openness and the growth rate of the working-age share of the population.

GENERATING, EXPANDING, AND CAPTURING THE DIVIDEND

The economic benefits of the demographic transition do not arise automatically. They require policies—and circumstances—that take advantage of the transition and bring about a demographic dividend. The circumstances—often involving political, economic, and military relations with other countries and in some cases international organizations—can sometimes be beyond the control of an individual country. But a country's policies are at least in principle more subject to in-country decision making.

The policies needed to bring about or strengthen a demographic dividend depend on a country's progress through the demographic transition. For example, if a country has only started experiencing a decline in infant mortality, policy will need to focus on facilitating faster mortality decline by, say, strengthening prenatal and neonatal care and providing sanitation and clean drinking water. In Afghanistan, for example, even though IMR has fallen, it is still very high (about 150 per 1,000 live births)—about the same level as India's in the late 1950s.

In some countries, fertility has been falling, but accelerating the pace of decline would help speed the demographic transition and potentially catalyse the emergence of a demographic dividend. In Afghanistan, again, TFR is still very high at about 6.5 children per woman. In Pakistan, TFR started falling rapidly in the 1990s but was still, in 2010, at 3.8 children per woman, the second highest in the region. Within-country variation is also substantial. For example, numerous Indian states have seen very substantial fertility decline, while others have not. Some are now experimenting with payments to encourage couples to delay childbearing (Yardley 2010). More broadly, family planning programmes, for example in Bangladesh, have had a significant effect on the pace of fertility decline. Countries that choose to speed this decline may be able to learn from successful efforts elsewhere. The expansion of basic and secondary education, especially for girls, also tends to speed the fertility transition.

Sri Lanka and the Maldives both lie at the opposite end of the mortality and fertility spectrum: both have relatively low IMRs and TFRs.

In general, the countries in the region are seeing substantially lower fertility and mortality rates, and the ratio of working-age people to dependents is increasing. Thus they are at a point in their demographic transition where a focus on the policy environment will maximize the chances of capturing a demographic dividend. Factors and policies that may help bring about, or increase the size of, the demographic dividend include:

1. *Quality of governmental institutions.* The efficiency and effectiveness of governmental institutions has a large effect on the ability of a government to carry out programmes of every type. If a government is to design and implement policies that facilitate the absorption of labour into productive employment, it will need to have programmes, policies, and well-trained people in place to reach this objective. Corruption, which has afflicted a large number of governments around the world, can greatly impede government performance. Governments that ensure respect for property rights, the sanctity of contracts, and the rule of law are more likely to be able to construct an economic environment that will facilitate the realization of the demographic dividend. If a government is ineffective, it may not be able to bring about stronger economic growth by building on the opportunities inherent in the demographic transition.

2. *Labour legislation.* A key task of a government is to take actions that help create an environment in which people are productively employed. With a historically large share of the population being of working age, this task becomes particularly important. A large unemployed or underemployed segment of the population will be a liability economically and in other ways. The 'low road' for achieving high employment, characterized by a focus on expanding low-wage jobs, has led to continued poverty in many countries. A 'high road' approach, characterized by seeking to build up types of employment (in services, industry, or agriculture) that reward workers' skills with higher wages, is attractive but has proven difficult for many countries. Although there is no single path that works for all countries, some agreement about the relative power and role of labour in strengthening the economy is useful. Some countries have struggled with the power of unions in a few industries or in government employment and with the effects of enforcing high minimum wage laws. Such concerns and related arguments apply directly to only the small portion of the labour force that works in the formal sector. Nevertheless, worker organization and wages in the formal sector may have some effect

on the labour market in the informal sector, so the possible force of these arguments cannot be entirely discounted.

3. *Macroeconomic management.* A country that has persistently high inflation will find it difficult to grow rapidly. The uncertainty of the value of future cash flows tends to dampen savings and thus hinder investment in new productive assets. Similarly, a country that has taken on a large amount of debt relative to its GDP may find itself saddled with high interest payments that sap the government's ability to carry out effective programmes. In addition, government borrowing to make interest payments can cause interest rates to rise. A stable macroeconomic environment is in general a necessary part of the environment in which a demographic dividend can be realized.

4. *Trade policy.* Trade policy can have a substantial effect on a country's ability to capture a demographic dividend. Historical evidence suggests that neither autarky nor a fully open economy is the most likely route to achieving sustained economic growth—and that country-specific circumstances are an essential guide to policymaking in this area. In general, however, a country with a large working-age cohort can increase employment by encouraging export industries (though this need not be done at the cost of the local market). A point to note is that not all countries can be net exporters at the same time.

The import side of this issue is more complicated. Trade liberalization was hailed by many (academic researchers and international financial institutions), especially during the ascendance of the Washington Consensus, as a *sine qua non* for rapid economic growth. Unfettered imports, it was pointed out, can stimulate local development by spurring local producers to produce more efficiently, resulting in lower prices for consumers and potentially creating export industries. In practice, the importation of capital goods in particular has proved beneficial, especially when such imports are accompanied by technology transfer that results in more efficient production.

But a wide range of experiences has led to considerable doubt about the value of across-the-board liberalization. In particular, it appears that countries risk considerable damage to their economies and to the livelihoods (and employment prospects) of large numbers of their residents if they open their markets to widespread importation of consumer goods, many of which, ironically, are subsidized in their country of origin. The argument about protection of 'infant industries' is not yet settled.

Although some research has found that having few restrictions on trade is an important factor in bringing about a demographic dividend, other research has cast doubts on the importance of 'free' trade in bringing about economic growth, independent of questions related to the demographic transition. Both developed and developing countries that have experienced significant periods of rapid economic growth have done so while maintaining careful and extensive controls on imports.

5. *Education policy.* A burgeoning supply of working-age people can be employed in a wide range of activities. The economic value of those activities depends to a significant extent on the education and training of the workforce. When countries were primarily agricultural, and especially when agriculture depended primarily on unskilled manual labour, it was possible to suggest that education was not a major factor affecting a country's productivity. As countries have mechanized agriculture and as industry and services have come to have considerably larger roles in most economies, the need for an educated workforce has grown. As high value-added industries come increasingly to the fore (for example, information and communications companies in India), the demand for educated workers will grow. But even in a wide range of services and industries that do not rely on cutting-edge technologies, having well-educated workers who are easy to train for ever-evolving positions is important for countries seeking to benefit from the demographic transition.

POTENTIAL PITFALLS

Although demographic transition can lead to a demographic dividend, it can also bring significant challenges with it. Among these are those related to population ageing, economic inequality, and a failure to take measures to ensure that the population is productively employed.

The ageing of a country's population is an inevitable consequence of the post-demographic transition period. With lower fertility, new generations eventually come to be smaller than previous ones. At the other end of the life cycle, increased life expectancy (an indicator of better health across all ages) is in part reflected in large numbers of people living to older ages than in the past. Although population ageing is most associated with Japan and Europe, it will eventually affect many other countries, including those in South Asia.

Figure 2.12 shows UN projections for the size and share of the elderly population in India. The 60+ population has already grown significantly, but it is set to accelerate in the near future, reaching nearly

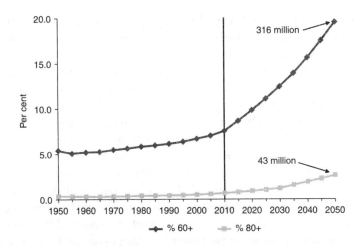

FIGURE 2.12   **Projections of Rapid Rise in India's Elderly Population**
Source: Based on data from United Nations (2009).

20 per cent of the population in 2050. The 80+ population is projected to reach 43 million people by 2050. For South Asia as a whole, the 60+ population is projected to reach 431 million in 2050 (19 per cent of the total population); the corresponding figures for the 80+ South Asian population in 2050 are 56 million and 2 per cent.

The rapid rise in the share of the elderly population has led many to wonder whether the burden imposed by a growing dependent group will inhibit the capture of the demographic dividend. This question arises in the broader context of concerns that population aging might slow economic growth. The concerns stem from several considerations. First, simply, older people tend to have considerably lower labour force participation and savings rates than prime working-age individuals. They very often depend on savings, government transfers, and family support. In these respects, they may be a collective drag on economic output and economic growth. In addition, the elderly need care and companionship, which take the form of financial and human resources that could otherwise go toward producing goods and services for the broader economy. These considerations and fears have led to considerable anxiety over the future of developed and developing economies alike. Among the various public policy questions raised have been the issues of retirement age and pensions. Although these points are relevant to South Asia, they have not risen very high on the policy agenda, perhaps because other economic considerations are so pressing. However, the ageing of the region's population will no doubt bring these issues into greater prominence.

Notwithstanding the reasons for concern about the economic consequences of population ageing, new research on this topic in relation to developing countries suggests that there is little reason for major worry. Bloom et al. (2010) find that in developing countries the effects of a higher old-age dependency ratio will be more than counteracted by a lower youth dependency ratio. In particular, the size of the labour force as a share of the total population is actually projected to rise, on a global basis, from 47 per cent in 2005 to 49 per cent in 2050. Table 2.1 shows that this ratio is projected to increase for all South Asian countries except Sri Lanka. This increase will be further augmented by greater participation of women in the labour force due to smaller family sizes. The effect of this rise will be that economies will be more, not less, able to produce the goods and services needed.

There are other reasons to think that population aging will not have the dramatic negative effects on economies that some have predicted. First, with improving health and longevity, more of the elderly are able to work well past traditional retirement ages. Even in South Asia, where most of the workforce is engaged in the informal sector, people are likely to work until later than in the past. This trend is abetted by a worldwide 'compression of morbidity', in which the portion of people's lives in which they are physically or mentally unable to work comes later and is shorter than in the past. Second, increased life expectancy will tend to lead towards greater savings for workers who anticipate

TABLE 2.1   Projected Rise in the Size of the Labour Force as a Share of Total Population (per cent)

	2005	2050
Afghanistan	34	43
Bangladesh	46	53
Bhutan	43	52
India	39	47
Maldives	40	50
Nepal	39	48
Pakistan	36	45
Sri Lanka	42	40

Source: Calculations by Bloom et al. (2010), based on United Nations (2009) and International Labour Organization Bureau of Statistics (2007).

a longer period of life after they stop working. Increased savings are normally channelled into increased investments, which has a positive effect on economic growth. Third, concern about a dearth of workers to replace large cohorts of retiring older workers may be allayed by the fact that most developing countries, including those in South Asia, have a large population of underemployed and effectively unemployed people who would like to have work. These people, currently living in both urban and rural areas, can be drawn into the labour market should shortages loom.[6] Fourth, part and parcel of population aging is a decrease in the share of children in the population. In particular, with fewer children on average in each family, both governments and families can afford to invest more in the health and education of each child. This investment can translate into a more productive workforce. Finally, business can play a role in responding to aging workforces by making changes that encourage older workers to remain in the labour force and that limit the fall in productivity that tends to come with an older workforce.

Inequality is another obstacle that potentially stands in the way of realizing the demographic dividend. None of the countries in South Asia are entirely homogeneous entities. Each contains numerous sources of powerful heterogeneity in such dimensions as language, religion, caste, income, and education. Sometimes heterogeneity can be a source of constructive synergy. At others, it can be the cause of social and political unrest and instability. Insofar as demographic cycles induce economic cycles by the arguments made earlier, the extraordinary degree of demographic heterogeneity within most South Asian countries suggests economic trajectories that are widely different. Policymakers must customize policies to local realities to address the possibility that geographic differences in economic growth rates could exacerbate internal inequality and political frictions and undermine realization of the demographic dividend.

Finally, it is important to consider the consequences of inaction. That is, what will happen if countries do nothing in response to demographic change? The most likely major effect will be that a large number of young, working-age people will be unemployed or underemployed. This is of course already the case in many countries, but this situation could easily become much worse than it is now. Large numbers of unemployed workers (of any age, but perhaps especially of relatively

---

[6] The case of China is considered in Banister et al. (2010).

young working-age people) can lead to increased internal conflict. In addition, unemployed young people will effectively increase the share of the population that is dependent on workers, slowing economic growth. And finally, the economic insecurity of the elderly can increase, because there will be fewer productively employed workers to generate the wealth on which both governments and families rely to support the elderly.

CONCLUSION

Demographic transition leads to the possibility of countries capturing a demographic dividend of substantial size. As the ratio of working-age people to dependents is currently increasing in South Asia, now is the time when the dividend is on offer.

It is important to focus on the fact that the demographic dividend does not automatically arise when demographic transition takes place. What countries do matters; the policies chosen can have a large effect on the outcome. Among the points to consider are the following:

1. The countries in South Asia stand at different points in the demographic transition. Some would benefit economically by speeding the decline in fertility. Failure to continue (or in some instances accelerate) fertility decline will result in a reduced or delayed demographic dividend.

2. A high share of working-age people is beneficial only if those people are employed. If they are unemployed, the outcome will likely be problematic. Labour market policies must encourage employment, but there are choices to be made about how this is to be accomplished.

3. Investment in access to healthcare and education and quality improvement in these areas is crucial for ensuring that working-age people are prepared for the demands of the economy. Advances in these areas are of course important independent of demographic change; the potential for reaping a demographic dividend is an extra spur for policymakers.

4. Sound macroeconomic management is key. An economy that has persistently high inflation is unlikely to be able to take the best possible advantage of a large segment of working-age people.

5. Contrary to longstanding development theory, new evidence, including that pertaining directly to South Asia, suggests that services, rather than manufacturing, are particularly effective in leading to sustainable growth (Ghani 2010b). This finding has implications for

the type of education that should be offered to students and young adults entering the workforce.

6. Trade policy matters. Many countries have benefited by expanding their exports, and a large working-age population can benefit by having a country's products succeed in the external market. Nevertheless, imports, unless carefully handled, have the potential to wreak havoc with the lives of millions of workers and their families.

7. Government institutions face a wide array of challenges. If governments are not up to the tasks they face—of providing infrastructure and other public goods and a legitimate and efficient policy environment, and addressing income and social inequality—a potential demographic dividend may be squandered.

8. Relations with other countries and with international financial organizations matter and can be important in potentiating economic growth.

The bottomline is that the economies of the countries in South Asia have been improving, and to some extent this change has been impelled by an increasing share of working-age people in the population. But full realization of the demographic dividend depends on the policies that countries choose and on their political, economic, and military relations with each other and with the rest of the world.

REFERENCES

Banister, Judith, David E. Bloom, and Larry Rosenberg. 2010. 'Population Aging and Economic Growth in China', Harvard Program on the Global Demography of Aging, Working Paper No. 53.2010. Available at http://www.hsph.harvard.edu/pgda/Working Papers/2010/PGDAvWPv53.pdf, accessed on 1 February 2011.

Bloom, David E. and David Canning. 2003. 'Contraception and the Celtic Tiger', *The Economic and Social Review*, 34 (3): 229–47.

———. 2010. 'The Graying of Global Population and Its Macroeconomic Consequences', *Twenty First Century: Journal of the Academy of Social Sciences*, 5 (3): 233–42.

Bloom, David E. and Jeffery G. Williamson. 1998. 'Demographic Transition and Economic Miracles in Emerging Asia', *World Bank Economic Review*, 12 (3): 419–55.

Ghani, Ejaz (ed.). 2010a. *The Poor Half Billion in South Asia: What Is Holding Back Lagging Regions?* New Delhi: Oxford University Press.

———. 2010b. *The Service Revolution in South Asia*. New Delhi: Oxford University Press.

Goldman Sachs. 2010. 'Global Economics Paper 201', 28 July, cited in *The Economist*, 5 August.

International Labour Organization Bureau of Statistics. 2007. ILO Database on Labour Statistics, International Labour Organization. Available at http://laborsta.ilo.org/

United Nations. 2009. *World Population Prospects: The 2008 Revision*. New York: Population Division of the United Nations Department of Economic and Social Affairs.

World Bank. 2010. *World Development Indicators*. Washington, DC: World Bank.

Yardley, Jim. 2010. 'India Tries Using Cash Bonuses to Slow Birthrates', *The New York Times*, 21 August.

3

The Rise of the Middle Class

Homi Kharas

South Asia has long been known as a region of poverty with a smattering of billionaires. According to the World Bank, more than a billion South Asians live on less than $2 per day. At the same time, there are reputed to be 69 dollar billionaires in India and a further seven in Pakistan.[1] That could change in the next 15 years. By 2025, when the total population approximates 2 billion, South Asia could be a predominantly middle class region.

This change is already under way. South Asia's[2] middle class has grown from about 24 million people in 2000 to 72 million today—a growth rate of 12 per cent annually. But it started as such a tiny fraction of the population that the change is barely noticeable. As a share of the total regional population of 1.6 billion, the middle class has expanded from 1.7 per cent to 4.5 per cent. South Asians have an even smaller share (3.8 per cent) of the global middle class of 1.9 billion consumers.

But the ranks of the South Asian middle class could be about to swell rapidly if rapid economic growth in India, in particular, is sustained. That, coupled with a large bulge of population that is emerging out of absolute poverty and is poised to enter the middle class, would create new dynamics in the region. Within 15 years, by 2025, South Asia could be a predominantly middle class region with 55 per cent of the

---

[1] See the Forbes 2010 list of global billionaires. Available at http://www.forbes. com/2010/03/10/worlds-richest-people-slim-gates-buffett-billionaires-2010land.html.

[2] For the purposes of this chapter, South Asia refers only to the relatively populous countries of Bangladesh, India, Nepal, Pakistan, and Sri Lanka.

population—or a billion people—in this category. This change would be almost entirely due to India, the largest and most rapidly growing country in the region. In fact, because its population growth is faster than that of China, India's middle class could be the largest in the world (in terms of numbers of people) by 2025.

India's rapid growth, coupled with urbanization, favourable demographic trends that will increase the proportion of the workforce in the total population, and relatively equal income distribution that should distribute the benefits of growth among a broad number, are setting the stage for a potentially massive expansion of the middle class. While many of the same trends are operating in other South Asian economies, their growth performance, given the current policy framework, is unlikely to match that of India.

The evolution of the Indian middle class is exciting because for the past decade it is private consumption, fuelled by the middle class, that has driven Indian growth. Private consumption in India is almost 60 per cent of the gross domestic product (GDP); it reached $750 billion in 2009, and private consumption growth has accounted for 70 per cent of Indian growth since 2000. Even though China's middle class is larger than India's and China's growth higher, private consumption accounts for a smaller fraction of growth. To put it in perspective, Indian total household final consumption expenditure is already higher than Russia's and close to that of Brazil. It is not an exaggeration to say that Indian growth will depend on the middle class and the evolution of the middle class will depend on Indian growth.

This chapter discusses the co-evolution of growth and the middle class in South Asia. The middle class is an ambiguous social classification, broadly reflecting the ability to lead a comfortable life. It usually enjoys stable housing, healthcare, and educational opportunities (including college) for its children, reasonable retirement and job security, and discretionary income that can be spent on vacations and leisure pursuits.

While recognizing this multidimensional nature of the middle class, I use an economic definition (in terms of the per capita expenditure of middle class households) in order to quantify the size of the middle class. This is not to suggest that expenditure is all that matters. Indeed, in real life, the non-economic attributes of the middle class are likely to be as important to growth dynamics as the economic attributes.

By 2025, India could be unrecognizable. The growth of the middle class is likely to be associated with a shift from large-scale informality that characterizes much of the services and manufacturing sectors today, to more formal, wage-earning, medium-scale businesses. Cities too will grow as job opportunities cluster there. The spread of growth across the population will be broader if there is sufficient migration between states and from rural to urban areas. The government is unlikely to be able to provide the quantity and quality of services that will be demanded, even in areas like health, education, and water that have evolved as public sector areas in other countries. India will have to adopt hybrid systems with private and public service providers.

But these changes are all in the realm of the possible, of the potential for change, not a forecast of what will happen in South Asia, or even what is likely. The transformations that are required are formidable and unprecedented. But they are not beyond imagination. If India, and other parts of South Asia, can replicate the experiences of Japan, the Republic of Korea, and China, then sweeping changes, such as those described later in this chapter, are possible. But there are more cases, historically, of countries like Brazil and Mexico that failed to sustain growth once they reached middle income levels.

The next section provides a definition of the middle class that can be used in a global comparative way. The section that follows measures the size of South Asia's middle class using this definition and shows how growth can swell the ranks of the middle class, while the final section discusses the reverse causality—how a growing middle class can help sustain growth.

DEFINING THE MIDDLE CLASS

The middle class is an ambiguous social category. Many diverse and overlapping groups belong to it. They share some common attributes. Being in the middle class implies having a comfortable standard of living, economic security, and self-reliance. The middle classes come from a range of occupations: government officials, college graduates, rich farmers, traders, business people, and professionals. They are in various management and clerical jobs. Many are self-employed in small businesses, crafts, and on commercialized family farms.

Because of the emphasis on 'comfortable living', the middle class can be defined in relative terms, meaning comfortable compared to others in the country, or in absolute terms, meaning comfortable compared to others regardless of where they live in the world. Easterly (2000) and Birdsall et al. (2000) take a relativist approach, defining the middle class as those between the 20th and 80th percentiles of consumption distribution and between 0.75 and 1.25 times median per capita income, respectively. In more recent work, Birdsall takes a mixed approach, defining the middle class as those between an absolute global threshold of $10 per day and a relative, local threshold of the 95th percentile of income or consumption (Birdsall 2010).

Bhalla (2002, 2007) takes an absolute approach, defining the middle class as those with annual incomes over $3,900 in purchasing power parity (PPP) terms. Banerjee and Duflo (2007) use two alternative absolute measures—those with daily per capita expenditures between $2 and $4 and those with daily per capita expenditures between $6 and $10. Milanovic and Yitzhaki (2001) implicitly use an absolute approach by discussing the distribution of income among world citizens. Ravallion (2009) takes a hybrid approach, defining a 'developing world middle class' as having one range of incomes (between the median poverty line of countries in the developing world and that of the US) and a 'Western world middle class' as having another range (above the US poverty line). The World Bank (2007) also uses an absolute definition, arbitrarily defining the middle class as those with incomes falling between the mean level in Brazil and Italy, or $4,000 and $17,000 in 2000 PPP terms.

Following my earlier work (Kharas 2010), I take an absolute approach in this chapter, choosing to lay down a global middle class standard. The idea is that everyone meeting this standard will have the same purchasing power regardless of where they live. I define the global middle class as those households with daily expenditures between $10 and $100 per person in PPP terms. The lower bound is chosen with reference to the average poverty line in Portugal and Italy, the two advanced European countries with the strictest definition of poverty. The poverty line for a family of four in these countries is $14,533 ($9.95 per day per capita in 2005 PPP terms). The upper bound is chosen as twice the median income of Luxemburg, the richest advanced country. Defined in this way, the global middle class includes those who are not considered poor in the poorest advanced countries and those who are not considered rich in the richest advanced country. The lower threshold also has some historical support.[3]

My definition is in line with many others, at least at the low threshold level that is the more important one for computing the size of the

---

[3] For reference, clerks in Victorian England in the middle of the 19th century had starting salaries of around 100 pounds per year, or about $11,800 in PPP equivalent terms today. Many historians believe these clerks formed the core of the 'great Victorian middle class'.

emerging middle class in developing countries. Not many people cross the upper threshold to the 'rich' category over, say, a 15-year time period, so the figures are not very sensitive to the choice of the upper threshold. For comparison, the National Council of Applied Economic Research (NCAER) in India defines the Indian middle class as households with a disposable income of Rs 200,000 to 1 million per year in 2000, or $14,675 to $73,370 in PPP terms. Of course, Indian households are somewhat larger than equivalent Western households with an average size of 4.8 family members, implying that the NCAER's lower threshold approximates $8.40 per day per person in PPP terms (Shukla et al. 2004).

To some extent, the choice of the threshold values that define the middle class range is rather arbitrary. If a lower value were to be chosen for the lower threshold (as in Banerjee and Duflo 2007 and Ravallion 2009), the current size of the South Asian middle class would be higher. Regardless, the trend towards a rapid expansion of the middle class if growth is sustained at current levels would be the same.

This is an important point because the estimate of the actual size of the middle class depends both on the choice of threshold values as well as sampling errors in household expenditure surveys, most notably in India, and additional measurement errors in converting these expenditure levels into PPP terms.

The issues with respect to India's National Sample Survey (NSS) are well known. The key fact is that the NSS estimate of aggregate household expenditure is just over half the estimate for household consumption in the national accounts (Ravallion 2003). This is thought, at least in part, to be because of undersampling of rich households in India.

At the same time, there can be considerable measurement errors in the price indices used to convert household survey data in national currencies into international PPP dollars. All absolute approaches to defining the middle class are in PPP terms. Here I use the latest results from the 2005 International Comparison Program (ICP), a joint exercise of the UN-OECD-World Bank-regional development banks. These estimates compare prices for 1,000 goods and services across 146 countries. The exercise has been described as 'the most extensive and thorough effort ever to measure PPPs across economies' (World Bank 2008: 9). But serious questions remain about the significant changes that have resulted from the 2005 measure as compared to previous estimates. In Asia, prices were adjusted upwards by almost 40 per cent on average, with price changes for large Asian economies being severe: China +38.7 per cent,

India +37.2 per cent, Bangladesh +47.3 per cent, Philippines +40.8 per cent, and Vietnam +31 per cent.[4] For developed countries, such as the US (+1.5 per cent), the changes were marginal.

There are many reasons to doubt the results of ICP 2005. In China, for example, prices were only collected from a handful of cities and, according to some reports, only from the most expensive areas within those cities. These prices are unlikely to be representative of China as a whole as most Chinese still live in rural areas where prices are likely to be much lower than in the urban areas from which ICP data were collected. On the other hand, prior to ICP 2005, China had never participated in a survey, and price levels were inferred from other data. The choice between inferred data and direct, if imperfectly measured, data is not easy to make.

One implication of the new series is that historical per capita GDP figures have also been revised down in PPP terms. This leads to implausible results. For example, if one takes the new PPP figures for Chinese GDP per capita in 2005, and works backwards using official Chinese real growth, one arrives at an estimated GDP per capita for China of less than $300 (2005 PPP) in the 1960s. That would mean that at that time China had one-fifth the income level of the average poor country today, or one-third that of Ethiopia or Malawi today. Such figures do not seem credible nor do they correspond with other estimates. For example, Angus Maddison (2009), in his detailed accounting of Chinese growth, estimates China's GDP per capita in 1960 at $660 in 1990 PPP terms, equivalent to $900 in 2005 prices.

The point being made is that globally comparable data are not very accurate. We can probably be more confident of changes over time than in levels of real expenditure when comparing across countries. It is therefore less interesting to place too much emphasis on a precise definition of the middle class range. The focus should be on changes over time of the number of individuals falling into a specific category, even if that has an element of arbitrariness about its boundaries.

SOUTH ASIA'S MIDDLE CLASS: CURRENT ESTIMATES AND TRENDS

Given that the middle class has been defined here in absolute terms, it is possible to estimate its size for each South Asian country if the mean and

---

[4] A positive sign means that prices were raised by the specified amount, also implying that real incomes in PPP terms are reduced by a corresponding amount.

distribution of household expenditures are known. In essence, I try to position each household in South Asia on a global expenditure scale and count the number of households that fall within the defined range.

To get statistics on the mean and distribution, I combine microeconomic household survey data with macro data. Rather than assuming that household surveys give accurate descriptions of the mean level of expenditure, I assume that the surveys capture income distribution, at least in the middle ranges, reasonably well, but systematically under-report expenditure. Some support for this can be found in the case of India where the NCAER consumer survey better approximates the national accounts estimate for aggregate consumption than the NSS survey.

For each of the five large South Asian countries that have household surveys, I obtain the distribution of household income by decile.[5] This is inputted into the World Bank's PovCal software to estimate the distributional parameters of a quadratic Lorenz curve.[6] This in turns allows us to generate a full income distribution describing expenditure levels for every household in the country and that distribution is then kept constant over time to develop a scenario of how the middle class could evolve over time.

Given that all countries have actually witnessed quite significant changes in income inequality recently, it might seem a heroic (and faulty) assumption to hold income distribution constant. Actually, this exercise does not strictly require holding the full income distribution constant but only the share of income of those around the middle class range. This is a weaker and much more realistic assumption. As shown by Palma (2006), actual changes in income distribution in developing countries have been dominated by changes in the top and bottom percentiles rather than in the share accruing to the middle eight deciles. The middle share has remained relatively constant over time.

To estimate the mean of distribution, the World Bank (2007b) uses the mean from household surveys while Sala-i-Martin (2002) uses GDP per capita. I choose to use the national income accounts measure of total

[5] The World Bank household survey data for developing countries are found in the PovCalNet database (http://go.worldbank.org/NT2A1XUWP0); data on advanced countries are found in 'Inequality around the World: Globalization and Income Distribution Dataset'(http://go.worldbank.org/0C52T3CLM0). Both accessed in December 2008.

[6] The PovCal software can be downloaded from http://go.worldbank.org/ YMRH2NT5V0. For a full discussion of the calculations involved, see Datt (1998).

household consumption expenditure in 2005 PPP dollars.[7] This best reflects the concept of purchasing power and the market for consumer goods and services which I have focused on as the key characteristic of the middle class. Mostly, the trends in these variables follow each other closely, so changes over time are not affected too much by the choice of mean. But in some cases, there can be a significant difference. India is one of those cases which has been analysed in detail by Deaton and Dreze (2002), who make adjustments to both household surveys and national accounts data to come up with comparable estimates of poverty changes over time.

Given the mean and distribution parameters, PovCal generates a headcount of those living below any given expenditure threshold. The number in the middle class is defined as the difference between the number of people with expenditures below the $100 per day threshold and of those with expenditures below the $10 per day threshold.

Using this approach, there were an estimated 72 million middle class people in South Asia in 2010. India, with 59.5 million middle class, not surprisingly, had the largest number, but that simply reflects India's large absolute population. Pakistan came next with 7 million. As a share of its total population, the Indian middle class is still less than 5 per cent. The highest incidence in South Asia is in Sri Lanka with the middle class forming 18 per cent of its population (Table 3.1).[8] South Asia's middle class has grown in absolute numbers by 11.6 per cent over the last decade, but it started from a very low base.

Table 3.1 shows that South Asia's middle class is just starting to become noticeable in global terms. Its 72 million people in this category comprise 3.8 per cent of the global middle class. Table 3.1 also shows why the middle class is so important to the American economy—fully three-quarters of all Americans belong to the middle class according to our definition.

These figures actually underestimate the global economic significance of the American middle class because each middle class person does not have the same individual purchasing power. The average US middle class consumer is closer to the top of the range, while the average developing-country middle class consumer is closer to the lower

---

[7] National income accounts data are from the World Bank's *World Development Indicators* (http://go.worldbank.org/U0FSM7AQ40). Accessed in August 2009 and updated to 2010 using the IMF's *World Economic Outlook*, October 2010.

[8] Note that Sri Lanka's middle class population share is larger than China's despite China having a higher per capita GDP. This is because more of Sri Lanka's GDP goes to households for their consumption.

TABLE 3.1   South Asia's Middle Class, 2010

	Number of People (million)	Global Share	Share of Country Population
Bangladesh	1.8	0.1%	1.1%
India	59.5	3.2%	4.9%
Nepal	0.3	0.0%	0.9%
Pakistan	7.1	0.4%	4.1%
Sri Lanka	3.6	0.2%	18.5%
South Asia	72.2	3.8%	4.5%
Memo: China	169.3	9.0%	12.5%
USA	232.0	12.3%	73.7%
World	1,889.1	100%	28.2%

Source: Author's calculations.

threshold. Actually the data suggest that the US accounts for over one-fifth of global spending by the middle class, while India accounts for only 1.8 per cent.

But this situation is fast changing as a consequence of diverging growth rates in South Asia and the developed world. According to the World Bank, South Asia was poised to grow by 6.9 per cent in 2010 and nearly 7.4 per cent in 2011 thanks to strong growth in India, good performance in Bangladesh, a post-conflict bounce in Sri Lanka, and recovery from the floods in Pakistan (World Bank 2010: 3). Medium-term growth scenarios for South Asia show most countries reverting to their pre-crisis growth rates, while India continues to accelerate to a new normal of up to 10 per cent thanks to a strong technological catch-up with advanced economies (Box 3.1).

The methodology described in Box 3.1 can be used to develop growth scenarios for each South Asian country.[9] These should be interpreted as scenarios, not forecasts or projections, based on current policies and trends. They are a look at what the future might hold for each country under one set of assumptions. Table 3.2 shows the outcomes of such an exercise.

The growth scenarios in Table 3.2 are mostly within the range of other commentators. There may well be other outcomes. Sri Lanka could recover strongly now that the war is over. Bangladesh has the potential to do better, especially if China—its main competitor in the global garments industry—moves up the value chain and becomes a more expensive locality for low-tech production. Pakistan has the potential to do better but has been distracted by political and security challenges.

---

[9] For the equations and data sources used to develop the scenario, see Kharas (2010).

Box 3.1   A Growth Scenario Methodology

The basic framework is a constant-returns-to-scale Cobb-Douglas production function with growth dependent on capital accumulation, labour force growth, and technological improvements. Capital accumulation is determined by investment which is assumed to remain at the average rate of the 10 years from 1998 to 2007. Labour force growth is taken from UN population projections of the working-age group of 15–64-year olds.

What remains is the estimation of technological improvements.

Following Goldman Sachs and others, I assume that the rate of technological improvement in each country has two components. First, the global technology frontier is shifting out with new advances in science, new products, and new processes. This is assumed to remain at its long-run historical level in the United States of 1.3 per cent per year. Second, most countries are operating within this global frontier. Some, with a proven policy track record like India, can catch up rapidly. I assume, like others, that the rate at which catch-up occurs is inversely proportional to the gap between the per capita income level of the country and that of the United States which is represented as the global leader in technology. Other countries, including Bangladesh, Nepal, Pakistan, and Sri Lanka, have no proven track record of convergence. I assume no change in policy and so simply assign a zero 'catch-up' rate for these countries. Of course, with a change in policy course, these countries too could become 'convergers', but the base scenario does not assume this will happen.

The modelling framework may appear overly deterministic and devoid of policy content, but several of the variables reflect policy choices. For example, some analysts, like Bhalla (2008) emphasize the role of undervalued exchange rates in promoting rapid growth over long periods of time. In our model, this same outcome is achieved as undervalued exchange rates lower a country's income level relative to that of the United States and induce more rapid technological growth. As another example, openness and other reform measures may show up in higher investment rates as businesses enter new sectors or may be captured by a demonstrated track record of convergence, boosting projected total factor productivity (TFP) growth. Implementation effectiveness, governance, and institutional development are captured by giving higher rates of technical progress to countries with demonstrated high levels of growth which are indicative of their institutional depth.

TABLE 3.2   GDP and Population Growth Assumptions,
2010–25 (per cent)

	GDPpc PPP Growth	Population Growth
Bangladesh	2.30	1.40
India	10.00	1.10
Nepal	2.50	1.80
Pakistan	3.00	1.80
Sri Lanka	1.80	0.30

Source: Author's calculations; United Nations, *World Population Prospects*.

Indeed, these are so severe that it could do even worse than its historical record would suggest.

A great question mark surrounds India. Here the growth scenario is at the top end of the range of most other analysts. The Eleventh Five-Year Plan, developed by the Planning Commission in November 2007 to provide a macroeconomic scenario for 2008–12, envisages growth of 9 per cent. But the Prime Minister has pushed for 10 per cent growth to accelerate reduction in poverty. India's former Chief Economic Adviser in the Ministry of Finance, Dr Arvind Virmani, proposes 9 per cent as the sustainable trend level for the next five years, but notes that the trend level has been rising (Basu 2008). As early as 2001 a McKinsey report on India indicated that a 10 per cent growth rate was achievable, driven by productivity improvements stemming largely from removing distortions in land and product markets (McKinsey Global Institute 2001). The International Monetary Fund (IMF), in a recent review of the Indian growth potential, shows that scholars have systematically been raising their estimates of India's long-run prospects: Rodrik and Subramanian (2004) to 7.3–7.6 per cent, Bosworth and Collins (2006) to 8–8.4 per cent, *World Economic Outlook* (Fall 2006) to 8.7–9 per cent, and Poddar and Yi (2007) to 9.5–9.8 per cent (Oura 2007). Actual Indian economic growth per capita for 2010 is forecast by the IMF at 9.75 per cent (IMF 2010: 23).

There are many reasons for being optimistic about India's growth prospects today.

1. Growth in Asia is strengthening, and India will benefit from neighbourhood effects—the fastest-growing markets in the world will be closer home. Already China is India's largest trading partner.

2. India recovered well, in fact almost unscathed, from the Great Recession, demonstrating the healthy underlying condition of its financial sector.[10]

3. Indian investment levels (foreign and domestic) and manufacturing growth have started to pick up, with record portfolio capital inflows recently.

4. India has turned the corner on public-sector debt—the share of interest in GDP that must be financed from budget resources has fallen since 2002, leaving more fiscal space for infrastructure spending.

5. Indian demographics and urbanization are favourable.

6. India's emerging middle class can drive growth in the same way as in other countries.

7. The shift in values that underpins the political economy of reforms appears to be well under way in India, suggesting that there will be sustained effort to continue along the path of good economic policies and structural reforms that was embarked upon in 1991.

Ultimately these advantages must be translated into real achievements, and India still faces a daunting array of constraints that should not be underestimated. But the potential for more rapid growth seems to be significant.

From a historical perspective, India would not be unique if it achieved this growth. In fact, China saw an increase of 11.3 per cent (in constant US dollars) in its per capita income from 1993 to 2008. The Republic of Korea saw an income growth of 10.7 per cent over 30 years between 1965 and 1995. These are, of course, different countries with different growth strategies and trajectories, but in reality India has tracked China very closely, with a 10-year lag, over the last 15 years (Figure 3.1). Should it continue to do so, the growth scenario depicted in the preceding discussion could come to pass.

With a specified growth scenario and income distribution parameters, it is possible to examine the implications for the evolution of the middle class over time. Table 3.3 shows what could happen in South Asia.

Table 3.3 shows the dramatic expansion in South Asia's middle class, driven by the expansion of the Indian middle class. From 72 million people, South Asia could have over a billion middle class consumers by 2025, representing one-quarter of the global total. South Asia would

---

[10] Warren Buffett is reputed to have quipped: 'You only know who's swimming naked when the tide goes out.' India is clearly well clad.

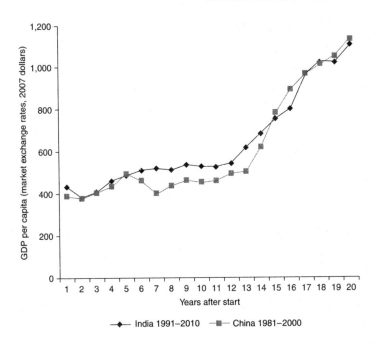

FIGURE 3.1   India and China Growth Trajectories

Source: Author's calculations; World Bank, *World Development Indicators*. Accessed July 2008, International Monetary Fund, *World Economic Outlook Database*, April 2008 Edition.

become a largely middle class region, with India's middle class having the same share of its population, as the United States does today. Sri Lanka too, even with relatively modest growth, would have a big expansion in its middle class, which would amount to 30.3 per cent of its population. But the other South Asian countries would lag behind.

A visual demonstration of why India's middle class could expand so rapidly is provided in Figure 3.2.[11] In this figure, the vertical axis shows the cumulative distribution of the population and the horizontal axis shows per capita GDP. Each point on the line shows the fraction of the population with income levels below the value represented by the horizontal axis. For example, the light grey line in the picture, representing incomes in 2005, shows that about 98 per cent of the population had incomes below $10 per day, while perhaps 35 per cent of the population

[11] Appendix A3.1 has similar figures for the other four major South Asian countries.

TABLE 3.3   South Asia's Middle Class, 2010–25

	Number of People: Global Share (million)				Share of Country Population	
	2010	2025	2010	2025	2010	2025
Bangladesh	1.8	4.9	0.1%	0.1%	1.1%	2.4%
India	59.5	1026.1	3.2%	24.8%	4.9%	70.9%
Nepal	0.3	0.8	0.0%	0.0%	0.9%	2.1%
Pakistan	7.1	28.9	0.4%	0.7%	4.1%	12.8%
Sri Lanka	3.6	6.2	0.2%	0.1%	18.5%	30.3%
South Asia	72.2	1066.9	3.8%	25.8%	4.5%	55.1%
Memo: China	169.3	844.5	9.0%	20.4%	12.5%	58.4%
USA	232.0	198.5	12.3%	4.8%	73.7%	55.9%
World	1,889.1	4,136.4	100%	100%	28.2%	53.4%

Source: Author's calculations.

had incomes below $2.50 per day. As economic growth happens, the lines shift to the right. The black line shows the scenario in 2015. Already, substantially fewer people (83 per cent of the population) have incomes below the $10 per day lower threshold for the middle class, but most

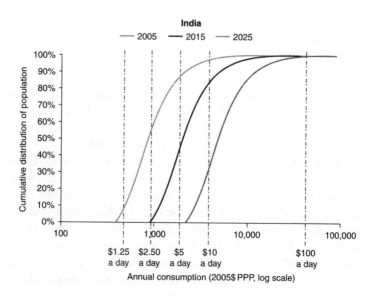

FIGURE 3.2   India's Passage towards Becoming a Middle Class Nation
Source: Author's calculations.

people will have overcome the $2.50 per day threshold. By 2025, the line will have shifted again to the right, and by then less than 30 per cent could have incomes below our middle class threshold of $10 per day.

These are stylized facts. Of course, because of the unevenness of growth, in spatial, ethnic, caste, and other terms, not everyone will share equally in India's growth. The shape of the tail of the distribution could change if some groups become marginalized. But that is unlikely to affect the large improvements in living standards for the bulk of the population that is already above $2.50 per day. Those are the people who will be joining the ranks of the Indian middle class in the next 15 years.

In this baseline scenario, with India and China having large middle class populations, the world would become increasingly middle class. But the United States would have a lower number of middle class people in absolute terms and a rapidly declining share of the global total. This is not because the United States is becoming poorer; quite the opposite, it is because it is becoming richer. The children of today's middle class are more likely to be rich, with higher education levels and large inheritances from their baby boomer parents.

A noteworthy feature is the differential performance of India and its neighbours. Until now South Asian income levels have been approximately the same. Within-country income differentials have far exceeded across-country ones. That could change if the growth scenario shown here comes to pass. A middle class India would stand in sharp contrast to its much poorer brethren to the east and west.

HOW THE MIDDLE CLASS CAN SUSTAIN GROWTH

While it is clear that growth can create a middle class, the reverse is also true, that is, a large middle class can help sustain growth. The middle class has played a special role in economic thought for centuries. Emerging as the bourgeoisie in the late 14th century, while derided by some for its economic materialism, it provided the impetus for expansion of a capitalist market economy and trade between nation states. Ever since, the middle class has been considered a source of entrepreneurship and innovation, setting up the small businesses that make a modern economy thrive.

Banerjee and Duflo (2007) list four specific contributions that the middle class can make to economic growth.

First, they note the links between the middle class and democracy. Researchers have found broad international support for many key features of democracy, such as individual rights and free and fair elections, in poor countries as well as in rich countries. Still, members of the global middle class tend to have a more intense desire for democracy than their fellow citizens, and governments of middle class countries will be more inclined to allow democratic expressions to flourish (Pew Global Attitudes Project 2009). Usually the middle class is disinclined towards radical reforms. A large middle class generates a shift towards the centre and reduces the risk of sudden changes in rules and regulations. This certainty reassures investors.

While intuitively appealing, evidence for the strength of the causal link from democracy to growth is mixed. Barro (1996) found a weak (and slightly negative) impact of democracy on economic growth in a panel regression of 100 countries from 1960 to 1990, but his results are conditional on maintenance of the rule of law, free markets, small government consumption, and high human capital. He does not go further to ask whether these outcomes themselves are associated with democracy or indeed a large middle class. Lehoucq (2008) goes further and explicitly links better growth performance in Costa Rica with democracy and political competition. His conclusion: 'stable democracy unambiguously helps development' at least in Latin America.

Second, Acemoglu and Zilibotti (1997) emphasize the role of the middle class as a source of entrepreneurs. This follows the original tradition of defining the middle class in terms of occupation and differentiating it from the nobility or peasants who characterized the feudal economy. It is often claimed that small businesses and family farms—the heart of the middle class—made America great. But Banerjee and Duflo (2007) find that the average middle class person is not an entrepreneur in waiting. If they do run a business, it is usually small and not very profitable. This finding does not necessarily contradict the commonly held view that entrepreneurs come from the ranks of the middle class. After all, there are many middle class people (at least in successful economies) and much smaller numbers of entrepreneurs. So it can still be the case that most entrepreneurs come from the middle class, even if most of the middle class are not entrepreneurs.

Third, Doepke and Zilibotti (2007) emphasize the contribution of the middle class to human capital and saving. But Kenny (2008) finds evidence of beta convergence in most human capital variables—education, infant mortality, and life expectancy—implying that the lower the starting point the more rapid the rate of accumulation of human capital. This is the opposite of what would be expected if saving rates and the willingness to invest in human capital were higher among middle class households. Similarly, studies on countries like China find that households save a considerable portion of their income even when they are near poor (World Bank 2009). Thus there is nothing special about the middle class in terms of its contribution to human capital. If anything, the evidence points to a slowing down in the rate of human capital formation (albeit from a much higher base) as households enter the middle class.

However, there is clear evidence that values and behaviours do change as families attain middle class status. Already a shift is taking place in India. Various rounds of the World Values Survey provide some information about how Indian society is changing. Perhaps the most interesting questions from the perspective of this chapter are those dealing with the political system, with jobs, and with qualities for the next generation.

In 1995, only 26 per cent of the Indian sample of 1,275 respondents was prepared to say 'no' when asked if democracy was bad for the economy, implying they thought democracy could be good for growth (Table 3.4). Six years later, in 2001, the share had risen to 38 per cent. By 2006, 70 per cent of respondents thought a democratic political system was fairly or very good for governing the country.

In 1995, only 47 per cent of respondents felt that it was important that their jobs be interesting. The vast majority valued pay and security as the only important elements of a job. By 2001, while pay and security remained important, job interest was identified as important by 74 per cent (Table 3.4). The percentage of respondents who felt that the opportunity to use initiative in a job was important rose from 46 to 64 per cent between 1995 and 2001. These data suggest a changing ethos towards work. Where interest levels and initiative are important, it is likely that labour productivity and job satisfaction will also be high. By the time of the 2006 survey, 70 per cent said that work should come first even if it meant less spare time.

The qualities that parents feel that their children will need to get ahead have also changed. On these questions it is possible to compare 1990 with 2001 and 2006: independence (30 per cent to 56 per cent to 67 per cent); hard work (67 per cent to 85 per cent to 82 per cent); thrift and saving (24 per cent to 62 per cent to 56 per cent); and determination and perseverance (28 per cent to 46 per cent to 41per cent). By 2006, 68 per cent of the parents felt that a feeling of responsibility was important for their child to get ahead. In other words, the changing values associated with middle income families are already visible in India.

The fourth hypothesis about what makes the middle class special focuses on consumption. Business houses such as Nomura (2009) argue that there is a kink in consumer demand curves around $6,000 per capita.

TABLE 3.4   Shifting Values as the Indian Middle Class Expands

Values	1990	1995	2001	2006
Is democracy bad for the economy? (% No)		26	38	
Having a democratic political system for governing the country (% very good, fairly good)				70
Is a prospering economy an essential characteristic of a democracy?				
(% Yes)				42
(% No)				10
First choice for aims of the country for the next 10 years				
A high level of economic growth				40
Strong defence forces				12
People have more say in how things are done				11
Trying to make our cities and countryside more beautiful				18
Is it important that your job be interesting ? (% Yes)		47	74	
Is it important to be allowed initiative in your job? (% Yes)		46	64	
Work should come first even if it means less spare time				
% Agree, strongly agree				70
% Disagree, strongly disagree				11
What is most important for your child to get ahead? (2010 version: Which of these qualities are especially important for children to learn at home)				
Independence (% Yes)	30		56	67
Hard work (% Yes)	67		85	82
Thrift and saving (% Yes)	24		62	56
Determination and perseverance (% Yes)	28		46	41
Feeling of responsibility (% Yes)				68

Source: World Values Survey, Rounds 1990, 1995, 2001, and 2006.

Above this level, the income elasticity for items like consumer durables as well as for services like insurance increases well above one. This remains the case until income levels surpass $25,000.[12] At that point, the income elasticity drops again.

---

[12] Actually, the Nomura analysis plots 'per capita expenditure of almost anything' against GDP per capita. Note that a GDP per capita of $6000 corresponds quite closely with a per capita household expenditure figure of $3650 (or $1/day).

The expanding demand for consumer durables—cars, motorcycles, televisions, air conditioners, mobile phones, and refrigerators—is already leading to an acceleration in manufacturing in India. Unlike East Asian countries that built their manufacturing industries as export platforms, South Asian manufacturing is largely domestically oriented (except for Bangladeshi garments).

The middle class is also demanding housing, shopping malls, and other infrastructure, and can afford to take an annual vacation, boosting domestic tourism. It saves for its own retirement, for housing, and for children's education, providing the resources for fixed capital formation, especially when there are two-income families. In short, most examples of rapid sustained economic growth coincide with the development and expansion of the middle class.

Murphy et al. (1989) concretize this argument. According to them, industrialization has fixed costs. Because international trade is costly, there must be a domestic market of a certain size to overcome these costs. The domestic market, in turn, is a function of the number of people with sufficient income to buy a product. In poor countries, if there is too much equality, individual income levels do not rise to a level which leads to a high demand for manufactures—most income being spent on basic necessities. On the other hand, if there is too much inequality, there are not enough people in the market to cover the fixed costs of a manufactured product. If instead there is a sizeable middle class, then a large enough number of potential customers to support industrial development exists.

Others have also emphasized the consumption role of the middle class. Schor (1999) has argued that it is a 'new consumerism' that defines the middle class: a constant, 'upscaling of lifestyle norms; the pervasiveness of conspicuous, status goods and of competition for acquiring them; and the growing disconnect between consumer desires and incomes'.

Middle class consumers are willing to pay a little extra for quality. That encourages product differentiation and firms that are successful in meeting these new demands will have higher profit margins. They also invest more in production and marketing of new goods. In this model, once the middle class passes a threshold size, a virtuous cycle is initiated: a bigger middle class spends more, leading to higher business profits, savings and investment, higher growth, and a larger middle class.

Due to its good economic performance lately, a new middle class has started emerging in South Asia. This middle class has a comfortable lifestyle, even by global standards. This is most evident in India and Sri Lanka.

However, the Indian economy alone in South Asia appears poised for growth at 'miracle-like' rates, that is, at rates that emulate the few countries in East Asia that have had successful development over many years. If this growth is sustained over the next 15 years, South Asia could be transformed. India would emerge as a region with a middle class that is proportionately as large as that of the United States today.

The implications of such a shift are far-reaching and go well beyond the economics of a larger consumer market in the region. They extend to shifting values, politics, and attitudes. There is already evidence that this is changing the face of Indian society. If it does not also occur elsewhere then the rough parity between countries on the subcontinent will give way to more dramatic differences.

This chapter has argued that a massive shift in India towards a middle class society is in the making. Others have made similar claims, but with different quantification methods. In the final analysis, the precise numbers are less relevant than the trends—and those seem to be strong at present. Growth, urbanization, education, home ownership, formal-sector jobs, and better economic security are a cause and consequence of India's expanding middle class. A more prosperous South Asia, with democratic governance and a demand for liberal economic policies, could be taking shape. If it does, it will finally spell the end of the 'Licence Raj'.

APPENDIX A3.1 THE EVOLUTION OF THE MIDDLE CLASS IN SOUTH ASIAN ECONOMIES

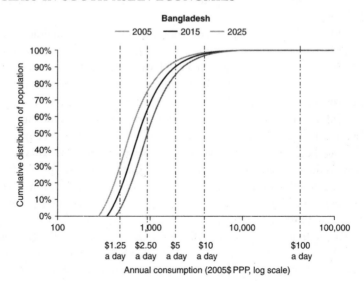

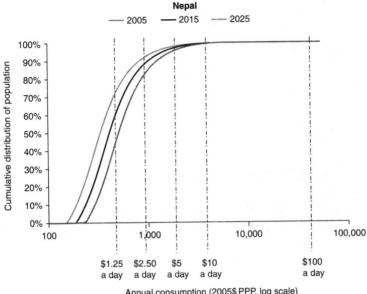

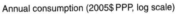

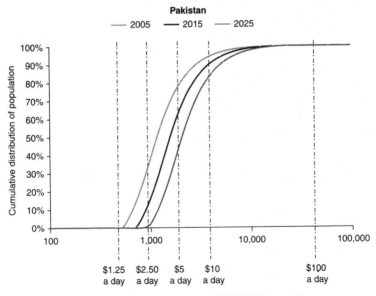

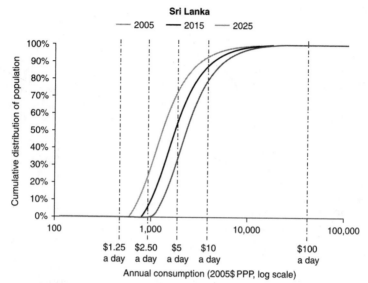

Source: Author's calculations.

REFERENCES

Acemoglu, D. and F. Zilibotti .1997. 'Was Prometheus Unbound by Chance?', *Journal of Political Economy*, 105 (4): 709–51.

Banerjee, A. and E. Duflo. 2007. 'What is Middle Class about the Middle Classes around the World?', MIT Department of Economics Working Paper 07-29. Cambridge, MA.

Barro, R. 1996. 'Determinants of Economic Growth: A Cross-country Empirical Study', NBER Working Paper 5698, National Bureau of Economic Research Inc., Cambridge, MA.

Basu, K. 2008. 'The Enigma of India's Arrival: A Review of Arvind Virmani's Propelling India: From Socialist Stagnation to Global Power', *Journal of Economic Literature*, 46 (2): 396–406.

Bhalla, S. 2002. *Imagine There's No Country: Poverty, Inequality and Growth in the Era of Globalization*. Washington, DC: Peterson Institute for International Economics.

———. 2007. *The Middle Class Kingdoms of India and China*. Washington, DC: Peterson Institute for International Economics. Available at http://www.oxusinvestments.com/files/pdf/NE20090106.pdf.

———. 2008. 'Indian Economic Growth 1950–2008: Facts & Beliefs, Puzzles & Policies', Oxus Research & Investments, New Delhi.

Birdsall, N. 2010. 'The (Indispensable) Middle Class in Developing Countries', in R. Kanbur and M. Spence (eds), *Equity and Growth in a Globalizing World*. Washington, DC: Commission on Growth and Development.

Birdsall, N., C. Graham, and S. Pettinato. 2000. 'Stuck in Tunnel: Is Globalization Muddling the Middle?', Working Paper 14, Brookings Institution,
Washington, DC.

Bosworth B. and S. Collins. 2006. 'Accounting for Growth: Comparing China
and India', NBER Working Paper No. 12943, National Bureau of Economic
Research, Cambridge, MA.

Datt, G. 1998. 'Computational Tools for Poverty Measurement and Analysis',
FCND Discussion Paper 50, International Food Policy Research Institute,
Washington, DC.

Deaton, A. and J. Dreze. 2002. 'Poverty and Inequality in India: A
Reexamination', Working Paper 107, Centre for Development Economics,
Delhi School of Economics.

Doepke, M. and F. Zilibotti. 2007. 'Occupational Choice and the Spirit of
Capitalism', NBER Working Paper 12917, National Bureau of Economic
Research Inc., Cambridge, MA.

Easterly, W. 2000. 'The Middle Class Consensus and Economic Development',
Policy Research Working Paper 2346, World Bank, Washington, DC.

International Monetary Fund (IMF). 2006. *World Economic Outlook*, September.
Available at http://www.imf.org/external/pubs/ft/weo/2006/02/pdf/
weo0906.pdf

————. 2010. 'Asia and Pacific Consolidating the Recovery and Building
Sustainable Growth', *Regional Economic Outlook*, October. Available at http://
www.imf.org/external/pubs/ft/reo/2010/apd/eng/areo1010.pdf

Kenny, C. 2008. 'What's Not Converging? East Asia's Relative Performance in
Income, Health, and Education', *Asian Economic Policy Review*, 3 (1): 19–37.

Kharas, H. 2010. 'The Emerging Middle Class in Developing Countries',
Working Paper No. 285, OECD Development Center.

Kroll, L. and M. Miller. 2010. 'The World's Billionaires', Forbes Special Report.
Available at http://www.forbes.com/2010/03/10/worlds-richest-people-slim-
gates-buffett-billionaires-2010_land.html

Lehoucq, F. 2008. 'Policymaking, Parties and Institutions in Democratic Costa
Rica', Working Paper Number 7, Commission on Growth and Development.
Available at http://www.growthcommission.org/storage/cgdev/documents/
gc-wp-007_web.pdf.

Maddison, A. 2009. 'Statistics on World Population, GDP and per capita GDP,
1-2006 AD'. Available at http://www.ggdc.net/maddison/.

McKinsey Global Institute. 2001. 'Unlocking Potential: Remove Barriers to
India's Growth', *The Wall Street Journal*, 11 September.

Milanovic, B.L.and Yitzhaki. 2001. 'Decomposing World Income Distribution:
Does the World Have a Middle Class?', World Bank Policy Research Working
Paper 2562. Available at http://www-wds.worldbank.org/external/default/
WDSContentServer/IW3P/IB/2001/03/26/000094946_0103200744564
0/Rendered/PDF/multi0page.pdf

Murphy K.M., A. Shleifer, and R. Vishny.1989. 'Income Distribution, Market Size, and Industrialization', *The Quarterly Journal of Economics*, 104 (3): 537–64.

Nomura International. 2009. 'China: A Secular Shift', *Asian Bank Reflections*, 3 (August).

Oura, H. 2007. 'Wild or Tamed? India's Potential Growth', International Monetary Fund Working Paper WP/07/24. Available at http://www.imf.org/external/pubs/ft/wp/2007/wp07224.pdf

Palma, J.G. 2006. 'Globalizing Inequality: Centrifugal and Centripetal Forces at Work', DESA Working Paper No. 35. Available at http://www.un.org/esa/desa/papers/2006/wp35_2006.pdf

Pew Global Attitudes Project. 2009. 'The Global Middle Class', February. Available at http://pewglobal.org/2009/02/12/the-global-middle-class/

Poddar, T. and E. Yi. 2007. 'India's Rising Growth Potential', Global Economics Paper 152, Goldman Sachs, New York.

PovcalNet. Online Poverty Analysis Tool—World Bank Household Survey Data for Developing Countries. Available at http://go.worldbank.org/NT2A1XUWP0.

Ravallion, M. 2003. 'Measuring Aggregate Welfare in Developing Countries: How Well Do National Accounts and Surveys Agree?', *Review of Economics and Statistics*, 85 (3): 645–52.

————2009. 'The Developing World's Bulging (but Vulnerable) "Middle Class"', Policy Research Working Paper 4816. Washington, DC: World Bank.

Rodrik, D. and A. Subramanian. 2004. 'Why India Can Grow at 7 Percent a Year or More: Projections and Reflections', IMF Working Paper No. 118.

Sala-i-Martin, X. 2002. 'The World Distribution of Income (Estimated from Individual Country Distributions)', Economics Working Paper 615, Department of Economics and Business, Universitat Pompeu Fabra.

Schor, J. 1999. 'The New Politics of Consumption', *Boston Review*, Summer. Available at http://www.bostonreview.net/BR24.3/schor.html

Shukla, R.K., S.K. Dwivedi, and A. Sharma. 2004. *The Great Indian Middle Class: Results from the NCAER Market Information Survey of Households*. New Delhi: National Council of Applied Economic Research.

World Bank. 2007a. 'Global Economic Prospects 2007: "Managing the Next Wave of Globalization"', Washington, DC: World Bank.

————2007b. *World Development Indicators*. Washington, DC: World Bank.

————2008. 'Global Purchasing Power Parities and Real Expenditures', Working Paper 45196. Washington, DC: World Bank.

————2009. 'China—From Poor Areas to Poor People: China's Evolving Poverty Reduction Agenda—An Assessment of Poverty and Inequality', Report 48058. Washington, DC: World Bank.

————. 2010. 'Global Economic Prospects 2010: Crisis, Finance, and Growth', World Bank, Washington, DC. Available at http://siteresources. worldbank.org/INTGEP2010/Resources/GEP2010-Full-Report.pdf

World Values Survey. 1990, 1995, 2001, and 2006. Available at http://www. worldvaluessurvey.org/

4

Harnessing Globalization

Weishi Grace Gu and Eswar Prasad

The integration of the world economy through increasing trade and financial linkages took a hit during the global financial crisis. Now that recovery is underway, the rapid growth of global trade and financial flows has resumed, indicating that the crisis resulted in only a temporary setback to the forces of globalization.

Of course, globalization is not an end in itself; nor is it an unqualified benefit. The literature seems to have moved towards a consensus that trade liberalization promotes growth, although it can have distributional consequences that favour some groups over others. At a macroeconomic level, however, trade is seen as clearly beneficial.[1] Indeed, there is also some evidence that developing economies that are more open to trade are less susceptible to crises and recover faster from crises that do occur (see Frankel and Cavallo 2004 and Cavallo 2005).

The literature on the costs and benefits of financial integration is more controversial. Theory suggests that financial openness should benefit all countries by promoting more efficient international allocation of capital, and also consumption smoothing via international risk-sharing. The strong presumption was that these benefits ought to be large, especially for developing countries that tend to be relatively capital poor and have

---

[1] For empirical evidence showing that trade openness has a direct and positive effect on economic growth, see, for example, Frankel and Romer (1999) and Dollar and Kraay (2003). Rodriguez and Rodrik (2002) present a contrarian view but, as summarized in recent surveys by Krueger and Berg (2003), Baldwin (2004), and Winters (2004), the weight of the evidence supports the by now conventional wisdom that trade is good for growth.

more volatile income growth. However, the empirical literature is far from conclusive. Indeed, Prasad et al. (2003) conclude that, taken as a whole, the vast empirical literature provides little robust evidence of a causal relationship between financial integration and growth. Moreover, they conclude that among developing countries, the volatility of consumption growth relative to income growth appears to be positively associated with financial integration, the opposite of what canonical theoretical models would predict. In theory, access to international markets should allow all countries to smooth consumption by insuring against country-specific income risk.

Kose et al. (2009a) provide a framework that yields some more nuanced perspectives on financial globalization. These authors argue that far more important than the direct growth effects of access to more capital is how capital flows generate a number of what they label 'potential collateral benefits' of financial integration. There is now a rapidly growing literature showing that financial openness can, in many but not all circumstances, promote development of the domestic financial sector, impose discipline on macroeconomic policies, generate efficiency gains among domestic firms by exposing them to competition from foreign entrants, and unleash forces that result in better government and corporate governance.

Kose et al. (2009b, 2009c) point out some complexities in managing the cost-benefit trade-off. For developing countries, financial globalization appears to have the potential of playing a catalytic role in generating this array of collateral benefits that may help boost long-run growth and welfare. At the same time, opening the capital account without having some basic supporting conditions in place can delay the realization of these benefits, while making a country more vulnerable to sudden stops of capital flows. This is a fundamental tension between the costs and benefits of financial globalization that may be difficult to avoid and ultimately the balance depends on country-specific conditions, including institutional and financial development.

In this chapter, we evaluate the extent and nature of integration of South Asian economies with world trade and financial systems, using this vast academic literature as a reference point. Our analysis covers Bangladesh, Bhutan, India, Nepal, Pakistan, and Sri Lanka. These South Asian economies have participated in the phenomenon of globalization to varying extents. As noted earlier, globalization is not an end in itself and the benefit-cost calculus depends to a significant extent on the structure of a particular economy and the nature of its integration into world trade and finance.

Hence, in the next section of this chapter, we begin our analysis by providing an empirical characterization of growth patterns in South Asia. On average, economies in this region have experienced decent gross domestic product (GDP) growth of 5.5 per cent over the last decade. We also examine the composition of growth in these economies, an issue that is particularly relevant in the context of recent discussions on global rebalancing of growth (see Prasad 2011). We find that in these economies consumption is in fact the main driver of growth and the trade balance is generally negative. Thus growth looks a lot more balanced and less dependent on external demand than is the case with some East Asian economies such as China. Employment growth, however, remains a challenge even for some fast-growing economies in the South Asian region. We also look at the region's dependence on external trade from different perspectives.

In the next section, we focus on service sector growth and services exports of South Asian economies. One of the interesting findings from this analysis is that growth in the services sector among economies in the region has already outpaced that of many other emerging markets and has led to a diverging growth path from the rest of Asia. The importance of services exports to economies in the region may in fact have played a role in allowing these economies to recover more quickly from the global financial crisis than countries whose exports are dominated by manufactured goods, as services exports held up a lot better during the crisis and in the early stages of the global economic recovery.

In the following section, we provide another perspective on the balance of growth that ties together the domestic and international implications by examining patterns of national savings and investment. An analysis of the evolution of savings–investment balances is especially relevant for understanding the dynamics of global imbalances. In the penultimate section we broaden this discussion by examining capital inflows to South Asia and the accumulation of foreign exchange reserves. In general, South Asia has had increasing openness to capital inflows but the de facto financial integration of each of its economies with the world economy, as measured by financial flows relative to the size of their domestic GDP, has remained modest. The countries in the region maintain relatively large levels of foreign exchange reserves and this should reduce the vulnerability of these economies to external crises. The concluding section contains a summary of the main findings and a discussion of policy implications.

COMPOSITION OF GROWTH

In this section, we characterize some of the key patterns of growth in the South Asian economies and also examine related outcomes, such as employment growth. It is useful to start off with a description of the evolution of the structure of GDP from a national accounts perspective. Table 4.1 shows the shares of different components of GDP for three years—1995, 2000, and 2009. We show the data for each South Asian economy, averages for the group, and some comparative data for other countries and country groups.[2]

The median share of private (household) consumption in South Asian countries' GDP fell from 76.6 per cent in 1995 to 65.2 per cent in 2009. The median shares of government consumption and investment increased from 9.5 and 23.7 per cent respectively in 1995 to 11.9 and 28.8 per cent in 2009. The median share of net exports in GDP was relatively stable at around −7.7 per cent.

Of course, these averages mask substantial differences across countries. Among the major South Asian economies, the most dramatic shift in the share of private consumption swas recorded by Bangladesh. Its share in GDP fell from 73 per cent in 2000 to 66 per cent in 2009. Bhutan is the only South Asian economy where private consumption now accounts for less than half of its GDP (48.5 per cent), while its government consumption is over a quarter of its GDP, much higher than other Asian and developed countries in our sample. In Bangladesh, the shares of both investment and net exports rose markedly—by about 4 and 3 percentage points respectively—from 2000 to 2009. There is a significant decline in the share of private consumption in India's GDP as well—from 64.2 per cent in 2000 to 59.5 per cent in 2009—with investment taking up the slack. The share of private consumption and investment in Sri Lanka's GDP declined as well—from 72.1 and 28 per cent respectively in 2000 to 64.3 and 23.8 per cent in 2009—while government consumption and net exports increased. In Nepal, there was a surge in the share of investment, which was offset by a corresponding expansion of the trade deficit. Overall, South Asian countries' private consumption, investment, and net exports shares similar to the averages of Asian developing countries, while their government consumption

---

[2] We show medians rather than means in these calculations to mitigate the effects of outliers in these small samples. In any event, using means rather than medians made little difference to the patterns we discuss in the text. The reported averages treat each country as a unit; there is no weighting for country size.

TABLE 4.1 Shares of Real GDP (per cent)

Country	1995 Consumption Pvt.	Govt	Invst	Net X	2000 Consumption Pvt.	Govt	Invst	Net X	2009 Consumption Pvt.	Govt	Invst	Net X
Bangladesh	84.5	4.6	18.9	-6.4	73.1	4.2	23.8	-3.8	66.1	5.2	27.0	-0.8
Bhutan	–	–	–	–	51.1	23.5	51.6	-26.2	48.5	25.6	34.8	-9.4
India	66.3	11.1	24.6	-1.5	64.2	12.9	25.9	-1.9	59.5	11.5	34.9	-6.1
Nepal	79.1	8.4	23.2	-12.0	80.2	8.1	22.3	-10.7	76.6	12.4	30.7	-22.0
Pakistan	–	–	–	–	75.4	8.6	17.2	-1.2	69.6	11.0	16.0	1.9
Sri Lanka	74.1	10.5	24.2	-8.9	72.1	10.5	28.0	-10.6	64.3	17.6	23.8	-6.5
South Asia Median	76.6	9.5	23.7	-7.7	72.6	9.6	24.9	-7.2	65.2	11.9	28.8	-6.3
Regional and International Comparisons												
China	44.9	13.3	40.3	1.6	46.4	15.9	35.3	2.4	35.3	13.3	43.5	7.9
Asian Emerging Markets	58.9	10.7	30.5	-3.4	60.4	10.2	25.4	2.7	57.4	11.4	20.5	8.2
Asian Developing Countries	74.1	8.2	24.2	-8.9	72.6	5.9	25.9	-7.2	67.1	5.9	25.4	-8.0
Germany	59.5	19.6	22.1	-0.9	58.9	19.0	21.8	0.4	58.0	20.0	17.9	3.9
Japan	56.7	15.5	27.7	0.4	56.2	16.9	25.5	1.5	58.1	18.7	19.7	3.0
US	67.7	16.2	17.2	-0.9	68.7	14.4	20.8	-3.9	71.1	16.4	15.2	-2.7

Source: CEIC Data Company Ltd (CEIC), IMF's *World Economic Outlook* (WEO), Economist Intelligence Unit (EIU), and authors' calculations.

Note: GDP contribution shares (in percentage points). Asian emerging markets include China, Hong Kong, India, Indonesia, Korea, Malaysia, Pakistan, the Philippines, Singapore, Taiwan, and Thailand. Asian developing countries include Bangladesh, Cambodia, Sri Lanka, and Vietnam.

ratios are mostly higher than those of Asian developing countries (except Bangladesh) and close to that of Asian emerging markets.

Table 4.2 shows average GDP growth rates over the period 2000–9 for each country in the sample. The next five columns to the right of GDP growth show the contributions of different components to GDP growth. They are total consumption (which is further broken down into private and government consumption), investment, and net exports. All of them should add up approximatedly to the overall GDP growth. The last column of the table shows employment growth in the formal sector.

Consumption is typically the largest component of GDP, so it is usually the case that consumption growth tends to track overall GDP growth. On average, total consumption growth (private and public) contributes about 4.2 percentage points to GDP growth, relative to median GDP growth in the sample of about 5.5 per cent per annum. In other words, consumption growth on average accounts for over three-quarters of GDP growth among the six countries in the sample.

There are two economies—Nepal and Sri Lanka—for which the contribution of consumption growth amounts to 90 per cent of GDP growth, well above the sample average. At the other extreme is Bangladesh, where consumption growth contributes about 3.6 percentage points out of 5.8 per cent GDP growth.

What is the relative importance of private versus government consumption in driving GDP growth? Private consumption growth strongly dominates total consumption growth in most sample countries, with the notable exception of Bhutan (where private and government consumption weight almost equally, with the former being 40 per cent and the latter 30 per cent; note that Bhutan also has a higher government consumption share in GDP than other countries in Table 4.1). On average, private consumption growth accounts for four-fifths of the total growth contribution of consumption.

Investment growth on average accounts for about 1.7 percentage points of GDP growth. Both India and Nepal get relatively high contributions from investment growth, nearly 4 percentage points per annum in the case of India and close to 2.3 in Nepal. It is worth noting that only in Nepal does investment growth contribute more than 50 per cent of GDP growth. Another key fact about India's investment growth is that it is heavily financed through foreign capital (as we will see later, India now runs a large current account deficit).

Another aspect of the balance of growth is related to dependence on external trade for growth. Here it is important to be careful about the

TABLE 4.2 Contributions to Growth and Employment Growth, 2000–9 (per cent)

Country	GDP Growth	GDP Growth Contributions					Employment Growth
		Consumption		Investment	Net Exports		
		Total	Private	Government			

Country	GDP Growth	Total	Private	Government	Investment	Net Exports	Employment Growth
Bangladesh	5.8	3.6	3.2	0.4	1.9	0.2	3.3
Bhutan	6.8	4.9	3.0	1.9	1.5	0.8	–
India	8.4	6.0	5.0	1.0	3.6	–1.4	1.9
Nepal	4.0	3.6	2.8	0.8	2.3	–2.0	–
Pakistan	4.7	3.5	2.8	0.7	0.8	0.4	3.1
Sri Lanka	5.2	4.8	3.8	1.0	1.3	–0.8	1.9
South Asia Median	5.5	4.2	3.1	0.9	1.7	–0.3	2.5
Regional and International Comparisons							
China	10.2	4.1	2.8	1.3	5.0	1.1	0.9
Asian Emerging Markets	4.6	3.2	2.6	0.6	0.8	0.7	1.7
Asian Developing Countries	6.5	5.0	4.3	0.4	2.2	–0.7	2.8
Germany	0.8	0.5	0.3	0.2	–0.2	0.5	0.4
Japan	1.5	1.0	0.6	0.4	0.2	0.5	–0.3
US	1.9	2.0	1.7	0.3	–0.1	0.0	0.3

Source: CEIC, IMF's WEO, ADB, EIU, and authors' calculations.

Note: GDP growth rates (in per cent) are annual averages over the period 2000–9. GDP growth contributions (in percentage points) are averages over the same period. Contributions may not sum exactly to GDP growth due to rounding error because the statistical discrepancy is large. Investment includes private and public investment. Employment growth rates (in per cent) are also annual averages over the period 2000–9, except for Bangladesh (only 2000, 2003, and 2006). India's employment data are only available for 2000 and 2005 from the ADB. See Table 4.1 for list of countries classified as Asian emerging markets and Asian developing economies.

use of the term 'export-led growth'. Even if a country has a very high level of exports relative to GDP, it could have a balanced trade account, which would mean that *net* exports were not contributing much to the bottomline in terms of GDP growth (Prasad 2011).

The penultimate column of Table 4.2 shows that, on average, net exports make a slightly negative contribution (–0.3 percentage points) to overall GDP growth among the countries in the region. For three of the six economies in the sample, net exports contributed –0.8 percentage point or below to GDP growth. The average contribution of net exports to growth is positive in the cases of Bangladesh, Bhutan, and Pakistan.

Overall, South Asia is on a reasonably balanced growth path on average, with about 70 per cent growth contributed by consumption, 20 per cent by investment, and 10 per cent by net exports, similar to other Asian and developed countries.

EMPLOYMENT GROWTH

A different way of thinking about the composition of growth is how much employment is generated in the process of achieving that growth rate. The last column of Table 4.2 shows that the cross-sectional median of employment growth over the period 2000–9 was about 2.5 per cent. The two economies with the lowest average rate of employment growth were India and Sri Lanka. It is striking that in India net employment growth, at 1.9 per cent per annum, was only about one-fifth the pace of output growth. This is consistent with the findings of Bosworth et al. (2007) and Gordon and Gupta (2004). They both show that to date, the increase in India's output growth has been associated with little increase in overall rates of job creation. Moreover, while agricultural output has fallen as a share of GDP, agriculture's share in total employment remains surprisingly high. The authors point out that there could be significant productivity gains from further sectoral reallocation of labour, moving from agriculture to other sectors.

DEPENDENCE ON TRADE

Returning to the issue of dependence on export-led growth, we present some additional trade data in Table 4.3. The first three columns show, the ratio of total trade (imports + exports), exports, and trade balance (exports – imports) to GDP for 2000.[3] The measure of exports and

---

[3] Data on the trade balance ratio to GDP should in principle match the data reported in Table 4.1. There are some discrepancies due to the fact that data in Table 4.1 are taken from the national income accounts while the data in Table 4.3 come from the balance of payments.

TABLE 4.3 Openness to Trade (per cent of GDP)

Country	2000			2009		
	Total Trade	Exports	Trade Balance	Total Trade	Exports	Trade Balance
Bangladesh	33.2	14.0	−5.2	46.7	19.3	−8.1
Bhutan	69.2	27.1	−15.1	95.4	40.3	−14.7
India	27.4	13.2	−0.9	46.3	20.4	−5.5
Nepal	41.3	13.5	−14.2	41.6	6.8	−28.0
Pakistan	28.1	13.4	−1.2	34.7	13.6	−7.5
Sri Lanka	88.6	39.0	−10.6	64.7	25.5	−13.7
South Asia Median	37.2	13.8	−7.9	46.5	19.8	−10.9
Regional and International Comparisons						
China	39.6	20.8	2.0	51.4	28.0	4.6
Asian Emerging Markets	80.0	40.0	0.5	56.6	25.7	−4.0
Asian Developing Countries	108.9	54.4	2.1	144.7	71.2	5.9
Germany	66.4	33.5	0.5	80.3	42.5	4.8
Japan	21.2	11.3	1.5	26.1	13.3	0.4
US	25.7	10.9	−3.8	24.4	10.9	−2.7

Source: CEIC, ADB's Statistical Database System (SDBS), EIU country data, and authors' calculations.

Note: Exports include both goods and services; total trade refers to the sum of exports and imports of goods and services. See Table 4.1 for list of countries classified as Asian emerging markets and Asian developing economies.

imports used here includes goods and non-factor services. The next three columns show the same three ratios, but for 2009. The median ratio of exports to GDP increased from about 14 per cent to 20 per cent during this decade, suggesting a higher level of dependence on exports. But the median ratio of trade balance (or net exports), which is of relevance to the GDP bottomline, has in fact become much more negative and, on average, was about −11 per cent of GDP in 2009. This is down from a median of about −8 per cent of GDP in 2000, reflecting a faster rise of imports into the region during the past decade.

For all the countries in the sample, the trade balance has on average been negative during the 2000s. But there are wide disparities in the region. The largest average trade deficits are recorded by Nepal, Bhutan, and Sri Lanka. Nepal's trade deficit increased from 14 per cent of GDP in 2000 to 28 per cent in 2009, resulting in about equal parts from declining exports and rising imports. India's and Pakistan's trade deficits also grew over the past decade, even though their exports increased. While trade openness has increased in most South Asian economies during 2000–9, the increase in volume of trade has not kept pace with GDP growth in Sri Lanka. Overall, trade growth among South Asian economies appears similar to the patterns observed in the broad group of Asian emerging markets.

SERVICE INDUSTRY AND TRADE IN SERVICES

Although overall trade data suggest that growth in South Asian economies' trade is similar to that in a broader sample of Asian emerging markets, there are still significant disparities in the structure of trade patterns across these two groups. One of the distinctive features of South Asian economies is that they have undergone what some authors have characterized as a services revolution over the past three decades (Ghani 2010).

How big is the services sector in South Asia? Ghani and Kharas (2010) show that among the countries in the region, the services sector's share in GDP has been steadily growing from 40 per cent in 1980 to 55 per cent in 2005, while the share of manufacturing has stayed relatively stable at around 20 per cent. Among the countries in our sample, in 2005, Sri Lanka's services sector accounted for about 60 per cent of the GDP, while that ratio is about 55 per cent for India and Pakistan and 43 per cent for Nepal. Among East Asian economies, by contrast, the share of manufacturing in GDP is about 45 per cent, with a growing services sector that on average still accounts for only about 45 per cent of GDP.

Ghani and Kharas (2010) also report the contributions of the services sector to GDP growth in Bangladesh, China, India, Korea, Pakistan, and Sri Lanka for the periods 1980–5 and 2000–7. In the early 1980s, four South Asian countries and Korea had a relatively large contribution to the GDP from their services sector, of about 40 to 55 per cent. In India, the services sector contributed about 40 per cent of GDP growth during that period while the corresponding figure for China was only 30 per cent. By the 2000s, services sector growth contributed about 60 per cent of GDP growth in India. The growth contribution of the services sector remained low in China, at around 40 per cent.

Clearly, there has been a divergence in the sectoral distribution of growth between South Asian countries and China. Ghani (2010) concludes that South Asia has witnessed a services-led growth that is very different from the manufacturing-led growth in China or, more generally, the emerging markets of East Asia. More recently, the growth patterns of these two groups have been converging in terms of the sectoral distribution of growth and the relative shares of services and manufacturing in GDP. The share of services output in GDP has increased significantly in China in recent years, while manufacturing growth has picked up in many South Asian economies, including Bangladesh, India, and Pakistan.

It is worth further examining the evidence on what kinds of services are growing faster—modern services (including banking, insurance, financial, and communication-related services) or traditional services (including trade, hotels and restaurants, personal, cultural and recreational services, community and social services, transportation, storage, real estate dwellings, and government and public administration services). Ghani (2010) shows that modern services experienced average annual growth of more than 9 per cent per annum in Bangladesh, India, Pakistan, and Sri Lanka during 2000–6. Traditional services grew at lower rates in all the sample countries. These trends suggest that the tradable portion of the services sector is expanding relatively fast in these economies, suggesting another channel through which these economies are likely to expand their integration into global trade and finance.

This conjecture is supported by data. Countries that had faster services sector value-added growth also experienced faster growth in services sector exports over the last three decades. India's services exports grew at an annual rate of 27 per cent during 2001–8; over the same period, the corresponding figures were about 17 per cent for Pakistan and about 10 per cent for Bhutan, Nepal, and Sri Lanka. Overall, South Asia's services exports grew by about 22 per cent annually according to Ghani and Anand (2009); this exceeds even the rapid growth of East Asian manufactured exports. The share of services exports (in value terms) in GDP in India increased from about 3 per cent in 2000 to 8 per cent in 2008; while their share in total exports increased from 27 per cent to 36 per cent over the same period (Table 4.4). In the case of Sri Lanka, the ratio of services exports to total exports rose by 5 percentage points from 2000 to 2008 but the share of services exports in GDP fell slightly over this period.

Most important, services exports served as a buffer for South Asian countries during the 2007 financial crisis. While most countries around the world experienced huge declines in goods exports, Bhutan, India, Nepal, Pakistan, and Sri Lanka achieved better balance of their trade accounts during this period largely as a consequence of an average increase of about 19 per cent in services exports in both 2007 and 2008. Ghani and Anand (2009) come to the same conclusion, noting that services exports are less volatile than goods exports. They also note that globalization of services is still at an early stage and it is likely to grow and/or recover faster even during crises.

SAVINGS–INVESTMENT BALANCES

Having examined the structures of South Asian economies and their trade patterns, we now shift to an analysis of where these economies fit into the debate about global imbalances and the rebalancing of domestic growth. The connection between domestic and global imbalances is through the current account, which represents the difference between national

TABLE 4.4   Services Exports

Country	2000		2008	
	As per cent of GDP	As per cent of Total Exports	As per cent of GDP	As per cent of Total Exports
Bhutan	7.8	–	4.4	–
India	3.4	26.7	8.2	36.1
Nepal	8.8	–	6.2	–
Pakistan	1.9	13.3	2.5	16.9
Sri Lanka	5.8	14.9	4.9	19.8

Source: United Nations Service Trade Statistics Database, EIU country data, and authors' calculations.
Note: Exports include both goods and services.

savings and national investment. It is of interest to examine not just the evolution of the current account but its components as well.

Table 4.5 presents 2009 nominal GDP, current account balances, and national savings, both in terms of value (to facilitate cross-country comparisons of magnitudes) as well as ratios to GDP. Most South Asian economies had current account deficits in 2009, with the exception of Bangladesh. At the same time, domestic savings rates in the region were quite high. The ratio of gross national savings to GDP ranged from 17–18 per cent in Pakistan and Sri Lanka to 31–2 per cent in India and Bhutan.

In India, the household savings rate has increased over the last decade, as documented by authors, such as Athukorala and Sen (2004), and Panagariya (2008). Households tend to hold about half of their savings in physical savings (including livestock, landholdings, and jewellery), with various forms of financial savings accounting for the other half (Prasad 2011). Moulick (2008) provides some qualitative evidence on how lack of access to the formal financial system affects savings patterns among poor people in the north-east region of India, including the level of household savings and the forms in which savings are held. Basu and Maertens (2007) suggest that expansion of nationalized bank branches during the 1970s might have helped the rise in financial savings. Mohan (2008), however, also notes that while gross financial savings of the household sector have increased in recent years, households' financial liabilities have also been rapidly increasing, albeit from a low base. He points to data showing that households' gross financial savings rose from 13.8 per cent of GDP in 2004–5 to 18.3 per cent in 2006–7, while their financial liabilities increased from 3.8 per cent of GDP during 2004–5 to 6.8 per cent during 2006–7. He attributes both phenomena to financial development as well as the broadening of access to the financial system. In addition, life cycle factors may affect India's saving behaviour. As Prasad (2011) points out, the share of the working-age population is projected to increase slightly over the next three decades in Bangladesh, India, and Pakistan, and this could have positive effects on savings, other things being equal, according to the life cycle model (see Ang 2009, for some empirical evidence).

Overall, South Asia's current account and national savings ratios to GDP are close to those of Asian developing countries. South Asian economies do have one significant difference relative to other Asian emerging markets. Economies in East Asia, in particular, tend to have high savings rates but also current account surpluses rather than deficits.

TABLE 4.5   GDP, Current Account Balance, and National Savings, 2009

Country	Nominal GDP (US$ billion)	Current Account Balance Value (US$ billion)	Current Account Balance As per cent of the GDP	Gross National Savings Value (US$ billion)	Gross National Savings As per cent of GDP
Bangladesh	89.5	2.9	3.3	24.5	27.4
Bhutan	1.1	−0.1	−12.0	0.4	32.3
India	1,296.2	−31.5	−2.4	403.1	31.1
Nepal	12.4	−0.3	−2.1	2.6	21.1
Pakistan	162.0	−2.7	−1.6	26.9	16.6
Sri Lanka	42.0	−1.6	−3.9	7.9	18.9
Regional and International Comparisons					
China	4,909.0	297.1	6.1	2,567.4	52.3
Asian Emerging Markets	264.0	20.3	6.1	78.0	31.0
Asian Developing Countries	65.7	−1.3	−5.3	16.2	23.2
Germany	3,356.5	135.0	4.0	708.5	21.1
Japan	5,067.0	140.6	2.8	1,171.9	23.1
US	14,256.3	−378.5	−2.7	1,208.9	8.5

Source: EIU and authors' calculations.

Note: See Table 4.1 for list of countries classified as Asian emerging markets and Asian developing economies.

To understand the implications of these differences, it is necessary to delve more deeply into the components of the savings–investment balance.

Figure 4.1 shows savings and investment balances for each of the South Asian economies in our sample. Figure 4.2 shows the corresponding evolution of current account balances. For instance, the top left panel of Figure 4.1 shows that savings and investment have both slowly been increasing in Bangladesh since the early 2000s. The rate of increase in savings has been higher than that of investment, leading to a rising current account surplus, which had increased to 3.3 per cent of its GDP by 2009. By contrast, Pakistan and Sri Lanka show no clear trend in savings and investment, but the difference between the two measures widened during 2003–8, leading to large current account deficits. Pakistan in fact used to run current account surpluses in the early 2000s. Sri Lanka has persistently run current account deficits during this period. Both countries experienced a sharp contraction in their current account deficits in 2009, partly because external financing dried up during the crisis. The case of Bhutan is an interesting one. Its investment to GDP

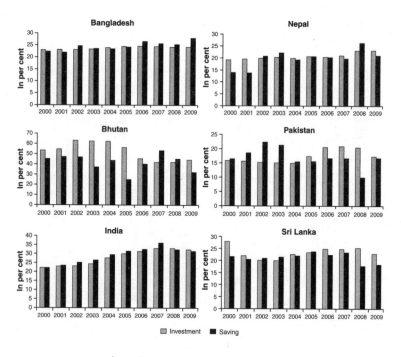

FIGURE 4.1   Savings–Investment as Ratios to GDP

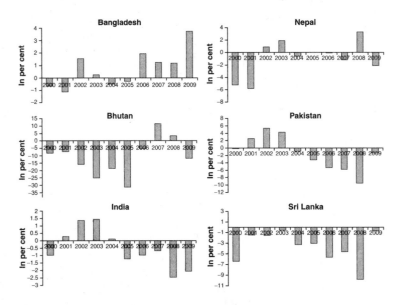

FIGURE 4.2   Current Account Balances as Ratios to GDP

Source: CEIC database and the authors' calculations.

ratio was more than 60 per cent in 2002–4, while its savings rate was substantially lower, implying massive current account deficits. This turned into a current account surplus in 2007–8, before reverting to a sizable deficit in 2009.

India experienced a gradual increase in both savings and investment to GDP ratios over 2000–7, before both levelled off during the crisis. Investment growth exceeded growth in savings for much of this period, resulting in a shift from a current account surplus in 2001–4 to a modest current account deficit of about 2 per cent of GDP in 2008–9. In other words, despite its high domestic savings rate, India still relies, to a modest extent, on foreign financing to plug the gap in its savings–investment balance.

One key question is whether current account deficits finance investment or consumption. In the former case, they are more likely to be sustainable as they add to an economy's productive capacity over the long term. By contrast, deficit-financed consumption booms of the sort experienced by some Latin American economies in previous decades can end in tears, especially if the foreign financing is in the form of foreign currency-denominated debt.

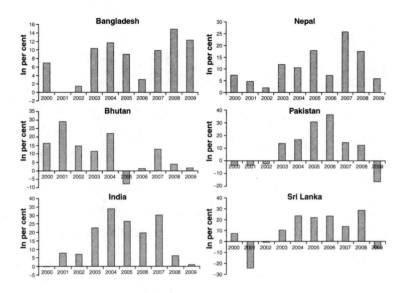

FIGURE 4.3   Gross Fixed Investment (Annual Growth Rates)
Source: CEIC database and the authors' calculations.

Figure 4.3 provides a complementary perspective to the overall savings–investment balance by showing annual growth rates of gross fixed investment. Across the region, investment growth is on average high but tends to be very volatile. In Bhutan and Pakistan, investment growth rates have plummeted in recent years, even before the crisis hit. By contrast, investment growth in Bangladesh has held to a moderate but steady pace even during the height of the global financial crisis. One consequence is that Bangladesh continued to experience strong overall GDP growth during the crisis while Bhutan had negative growth in 2009. As expected, there is generally a positive correlation between investment growth and GDP growth over time for the countries in our sample. Interestingly, while the investment to GDP ratio stayed at a high level, investment growth in India declined in 2008–9 during the worst of the financial crisis.

CAPITAL INFLOWS AND FOREIGN RESERVES

In the past decade, South Asia has gradually become open to capital inflows. We now examine in greater detail the levels of financial integration of these economies with the world economy and also the form

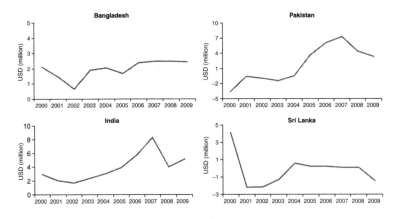

FIGURE 4.4   Net Capital Inflows

Source: CEIC database and the authors' calculations.

that this integration has taken. Figure 4.4 shows the evolution of overall net capital inflows into Bangladesh, India, Pakistan, and Sri Lanka.

The level of net inflows into Bangladesh has remained relatively stable over 2000–9. Net inflows into India and Pakistan increased sharply over the 2000s until the crisis hit, when they shrank significantly but did not collapse. Sri Lanka experienced low or slightly negative net inflows for much of the 2000s.

Table 4.6 looks at total net inflows expressed as ratios to GDP, for 2000 and 2009, for each of these countries. Table 4.6 also shows the distribution among different types of capital inflows, as this has implications for judging the potential benefits and volatility of overall capital inflows. The level of net inflows into Bangladesh as a ratio to GDP was roughly the same in 2000 as in 2009, with the other investment category accounting for the major portion. In India's case, both foreign direct investment (FDI) and equity investment increased sharply and now dominate overall net inflows. FDI inflows as a share of GDP rose from 0.8 per cent to 2.7 per cent while equity inflows rose from 0.5 per cent of the GDP to 1.6 per cent. While portfolio equity flows are considered to be more volatile than FDI, both types of inflows are presumed to have advantages compared to other types of flows in terms of their contributions to both productivity growth and risk sharing (see Kose et al. 2009b, 2009c). By contrast, the biggest increase in the case of Pakistan was accounted for by other

TABLE 4.6 Capital Inflows into South Asian Economies (per cent of GDP)

Country	2000					2009				
	Total	FDI	Equity	Debt	Other	Total	FDI	Equity	Debt	Other
Bangladesh	2.1	0.6	0.0	0.0	1.5	2.4	0.8	-0.2	0.2	1.6
India	2.9	0.8	0.5	0.0	1.6	5.1	2.7	1.6	0.0	0.8
Pakistan	-3.6	0.4	0.0	-0.7	-3.4	3.3	1.5	0.0	-0.3	2.2
Sri Lanka	4.1	1.1	0.0	-0.4	3.4	-1.4	1.0	-0.9	0.0	-1.5

Source: CEIC, EIU country data, and authors' calculations.
Note: The numbers here are net inflows.

investment, which, according to the International Monetary Fund (IMF) classification of capital flows, includes currency and deposits, loans, and trade credits. Sri Lanka experienced sharp net outflows of portfolio equity as well as other investment in 2009, moving from a situation of net inflows of 4.1 per cent of GDP in 2000 to net outflows of 1.4 per cent of GDP in 2009.

Overall, South Asia has had increasing openness to capital flows, but de facto financial openness as measured by the ratio of flows to GDP remains small. In terms of potential benefits from these flows, the composition of inflows has become increasingly favourable for India and, to some extent, for Pakistan. Ghani and Anand (2009) show that foreign capital inflows to South Asia—remittances, international syndicated bank lending, private capital investments, and issue of bonds—surged during the early to mid-2000s, but collapsed in the aftermath of the crisis. They argue that South Asia is unique in attracting capital flows that are less volatile, noting that the region relies more on remittances than traditional forms of inflows like direct investment, portfolio flows, and bank loans. According to them, remittances are less volatile and more persistent, although such flows were of course not totally immune to the global recession.

Nevertheless, greater financial openness does imply greater exposure to the vagaries of international capital flows and the whims of international investors. Foreign exchange reserves provide a way to self-insure against these risks, although such self-insurance can be quite costly.[4] Indeed, the recent crisis has provided emerging markets further impetus to consider self-insurance strategies. How do South Asian economies look in terms of their ability to fend off crises using reserves? To examine this, we look at how reserves stocks stack up relative to the size of the economy and the quantity of short-term external debt.[5]

---

[4] Rodrik (2006) estimates the social cost of self-insurance through holding reserves to be about 1 per cent of GDP for developing countries as a group. Hauner (2006) presents estimates of the quasi-fiscal costs of holding reserves. Prasad and Rajan (2008) discuss how China's currency policy, which has resulted in rapid reserve accumulation, has constrained domestic macroeconomic policies and hampered financial sector reforms, both of which could have long-term consequences for economic welfare.

[5] Obstfeld et al. (2008) argue that countries may have good reasons to use the ratio of reserves to M2 or the monetary base as a more suitable criterion, especially if they have weak banking systems. Prasad and Rajan (2008) argue that while foreign exchange reserves provide a useful cushion against financial and balance-of-payments crises, thus making capital account liberalization less risky, they also create problems of their own.

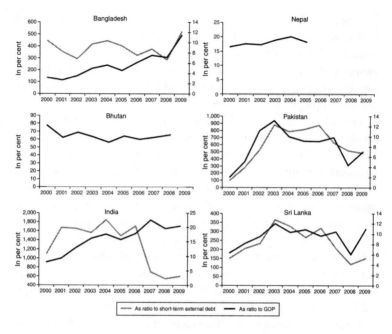

FIGURE 4.5   Total Foreign Exchange Reserves

Source: CEIC database and the authors' calculations.

Figure 4.5 shows individual countries' foreign exchange reserves as a ratio of GDP or of short-term external debt. The left axis of each panel and pink line show the reserves to short-term debt ratio and the right axis and blue line show the reserves to GDP ratio. Bhutan had a stable ratio of reserves to GDP of about 60 per cent during the past decade, which is also the highest reserves–GDP ratio among the sample countries. Both Bangladesh and India have had a growing reserves–GDP ratio over the years, while Pakistan's and Sri Lanka's ratios first increased in the early 2000s and then declined during the financial crisis.

Many emerging market economies, including India, are finding it increasingly difficult to 'sterilize' (using government bonds) the liquidity created by inflows; therefore pressures for domestic currency appreciation are building. Further, governments are increasingly questioning the benefits of a policy that, in essence, involves purchasing more low-yield securities from foreign governments financed by higher-yield domestic debt. Also see Jeanne (2007) for a discussion of the costs and benefits of reserves.

The evolution of the ratios of reserves to short-term debt looks similar to that of the reserves to GDP ratios, except in the case of India, where the former ratio declined sharply in 2007 due to a huge increase in short-term debt in 2007 (from US $10 billion to US $38 billion). More importantly, even though there was a dramatic increase in short-term debt, reserves still account for many multiples of short-term debt. In fact, reserves are still close to the level of total external debt of all maturities (short-term debt accounts for only 20 per cent of India's external debt; see Prasad 2009). Hence reserve adequacy based on standard benchmarks is certainly not a concern for India and other South Asian economies.

One other concern among developing economies about greater capital account openness is related to fluctuations in the exchange rate, which these economies view as detrimental to their export sectors. To look at this, we examine the trade-weighted real effective exchange rates for a subset of the countries in our sample. There is no evidence of excessive volatility in these exchange rates, although there is an unmistakable trend towards real exchange appreciation in India and Sri Lanka starting in the mid-2000s and similar forces in the other two economies more recently in Figure 4.6. In any event, there is no evidence of sharp year-to-year fluctuations in real effective exchange rates.

As is the case for the rest of the world, South Asian economies are increasing their global trade linkages, a process that looks set to continue and that has significant benefits for these economies. The picture on financial integration is more complex. Despite the relatively

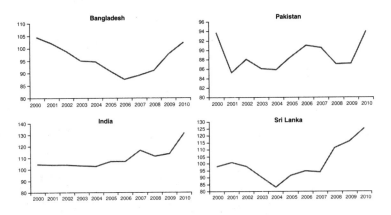

FIGURE 4.6   Real Effective Exchange Rates

Source: CEIC database and the authors' calculations.

modest numbers, the reality is that the wave of financial globalization has probably only temporarily receded from the shores of South Asian economies as a result of the global financial crisis. Indeed, countries do not have much of a choice but to manage rather than resist capital account liberalization over time as capital accounts are becoming de facto more open over time irrespective of government attempts to control them (Prasad and Rajan 2008).

This creates a conundrum for countries with low levels of financial and institutional development (see Kose et al. 2011). But even more generally, the costs and benefits of financial openness are far from obvious, as alluded to earlier. For instance, Prasad et al. (2007) have documented that non-industrial countries with smaller current account deficits or current account surpluses have, on average, registered higher growth rates than those non-industrial countries that have run larger current account deficits. Further, Aizenman et al. (2007) show that developing countries that tend to rely more on domestic rather than foreign finance for their investment do better in terms of growth. However, there are also many benefits that can be brought by financial integration, such as to growth, financial sector development, and institutional quality (Kose et al. 2009a; Kose and Prasad 2010).

Indeed, the right approach might be to manage capital account opening in a manner that delivers potential direct and indirect benefits while controlling the risks. For instance, Kochhar et al. (2006) argue that India needs to rethink its capital account framework in the light of the need for infrastructure investment. This requires a rapid expansion of the country's real and financial absorptive capacity, including developing the corporate bond market, raising the limits on foreigners' participation in this market, and permitting greater capital outflows. On the other hand, increasing exposure to international capital flows could make countries more vulnerable to sudden stops, especially countries with significant current account deficits, including India. Therefore, it is important to systematically develop a strategy for opening up a country's capital account in a manner that maximizes the potential benefits while keeping under control the inevitable costs, which may be especially large during the initial phases of the transition to a more open capital account (Kose et al. 2009; Prasad 2009a).

REFERENCES

Aizenman, Joshua, Brian Pinto, and Artur Radziwill. 2007. 'Sources for Financing Domestic Capital—Is Foreign Saving a Viable Option for

Developing Countries?', *Journal of International Money and Finance,* 119 (2): 613–46.

Ang, James. 2009. 'Household Saving Behaviour in an Extended Life Cycle Model: A Comparative Study of China and India', *Journal of Development Studies,* 45 (8): 1344–59.

Athukorala, Prema-Chandra and Kunal Sen. 2004. 'The Determinants of Private Saving in India', *World Development,* 32 (3): 491–503.

Baldwin, Robert E. 2004. 'Openness and Growth: What's the Empirical Relationship?', in Robert E. Baldwin and L. Alan Winters (eds), *Challenges to Globalization: Analyzing the Economics.* Chicago, IL: The University of Chicago Press, pp. 499–526.

Basu, Kaushik and Annemie Maertens. 2007. 'The Pattern and Causes of Economic Growth in India', *Oxford Review of Economic Policy,* 23 (2): 143–67.

Bosworth, Barry, Susan M. Collins, and Arvind Virmani. 2007. 'Sources of Growth in the Indian Economy', NBER Working Paper No. 12901, National Bureau of Economic Research, Cambridge, MA.

Cavallo, Eduardo A. 2005. 'Output Volatility and Openness to Trade: A Reassessment', manuscript, Kennedy School of Government, Harvard University, Cambridge, MA.

Dollar, David and Aart Kraay. 2003. 'Institutions, Trade, and Growth', *Journal of Monetary Economics,* 50 (1): 133–62.

Frankel, Jeffrey and Eduardo A. Cavallo. 2004. 'Does Openness to Trade Make Countries More Vulnerable to Sudden Stops or Less? Using Gravity to Establish Causality', NBER Working Paper No. 10957, National Bureau of Economic Research, Cambridge, MA.

Frankel, Jeffrey and David Romer. 1999. 'Does Trade Cause Growth?', *American Economic Review,* 89 (3): 379–99.

Ghani, Ejaz. 2010. 'Is Service-led Growth a Miracle for South Asia', in Ejaz Ghani (ed.), *The Service Revolution in South Asia.* New Delhi: Oxford University Press.

Ghani, Ejaz and Rahul Anand. 2009. 'How Will Changes in Globalization Impact Growth in South Asia', Working Paper 5079, World Bank, Washington, DC.

Ghani, Ejaz and Homi Kharas. 2010. 'The Service Revolution in South Asia: An Overview', in Ejaz Ghani (ed.), *The Service Revolution in South Asia.* New Delhi: Oxford University Press.

Gordon, James and Poonam Gupta. 2004. 'Understanding India's Services Revolution', Working Paper 04/171, International Monetary Fund, Washington, DC.

Hauner, David. 2006. 'A Fiscal Price Tag for International Reserves', *International Finance,* 9 (2): 169–95.

Jeanne, Olivier. 2007. 'International Reserves in Emerging Market Countries: Too Much of a Good Thing', *Brookings Papers on Economic Activity,* 1: 1–79.

Kochhar, Kalpana, Utsav Kumar, Raghuram Rajan, Arvind Subramanian, and Ioannis Tokatlidis. 2006. 'India's Pattern of Development: What Happened, What Follows?', *Journal of Monetary Economics*, 53 (5): 981–1019.

Kose, M. Ayhan and Eswar Prasad. 2010. *Emerging Markets: Resilience and Growth Amid Global Turmoil.* Washington, DC: Brookings Institution Press.

Kose, M. Ayhan, Eswar Prasad, and Ashley Taylor. 2011. 'Thresholds in the Process of International Financial Integration', *Journal of International Money and Finance*, 30 (1): 147–79.

Kose, M. Ayhan, Eswar Prasad, Kenneth Rogoff, and Shang-Jin Wei. 2009a. 'Financial Globalization: A Reappraisal', *IMF Staff Papers*, 56 (1): 8–62.

Kose, M. Ayhan, Eswar Prasad, and Marco Terrones. 2009b. 'Does Financial Globalization Promote Risk Sharing?', *Journal of Development Economics*, 89 (2): 258–70.

————. 2009c. 'Does Openness to International Financial Flows Raise Productivity Growth?', *Journal of International Money and Finance*, 28 (4): 554–80.

Krueger, Anne O. and Andrew Berg. 2003. 'Trade, Growth, and Poverty: A Selective Survey', Working Paper 03/30, International Monetary Fund, Washington, DC.

Mohan, Rakesh. 2008. 'The Growth Record of the Indian Economy, 1950–2008: A Story of Sustained Savings and Investment', Keynote Address at Reserve Bank of India at the Conference 'Growth and Macroeconomic Issues and Challenges in India', organized by the Institute of Economic Growth, New Delhi. Available at http://www.bis.org/review/r080218c.pdf, accessed on 8 November 2010.

Moulick, Madhurantika. 2008. 'Understanding and Responding to the Savings Behavior of Poor People in the North East of India', USAid, microREPORT, No. 103. Available at http://www.microlinks.org/ev/en. php?ID=24906/201&ID2=DO/TOPIC, accessed on 8 November 2010.

Obstfeld, Maurice, Jay C. Shambaugh, and Alan Taylor. 2008. 'Financial Stability, the Trilemma, and International Reserves', NBER Working Paper No. 14217, National Bureau of Economic Research, Cambridge, MA.

Panagariya, Arvind. 2008. *India: The Emerging Giant.* New Delhi: Oxford University Press.

Prasad, Eswar. 2009. 'Some New Perspectives on India's Approach to Capital Account Liberalization', NBER Working Paper No. 14658, National Bureau of Economic Research, Cambridge, MA.

————. 2011. 'Rebalancing Growth in Asia', *International Finance*, 14 (1): 27–66.

Prasad, Eswar and Raghuram Rajan. 2008. 'A Pragmatic Approach to Capital Account Liberalization', *Journal of Economic Perspectives*, 22 (3): 149–72.

Prasad, Eswar, Raghuram Rajan, and Arvind Subramanian. 2007. 'Foreign Capital and Economic Growth', NBER Working Paper No. 13619, National Bureau of Economic Research, Cambridge, MA.

Prasad, Eswar, Kenneth Rogoff, Shang-Jin Wei, and M. Ayhan Kose. 2003. 'Effects of Financial Globalization on Developing Countries: Some Empirical Evidence', Occasional Paper No. 220, International Monetary Fund, Washington, DC.

Rodriguez, Francisco and Dani Rodrik. 2002. 'Trade Policy and Economic Growth: A Skeptic's Guide to the Cross-National Evidence', in Ben S. Bernanke and Kenneth Rogoff (eds), *NBER Macroeconomics Annual 2000*, Vol. 15. Cambridge, MA: MIT Press, pp. 261–338.

5

International Migration and Demographic Divergence between South Asia and the West

Çağlar Özden and Christopher Robert Parsons

Migration and remittances play an important role in the economic growth and poverty reduction story currently unfolding in South Asia. Millions of highly skilled South Asian engineers, professionals, and other workers live and work in Western OECD (Organisation for Economic Co-operation and Development) countries and the Persian Gulf. These migrants form some of the crucial bonds that link South Asian economies to global markets and facilitate transfer of key knowledge and technologies. As importantly, the remittances that the migrants send back sustain higher living standards, enable children to attend schools, and provide capital for numerous small businesses without access to formal finance channels. In short, migrants and their remittances are already a big part of the economic growth picture in South Asia for millions of people regardless of their location in the social and economic spectrum.

This chapter argues that the current migration patterns and outcomes observed for South Asia, especially with respect to OECD countries, are actually just the tip of the iceberg as compared to the actual potential. The main source of potential benefits of migration flows from South Asia to OECD countries is the significant demographic divergence between the two regions. While OECD countries, especially those in Western Europe and Japan, are experiencing rapid declines in fertility rates and increases in dependency ratios, South Asia is on an almost opposite trajectory.

However, this divergence is only expected to last for one generation, so the window of opportunity for implementing any economically significant labour mobility agreements is actually quite narrow. After identifying the current migration and demographic patterns for the two regions, exploring politically and institutionally feasible arrangements is the second goal of this chapter.

Before proceeding to the demographic profiles and trajectories of OECD and South Asian countries, it is important to provide a brief snapshot of why migration and remittances are important for South Asia. A detailed analysis is provided in Mohapatra and Ozden (2010).

Currently, almost 24 million people born in South Asia are living outside their countries of birth. The details by destination and origin are presented in Table 5.1. This is around 1.5 per cent of the total population of the region. Indians constitute a majority of the migrants due to the sheer size of the country, but the rate of emigration is higher for smaller countries, such as Nepal, Sri Lanka, and Afghanistan. In terms of destinations, 35 per cent of the migrants are in the Middle-Eastern countries, close to 20 per cent are in the wealthy OECD countries, and 43 per cent are in the other countries in the region. Among the most important examples of the latter are Nepalis, Pakistanis, and Bangladeshis who are currently living in India. The second section of the chapter provides a detailed picture of migration patterns.

Remittances form a significant share of external financial flows to South Asian countries according to estimates compiled by Ratha and Mohapatra (2009). Officially recorded remittance flows to South Asia were expected to have reached $66 billion in 2008. Migrant remittances were more than half the size of private medium- and long-term capital

TABLE 5.1   **Migrants from South Asia, 2000 (in thousand)**

	EU	USA and Canada	Middle-East	Other South Asian	Rest of the World	Total
Afghanistan	94	70	2,338	44	106	2,652
Bangladesh	285	122	666	5,534	266	6,873
India	793	1,400	4,049	2,045	755	9,042
Nepal	19	14	188	911	63	1,195
Pakistan	513	313	28	1,422	178	2,454
Sri Lanka	197	118	967	278	147	1,707

Source: Ozden et al. (2011).

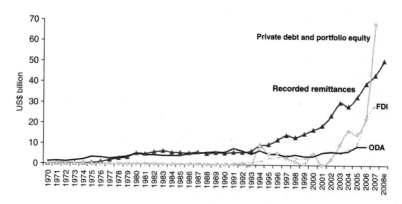

FIGURE 5.1   Remittances and Other Resource Flows to South Asia,
1999–2007

Source: Ratha and Mohapatra (2009).

flows received by South Asia in 2007, and more than four times the official development assistance (ODA) to the region in the previous year (see Figure 5.1). Remittances are the largest source of external financing after private capital flows to the region. The true size of the remittances is likely to be higher, due to significant unrecorded flows through formal and informal channels. The last section of this chapter provides a more detailed country-level picture of remittance flows to the region.

Current demographic trends in most OECD countries suggest that they are entering uncharted territories. Rapid declines in fertility rates and increases in life expectancy are leading to population and age dynamics that will have significant economic and social consequences in the very near future. The critical features of the new population profiles are the steadily declining under-30 and the rapidly growing above-65 years segments. Although these demographic patterns are the most evident in Western Europe, and Japan and Korea, similar trends are gradually emerging in Canada and the US, and in Australia and New Zealand as well. The projected changes in the population structures of Western Europe and Japan and Korea suggest that these regions will be facing labour shortages as early as 2025. Even if one accounts for immigration and changes in labour participation rates, the labour force is expected to decline in both regions and current labour shortages are likely to worsen over time. Of course, these will have many consequences for various components of the national economic and policy environment, such as fiscal balances, social protection, and welfare policies.

Meanwhile, developing regions are experiencing distinct demographic trends. Latin America and Eastern Europe, key suppliers of migrant labour to the US and Western Europe respectively, are in the process of completing their demographic transitions. Fertility rates are falling and life expectancy is increasing in both the regions, suggesting that growth in their labour supplies has already started to taper off. In stark contrast, countries in South Asia and Sub-Saharan Africa continue to experience rapid growth of their working-age populations, the outcome of a combination of improving life expectancy and continuing high fertility rates. Therefore, the populations in both the regions will remain extremely youthful and their labour force is projected to grow until around 2030.

The divergent trends of a shrinking labour force and an ageing population in OECD countries and growing labour supplies in South Asia and Sub-Saharan Africa provide compelling reasons for liberalizing the labour movement from both the regions to OECD countries. Moreover, the expected declines in the growth rates of the labour supply in both the regions within the next two decades lend urgency to facilitating the labour movement. Although the demographic profiles of South Asia and Sub-Saharan Africa suggest that both the regions could supply workers to OECD countries, the sheer size of South Asia's relatively well-educated labour force makes it a much more attractive source of labour than Sub-Saharan Africa.

Current demographic trends suggest that increased levels of immigration have already become an economic necessity in many OECD countries and will soon become so in the rest. However, strong and growing public opposition to higher migration flows will make it very difficult for OECD governments to pass legislations or reach agreements that facilitate the movement of workers from developing countries. OECD governments therefore need to search for alternative mechanisms that respond to their labour market pressures without triggering strong public and political opposition, especially in the shadow of the current economic crisis.

One potentially acceptable approach is to use temporary movement schemes of workers. This would help OECD countries meet their labour needs while addressing public fears which usually centre upon permanent movement of migrants. Ensuring temporariness of migration can be challenging but governments in host and source countries can use a range of incentive measures and policies to increase the likelihood of migrants' return. Such measures should involve various stakeholders, including employers and regulatory agencies in OECD countries and recruitment agencies and governments in South Asian countries. The objective of such measures would be to facilitate the movement of people through planned, safe, and lawful channels that make temporariness feasible and desirable for all parties involved—sending and receiving countries as well as the migrants themselves.

Some of the incentives that would facilitate temporariness include: (i) increasing workers' ability to reach their earning/saving targets, (ii) enhancing the advantages of using legal means to migrate and maintaining legal migration status, (iii) reducing the costs of temporary emigration by, among other things, lowering the cost of placement services and keeping costs of administrative procedures related to emigration to a minimum, (iv) increasing incentives for return by enhancing financial transfers: facilitating savings, social security, and remittances, and (v) providing portability of pensions and certain social security and health benefits through bilateral social security agreements. Regulatory agencies can also use sanctions to discourage permanent stay. Some of the sanctions that have been used by countries include an employer's loss of right to continue to recruit abroad, punitive measures that are applied to those who facilitate irregular emigration, and joint liability of destination-country employer and country-of-origin agent/recruitment agency in relation to temporary workers.

Many studies have chronicled the aberrant demographic trajectory of the world's population. Following the onset of the Industrial Revolution, many countries have completed their demographic transitions, while others have begun their journeys from high birth and death rates to sustainably lower ones. In tandem with significant advances in medicine— among other contributory economic and social factors—many of today's rich industrialized nations are now entering a period of unprecedented ageing. Figure 5.2 highlights the issue by plotting the total dependency ratio for the rich OECD nations[1] as well as for the countries of South Asia. Whereas in 1990 the dependency ratio for OECD was under 50, in 2050 this number is projected to be over 70. The news is not all bad. A healthier older generation tends to have high rates of saving and makes large intra-generational transfers. Ultimately, however, there do need to be sufficient numbers in the labour force to support those elsewhere, both in terms of required services and social protection.

---

[1] For the sake of comparability over time, 'rich OECD' comprises those nations that have been relatively well-off over the entire period. These are the OECD countries of North America, Oceania, Western Europe, and East Asia.

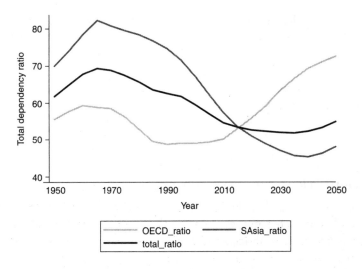

FIGURE 5.2   Historical and Projected Dependency Ratios in the OECD
and South Asia, 1950–2050

Source: United Nations (2009).

Since most regions in the world are at least on the path towards lower birth and death rates, there remain few in a position to provide labour abroad. In the case of OECD, the only source regions with sufficient numbers are Sub-Saharan Africa and South Asia. Although variations exist, as a broad region, Sub-Saharan Africa would still be classified as not yet having entered its demographic transition. Differences are also evident within South Asia, since Sri Lanka has completed its transformation while Afghanistan is yet to start its. Nonetheless, South Asia is the only region that has a sufficiently large population to be able to offset, in any meaningful way, this demographic deficit in the relatively richer 'North' and provide the labour to potentially reap the benefits of its 'demographic dividend'.

As can be seen from Figure 5.2, while in recent history the overall dependency ratio for the collective OECD has been increasing, the corresponding ratio for South Asia has been falling rapidly since the late 1960s. It is expected to continue to fall until 2040 and then gradually increase. The middle line is the weighted average dependency ratio of the two regions, representing therefore the theoretical (although somewhat infeasible) outcome that could be obtained with complete freedom of movement of labour between the two regions. This serves to highlight the potential demographic benefits of increased mobility of South Asians to OECD countries. It is also important to note that from around 2040, the dependency ratios in South Asia are projected to increase again, partly in response to falling fertility rates throughout the region. As such, the window of opportunity in which any benefits can be derived from this potential migration is relatively narrow. The time to prepare for change is now. The emphasis of this chapter is on the potential benefits of this migration, the beneficiaries of any migration programme, and the policies that need be put in place to reap these benefits.

POPULATION PATTERNS IN DESTINATION COUNTRIES

We begin our analysis by investigating the demographic patterns of the relatively rich countries of the North. We concentrate on six major receiving regions with relatively divergent demographic and migration patterns, especially with respect to South Asian migrants. These are: (i) the United States and Canada, (ii) Australia and New Zealand, (iii) the United Kingdom, (iv) the Rest of Europe,[2] (v) the Persian Gulf, and (vi) Japan and Korea. Figures 5.3a–f show the population dynamics among these regions and the relevant projections until 2050.[3] The total population in each country is divided into four groups—young (0–15), mid1 (16–39), mid2 (40–64), and old (65+). Each line in the figures represents the number of people whose age is under that age grouping's upper limit. For example, according to UN projections, there will be slightly over 72 million people in the United Kingdom in 2050 (top line in Figure 5.3a), around 56 million people at age 64 and below (second line from the top), 34 million people below age 39 (third line), and finally slightly below 12 million people below age 15 (bottom line). Interpreted in another way, the *area* between each line presents the population size of each of these age groups.

The Anglo-Saxon countries (Figures 5.3a–c) largely exhibit two patterns in the evolution of their populations. First, they evince considerable population growth with the United Kingdom being the least pronounced. Each age category is relatively flat, especially after

[2] The Rest of Europe basically refers to Western Europe and does not include Eastern European countries. It consists of the EU-15 countries (with the exception of the United Kingdom) as well as Norway, Iceland, and Switzerland.

[3] Note that all fundamental demographic data regarding population dynamics (such as age distribution, fertility levels, and dependency ratios) in this chapter are provided by the United Nations Population Division. Projections are based upon the medium fertility assumption.

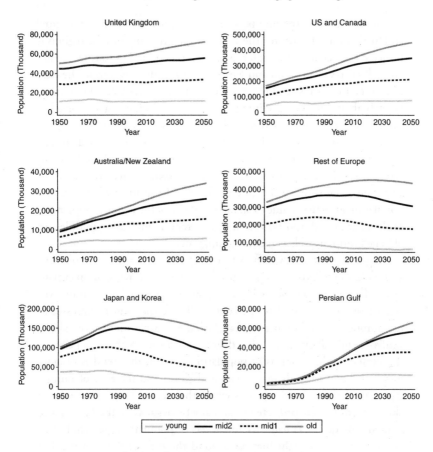

FIGURES 5.3a–f   Population Dynamics (Projected), 1950–2050, in
Various Destination Countries

Source: United Nations (2009).

1990, with the exception of the 'old'. This is the age bracket that is
widening and is projected to grow far more rapidly in the future. These
trends demonstrate that the increase in overall population is mainly due
to ageing, together with a certain amount of in-migration. The Rest of
Europe (Figure 5.3d) and Japan and Korea (Figure 5.3e) exhibit generally
similar demographic trajectories with a couple of differences. First, the
'young' constitute an ever-dwindling proportion of the population whose
decline began around the 1980s. This deterioration in the numbers of the
'young' is particularly striking in the Rest of Europe. Conversely, the 'old'
in both these latter regions constitute a considerably larger proportion of

the population and the numbers in this category are projected to grow still further into the future. The overall population in both the regions is projected to decline, although this process is expected to start far sooner and fall far faster in Japan and Korea. Importantly however, in the Rest of Europe the total size of the middle-aged group is projected to remain fairly high and to start declining around 2020. In Japan and Korea the number of the middle-aged started falling as early as 2000.

The Persian Gulf region (Figure 5.3f) exhibits very different demographics. The total population skyrocketed over 1950–2050. In terms of specific age groups, the number of young increased until 1990 and then levelled off in subsequent decades. In short, while the earlier population growth was due to an increased size of the young group, much of the later growth (post-1990) is due to rapidly increasing middle and old age groups as well as incoming migrants.

Figures 5.4 and 5.5 turn instead to the *growth* in total populations and evolution of fertility rates in these six regions. The population growth rate is the average exponential rate of growth of the total population over a given period[4] expressed as a percentage. The fertility rate is expressed as the number of children per woman.[5] All the destination regions exhibit similar trends albeit to differing degrees, with the notable exception of the Persian Gulf. In terms of population growth, the trend is broadly downward and towards zero. Japan and Korea and the Rest of Europe represent the most extreme cases where the current rates of growth are close to zero but are projected to actually be negative in the future. The United Kingdom has had very low levels of population growth, but in fact experienced a slight increase around the turn of the century. The Persian Gulf countries, in contrast, experienced huge population growth throughout the decade of the 1970s in response to the rapid increase in oil incomes. This process also led to rapid migration flows. Until 2050, the Persian Gulf countries are expected to sustain the highest levels of population growth among the six regions analysed here.

The Anglo-Saxon countries (United Kingdom, United States, Canada, Australia, and New Zealand) again exhibit very similar patterns in terms of fertility rates which fell until the mid-1980s, thereafter remaining flat, hovering around 2. In comparison, fertility rates in Japan and Korea and

---

[4] This is calculated as $\ln\left(\frac{P_t}{P_0}\right)/t$, where 0 refers to the beginning time period and t refers to the length of time over which the measure is calculated.

[5] This is the average number of children a hypothetical cohort of women would have at the end of their reproductive periods. They are assumed to be subject to the fertility rates of a given period during their whole lives and are assumed to live throughout the period.

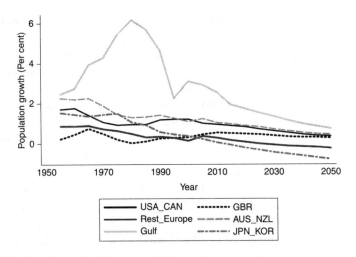

FIGURE 5.4   Population Growth Rates in Destinations, 1950–2050
(Projected)

Source: United Nations (2009).

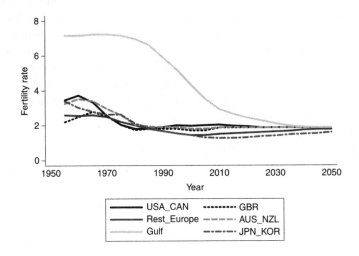

FIGURE 5.5   Total Fertility Rates in Destinations, 1950–2050 (Projected)

Source: United Nations (2009).

the Rest of Europe, which started from lower fertility levels in 1950, have fallen faster and more significantly over recent decades. Today, the fertility rates in both the regions are under 2, when a common rule-of-thumb measure of the replacement fertility rate for developed countries is somewhere around 2.1. These low rates help explain both the low numbers of the young in these regions as well as the projected declining population in the future (in the absence of migration).

Figures 5.6a–f show the total, child, and old dependency ratios for each of our six major destination regions,[6] which prove useful for assessing future demographic trends and their impact upon residents' lives, especially in terms of labour market patterns and social protection issues. Again, the Anglo-Saxon countries exhibit the most similar patterns. They have a gradually declining total dependency ratio up until around 2010, after which their ratios increase. Importantly, for all of these countries the dependency ratio of the old surpasses that of the young, immediately for the United Kingdom and around 2025 for countries in North America and Oceania. The dependency ratios in both Japan and Korea and the Rest of Europe are far more exaggerated, portending therefore the future global trend and what lies in store for the Anglo-Saxon countries after 2050. In these regions, the total dependency ratios have already started rising, dramatically so in Japan and Korea. In both these regions the old dependency ratio has already surpassed that of the young, reflecting increasing life expectancies in conjunction with rapidly falling rates of fertility. The projections for the Persian Gulf countries, however, represent the other extreme. Across this region, dependency ratios are forecast to continue to fall until around 2030 after which they are expected to increase, but only mildly. At no point is the dependency of the 'young' projected to overtake that of the 'old'. As we shall see dependency ratios in the Persian Gulf region are far more similar to those of South Asia.

POPULATION PATTERNS IN SOUTH ASIA

Now we turn to a comparable analysis in the six largest countries of South Asia, namely India, Pakistan, Afghanistan, Bangladesh, Sri Lanka, and Nepal. We omit a discussion of the Maldives and Bhutan since although they represent interesting case studies, collectively they comprise just a sliver of the total population in the region.

Figures 5.7a–f show the evolution of population in these countries. Populations have clearly been increasing sharply in recent decades.

---

[6] The child dependency ratio is calculated as the numbers aged 0–15, divided by the working population (15–64). The old dependency ratio is calculated as the numbers aged 65+, divided by the working population (15–64). The total dependency ratio is the ratio of (the sum of) the young and old to the working-age population. These ratios are expressed as the number of dependents per 100 persons of working age.

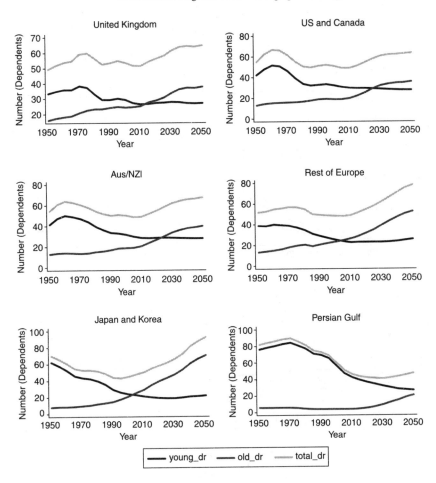

FIGURES 5.6a–f   Dependency Ratios in Destination Regions,
1950–2050 (Projected)

Source: United Nations (2009).

The formats of the figures are identical to the ones presented for the six main destination regions. India, Pakistan, Bangladesh, and Nepal exhibit very similar population trends. The populations of all the four countries were increasing until 1970, after which they grew even more rapidly. Importantly, for these countries the 'young' group (which is far broader when compared to that of the destination regions) remains flat, such that after 2010 further population increases will result from changes in life expectancy and not from ever greater numbers of births.

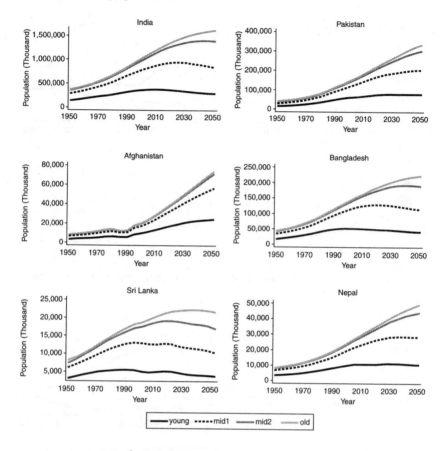

FIGURES 5.7a–f   **Population Dynamics in South Asia, 1950–2050**
(Projected)

Source: United Nations (2009).

This is exemplified by the projected widening of the remaining age brackets. However, even by 2050 the proportion in the 'old' bracket will be far narrower than in the cases mentioned earlier indicating lower life expectancies than in the other parts of the world. At the same time, the proportion of the young, although flat, also comprises a larger fraction of the population in 2050, demonstrating the fact that fertility rates will also remain *relatively* high for longer in these countries.

Afghanistan and Sri Lanka remain outliers. Afghanistan, having borne the brunt of military invasion, civil conflict, and political upheaval for decades, had relatively few people until 1990, when the population began to take off. Unlike the four countries mentioned earlier, the vast majority of this growth will result from births, causing the lower two age brackets to expand substantially. The numbers in the 'old' category will grow, although to a far lesser extent, demonstrating the low life expectancy which is expected to be prevalent in the coming decades. Sri Lanka, having traditionally adopted sophisticated health, education, and migration strategies, exhibits population trends that are different from the rest of the region and in the opposite direction. The numbers of the 'young' in Sri Lanka are already dwindling due to the country's rapid movement through its demographic transition and the significant out-migration that it has experienced. At the same time, a significant proportion of the population lives into old age, a far greater fraction as compared to the other countries in South Asia.

Figures 5.8 and 5.9 present the population growth and fertility rates of the six South Asian countries. These countries exhibit rising population growth rates until around the mid-1980s, after which the rates decline steadily. The only exception is Afghanistan, which demonstrates a sharp fall at the time of the Soviet occupation followed by a corresponding bounce. By 2050, it is projected that India's population growth rate will be close to zero, while Sri Lanka's will actually be negative. Rapid declines in fertility rates, both actual and projected, have, however, been truly startling. Sri Lanka's fertility rates started falling first (reflecting its early entry into the demographic transition) in 1960. However, by 2010, all

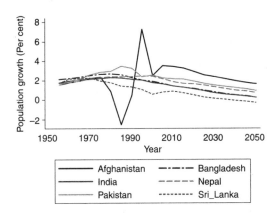

FIGURE 5.8   Population Growth Rates in South Asia, 1950–2050
(Projected)

Source: United Nations (2009).

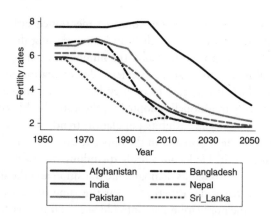

FIGURE 5.9   Total Fertility Rates in South Asia, 1950–2050 (Projected)

Source: United Nations (2009).

the countries exhibited sharp falls. Afghanistan lags behind the others, but its rates are eventually expected to converge with those of the other countries in the region.

Figures 5.10a–f show the parallel dependency ratio graphs for the six origin countries of interest in South Asia. Again four countries, India, Pakistan, Bangladesh, and Nepal, exhibit very similar patterns. In these countries the 'total' and 'child' dependency ratios have remained extremely high but have started falling rapidly and are projected to fall further. At the same time, the 'old' dependency ratio has remained fairly flat, but this is forecast to rise gently until 2050. Afghanistan, again an outlier, is projected to have an extremely flat 'old' dependency ratio and 'total' and 'child' dependency ratios that fall less swiftly. Sri Lanka, in contrast, exhibits a 'total' dependency ratio that is more U-shaped, and is actually very similar to that of the United Kingdom or United States. Here the 'total' dependency fell until the turn of the century after which it started increasing. At the same time, the child dependency ratio has been falling dramatically and this trend is expected to continue, reflecting the low numbers of young that are forecast for the future. What drives the upward section of the 'U' is the steep increase in the 'old' dependency ratio, which by the end of the period, is expected to have surpassed that of the 'young'. As different as it is, Sri Lanka portends the demographics of the region as a whole.

In summary, population growth rates across the major destination regions are declining or are on the verge of becoming negative. At the same

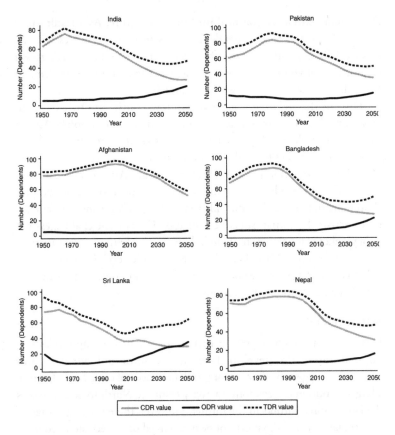

FIGURES 5.10a–f   Dependency Ratios in South Asia, 1950–2050
(Projected)

Source: United Nations (2009).

time, low fertility rates, which are currently close to the replacement level, together with higher life expectancies, are contributing to rapidly ageing populations. Fewer young people and greater numbers of old will inevitably result in significantly higher 'old' dependency ratios in these countries. Increasingly therefore, across these destination OECD countries, fewer workers will remain to support those not in the labour force, which will ultimately translate into a greater demand for labour from abroad.

In complete contrast, the countries in South Asia have experienced, or are experiencing, huge population growths. Relatively lower projected rates of life expectancy (with the notable exception of Sri Lanka), coupled with relatively high fertility rates, will ensure that their populations will also remain extremely youthful into the near future. As a result, until around 2030, the total dependency ratios in these countries will fall substantially. Up until then, therefore, across most of South Asia there will be a surplus of young workers at precisely the same time as the demand for global workers from the wealthier North increases.

During this relatively narrow window (until 2030), there will exist considerable potential for labour to migrate from South Asia to the wealthier North. The crucial point is that the time frame of this opportunity is rather limited. As cultural norms converge on lower rates of fertility, population growth rates across South Asia are also expected to fall. This, in combination with an ageing population, albeit at a far slower rate than in the North, will eventually result in rising dependency ratios across the Indian subcontinent too. The current challenges that policymakers face therefore include how best to harness this potential, how to maximize the benefits to both sending and receiving regions, and how to militate against the potential pitfalls that are commonly associated with large international migrations.

MIGRATION

It is mainly through migration that Asian labour can support ageing populations in the developed countries. Some policymakers and economists suggest that outsourcing and international trade can help move a large portion of the economic activity from the North to South Asia as the labour force shrinks in the former. However, there is a large range of non-tradable services that cannot be outsourced or traded and need to be locally supplied. Among these are healthcare and household services that will especially be in high demand as the populations in the North age.

Migration could also have huge consequences for relieving resource constraints in the origin countries in South Asia that will come under increasing pressure in the near future. Ultimately, we wish to assess the future benefits from these migration flows and discuss their potential in terms of the current policy environment. However, before doing so we examine current and past migration patterns in terms of geographic coverage as well as the age and education profiles of migrants.

Ozden et al. (2011) find that the proportion of global migration relative to overall population remained remarkably stable between 1960 and 2000, the last year for which comprehensive data exist. In addition, they find that the great increase in the *numbers* of migrants between 1960 and 2000 is the result of a far larger number of people emigrating from the relatively poor 'South' to the more affluent 'North'.

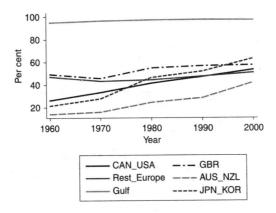

FIGURES 5.11   Percentage of Immigrants from All Developing
Countries to Major Destinations

Source: Ozden et al. (2011).

The trends in Figure 5.11 clearly demonstrate that in *every* destination region, there have been increasing migrant stocks from developing regions, although in varying degrees. In 2000, the immigrant stocks in Australia and New Zealand and Japan and Korea comprised three times as many migrants from developing countries as in 1960. Between 1960 and 2000, Australia and New Zealand maintained the lowest proportion of migrants from developing countries in their immigrant stock because of the large influx of migrants from Europe, predominantly the United Kingdom. Similarly, Japan and Korea attracted migrants mainly from other developed nations. However, over the period, large numbers from China, North Korea, and Brazil have changed the composition significantly, to the extent that in 2000 Japan and Korea had overtaken both Europe and North America in terms of the proportion of migrants from developing countries in their stock. The proportion of developing-country migrants in the United States and Canada has doubled. On the other hand, the proportions in the Rest of Europe have remained remarkably stable. It is the large inflows from the Philippines, India, Vietnam, China, and Cuba to the United States which account for the changing composition of the migrant stock in North America. In the countries of the Persian Gulf, the proportions of those from developing countries have always been extremely high, around 95 per cent.

Figure 5.12 shows the total number of immigrants in key destination regions as a fraction of their total populations. Japan and Korea have historically been the most isolationist countries in terms of the

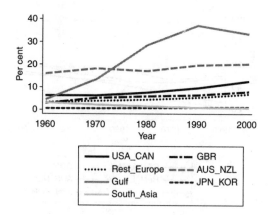

FIGURE 5.12   Immigrant Concentrations in Major Destinations
Source: Ozden et al. (2011).

proportions of migrants admitted, even though they face the most severe demographic challenges. The trend line for the share of migrants in South Asian countries, composed mostly of regional migrants, declines gradually over time. Most of these migrant stocks emerged during the partition and as that population aged, their overall ratio declined. The countries of Europe (including the United Kingdom), have since 1960 accepted an ever-growing fraction of immigrants relative to their home populations. This trend is largely replicated in the data for the two North American destinations, although they exhibit a flatter trend in the earlier decades. Data for Australia and New Zealand, the youngest countries in the group, reveal that the overall immigrant concentrations have remained fairly stable throughout the 40 years for which we have data. This is in spite of the specific immigrant policies adopted to promote international migration to these destinations throughout the period. The most interesting case study in this context is that of the Persian Gulf, where the immigration concentration soared from under 5 to over 33 per cent, reflecting the increase in oil wealth.

So how do the migrations from South Asia compare to those from developing countries as a whole? Figure 5.13 presents the fraction of South Asians in each of our destination country migrant stocks. In general, South Asians comprise a relatively small fraction of the total immigrant stocks—5 per cent in Japan and Korea, Australia and New Zealand, the Rest of Europe and the United States, and Canada. Historically United Kingdom has been the single country with the

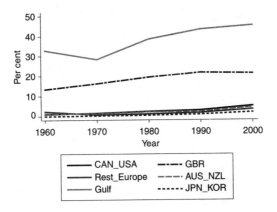

FIGURES 5.13   Immigrants from South Asia to Destinations, 1960–2000
Source: Ozden et al. (2011).

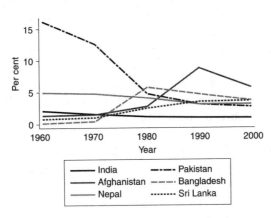

FIGURES 5.14   Emigrant Concentrations, South Asia, 1960–2000
Source: Ozden et al. (2011).

highest concentration of migrants from South Asia, around a fifth of the total in 2000. However, it is the Gulf that hosts the largest fraction of South Asians relative to the total stock. This arguably reflects the strong selection of mostly unskilled migrants from South Asia as well as from Egypt, Yemen, and the Philippines.

Figure 5.14 plots the ratio of origin-country emigrant stocks as a proportion of their total native populations. In terms of these emigrant concentrations, the early decades are dominated by political migrations during the partition of India. In 1960, over 16 per cent of the people born in Pakistan resided outside its borders. The corresponding figures are 5 per cent for Nepal and 2 per cent for India. These reflect both the size and growth of their domestic populations. Over time, the emigrant concentrations across all these countries have fallen due to the attrition in their migrant stocks, that is because of return migration and deaths of the original migrants from the partition. Bangladesh and Afghanistan both exhibit fairly flat trends until their respective conflicts, after which the percentage of emigrants relative to their total populations increased significantly. Sri Lanka, again the outlier, exhibits a steady increase in the concentration of emigrants throughout the period and no noticeable jump is obvious around the time of the start of the civil war in 1983.

All regions, therefore, demonstrated a greater propensity to accept migrants from abroad between 1960 and 2000, although there is significant variation. Over the same period, there has been increasing diversification in terms of the number of countries from which host nations accept migrants; with increasing numbers originating in developing countries. On the whole, however, the overall concentrations of migrants in the various destinations are reasonably low. Only the Persian Gulf and to a lesser extent the United Kingdom, have traditionally admitted significant proportions of South Asians relative to their total immigrant stocks, although large numbers are also hosted by North America. Despite the fairly large numbers of South Asians residing abroad—over 21 million officially recorded in 2000—the actual fractions of those migrating still remain fairly small due to their large domestic populations at home.

The next question is between which pairs of countries have migrations taken place to date, since this might give provide an insight into future migration patterns. In terms of regions, in 2000, and excepting South Asia itself, the Gulf, the United States (and Canada), and the United Kingdom were by far the most important destinations for South Asian migrants (as a whole). These countries were home to 4.6 million (45 per cent of the total immigrant stock), 2 million (5 per cent), and 1 million (21 per cent), South Asian migrants respectively. Collectively, the Rest of Europe also hosts 1 million South Asian migrants (3.3 per cent of the total), while Australia and New Zealand, and Japan and Korea are home to under a quarter of a million between them. It is important to note that here the data refer to the foreign born; in other words to first generation migrants. If we were instead able to use a definition based on an ethnicity dimension, the number of *ethnic* immigrants would be much higher in those countries since it would include the children born in the destinations.

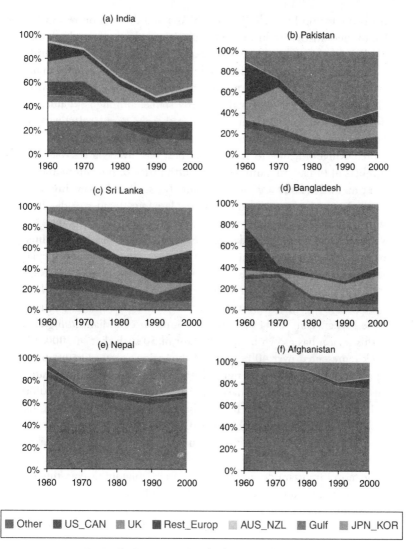

FIGURES 5.15a–f   Emigrant Stocks from South Asia, 1960–2000
Source: Ozden et al. (2011).

Figures 5.15a–f show the composition of emigrant stocks from each of our six South Asian countries to the rest of the world, while excluding South Asia as a destination. We begin our analysis with India, the most populous country in the region. The total number of Indian migrants increased by half a million between 1960 and 2000. This again—and this is the reason for excluding South Asia as a destination region—is due to the statistical influence of the partition. However, leaving intra-South Asian migrants aside, while the actual numbers of first-generation Indian migrants abroad has changed relatively little, the composition has changed fundamentally. The number of Indians in the rest of the world (classified as 'other') has remained fairly stable, although the fraction of the total that this represents has fallen sharply. Popular destinations included in this catch-all term include Singapore and Malaysia. The United Kingdom, due to its colonial ties, has always attracted high numbers of Indian migrants, over one-fifth in 1970. But this figure fell over time and in 2000 was just 9 per cent. The stock of Indian emigrants in the Rest of Europe tripled during the last four decades of the 20th century. By 2000 the region was almost as important a destination region as the UK (8 per cent). Canada and the United States, however, continue to attract ever greater numbers from India. These North American countries collectively attracted over 14 times as many migrants in 2000 as in 1960, over one-quarter of the total emigrant stock of Indians in the world. By far the most important destination for Indian migrants is the Persian Gulf. Data show that the number of Indian immigrants in this region has grown by over a factor of 50 such that in 2000 this stock represented over 40 per cent of the region's total migrant stock. Japan and Korea have experienced negligible migration from India. Australia and New Zealand have experienced an upsurge (from 18,000 to 113,000) in immigration from India, but they continue to focus on admitting only the most highly skilled.

Pakistan, the second most populous country in the region, exhibits fairly similar migration patterns to those of India. The United Kingdom is the most important destination for Pakistani migrants accounting for 14 per cent of the total stock, compared to just 13 per cent in the United States and Canada and 11 per cent in the Rest of Europe. Importantly then, although the number of Pakistanis in the US and Canada has increased by a factor of over 20, these countries are far less important for Pakistan than for the other countries in the region. Similar to the Indian case, the importance of the Rest of Europe significantly jumped for Pakistan between 1990 and 2000. Should the trend continue, it will likely overtake both the United Kingdom and the countries of North America as the most important destination region for Pakistanis. Seventy-five times as many Pakistanis were residing in the countries of the Persian Gulf in 2000 when compared to 1960. In terms of the share of total migrant populations, the Persian Gulf countries represent a more important destination for Pakistani migrants than for Indian migrants. Finally, few Pakistanis migrate to Oceania or East Asia.

Bangladesh demonstrates similar overall migration patterns to both India and Pakistan with slight differences. First, the Persian Gulf is by far the most important emigration destination, home to nearly three-quarter of all Bangladeshis abroad in 1990 and still well over half in 2000. This declining share has occurred in parallel with relatively more Bangladeshis migrating to both the United States and Canada and countries in the Rest of Europe, most notably France, Italy, and Germany. In comparison to North America and continental Europe, UK is a more important destination for migrants from Bangladesh. The share of migrants in UK stayed quite stable since 1980, while the overall number of immigrants from Bangladesh increased rapidly. Again, neither Australia and New Zealand nor Japan and Korea host significant numbers of migrants from Bangladesh.

Sri Lanka's migration history contrasts with that of the other South Asian countries already analysed. Although the Persian Gulf is an important destination for Sri Lankans, in terms of official data, greater numbers of Sri Lankans resided in the Rest of Europe in 2000. This is due, in large part, to the migration of ethnic Tamils from Sri Lanka, large numbers of whom reside in Germany, Switzerland, France, and to a lesser extent the Netherlands. Collectively, this region accounts for around one-third of all Sri Lankans abroad. The Gulf has also experienced large increases in the number of Sri Lankan migrants, nearly a 50-fold increase over the period, and according to official statistics, today around one-third of all Sri Lankans reside there. While the United Kingdom is an important destination for South Asians as a whole, this is not so in the case of Sri Lanka (or Nepal). America, Canada, Australia, and New Zealand have been relatively important destinations throughout the period. Japan and Korea again attract few from Sri Lanka, while other notable destination countries include Thailand and Malaysia.

Overall, there are far fewer Nepalese abroad when compared to the other South Asian nations and those who reside abroad exhibit fairly different migration patterns. First, the largest portion of Nepalese migrants lives in India. Outside the region, the Persian Gulf remains an important destination, hosting around one-fifth of recorded Nepalese emigrants in 2000. In stark contrast to the other origin countries, the United Kingdom hosts negligible numbers from Nepal. Some 2 per cent reside in North America, while some 4 per cent make their home in the Rest of Europe, predominantly in Germany, the Netherlands, and Switzerland. Interestingly, one-tenth of all Nepalese emigrants live in either Australia and New Zealand or Japan and Korea. Indeed, there was a noticeable increase in the relative importance of both these regions between 1990 and 2000. In the case of Nepal, however, the most popular destination region is our remainder category, with the largest numbers migrating to Thailand and Malaysia.

Last, we turn to the case of Afghanistan. Perhaps unsurprisingly, given its history, the most popular destinations for Afghans are the bordering countries of Iran and Tajikistan. North America and the Rest of Europe each host around 5 per cent of Afghans, the latter predominantly in the Netherlands, Germany, Italy, and France. The Persian Gulf attracts just over an eighth of all Afghans abroad, while few Afghans are hosted by the United Kingdom, Oceania, or East Asia.

Next we examine migrant characteristics, beginning with age. Figure 5.16 shows the number of migrants from each country in South Asia in OECD, by five-year age brackets. Correspondingly, Figure 5.17 shows the percentage of migrants in each five-year age bracket above the age of 15 and below the age of 70.[7] Clearly, the numbers from India and

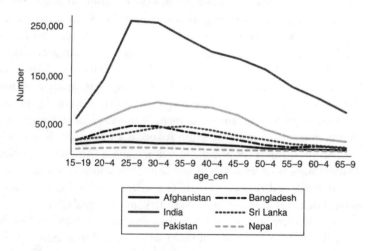

FIGURES 5.16   **Age Breakdown of South Asian Immigrants in the OECD (Numbers), 2000**

Source: OECD DIOC Database (2008).

[7] Data for these graphs have been taken from the OECD DIOC database. However, one of the limitations is in not having data on those aged less than 15 years. Moreover, since the age categories above 69 years are aggregated in the underlying data, we omit these from our analysis here since they serve to skew the figures.

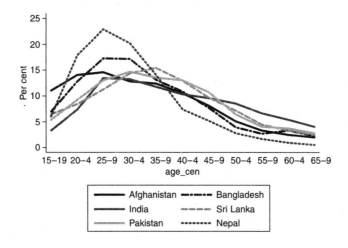

FIGURES 5.17   Age Breakdown of South Asian Immigrants in the
OECD (Percentage), 2000

Source: OECD DIOC Database (2008).

Pakistan dominate, with a majority of Indians being in their mid-20s and mid-30s. However, all the age brackets from India are well populated, including that of those aged above 50, which is conspicuously sparser in the other countries of South Asia, because they entered their demographic transitions later. Nepal has by far the youngest emigrant stock in OECD, since four-fifths are aged under 40, and approximately one-half under 30. In terms of ages, Afghani and Bangladeshi migrants are very comparable since around two-thirds of the emigrant population of each is under 40 and around two-fifths is under 30. Similarly, emigrants in OECD from Pakistan and Sri Lanka are very alike (over half of each under 40 and one-quarter under 30). India has the oldest emigrant population. Less than one half is aged less than 40 and less than one-quarter aged under 30.

Figures 5.18a–f, investigate the selection of South Asian migrants by age category. In others words, they compare the age distributions of a country's domestic and emigrant populations. Across all origin countries, the proportion of emigrants aged 25 or under is far lower than that of the domestic population; with the exception of Nepal, the country with by far the youngest emigrant stock. Similarly, and unsurprisingly, a higher proportion of older South Asians reside at home as opposed to abroad; with the exception of India—the country with by far the oldest emigrant stock. Interestingly, India has a greater proportion of emigrants in every age category with the exception of those aged under

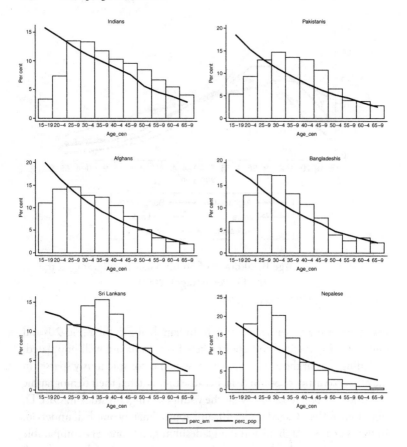

FIGURES 5.18a–f   Selection of South Asian Migrants by Age, 2000

Source: OECD DIOC Database (2008); United Nations Population Division, *World Population Prospects*, 2008 revision.

25. Bangladesh and Nepal have a greater propensity to send migrants aged between 25 and 40 to OECD, when compared to their domestic populations. Generally, Sri Lankans and Pakistanis in OECD are a little older, with the greatest differences (selections) occurring between those aged between 30 and 50.

Figures 5.19a–f compare the age distributions of migrants and natives across our destination regions[8] such that the gaps between the

---

[8] Due to data constraints, Rest of Europe is not directly comparable to its aforementioned namesake. Rather, this group comprises all those European countries that are members

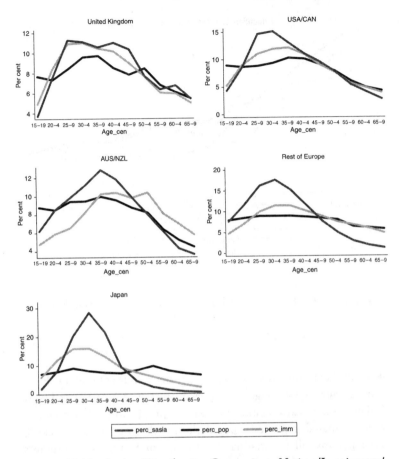

FIGURES 5.19a–f   Age Distribution Comparison: Natives/Immigrants/
South Asians in Major Destinations, 2000

Source: OECD DIOC Database (2008); United Nations (2009).

plotted lines highlight a greater/smaller proportion of natives vis-à-vis
immigrants, or vice-versa. The three lines represent the distribution of
natives, the distribution of all migrants, and finally the distribution

of the OECD—for which comparable data exist (as opposed to simply all members of
the EU-27 with the exception of the United Kingdom). The full list includes: Austria,
Belgium, the Czech Republic, Denmark, Finland, France, Greece, Hungary, Ireland, Italy,
Luxembourg, the Netherlands, Norway, Poland, Portugal, Slovakia, Spain, Sweden, and
Switzerland. Korea also had to be dropped from being twinned with Japan in this analysis,
again due to data constraints.

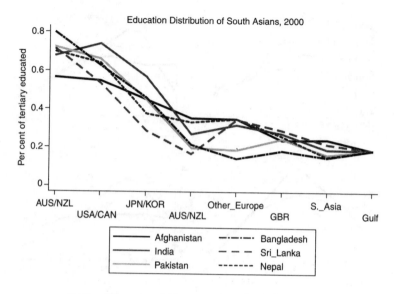

FIGURE 5.20   Educational Composition of South Asians in Major
Destinations, 2000

Source: Docquier et al. (2010).

of South Asian migrants. Several interesting trends are evident. First, across all our regions—again with the exception of Australia and New Zealand—there exist significantly higher proportions of immigrants when compared to domestic populations in the younger age brackets. Second, across all the destinations the age of South Asian migrants is disproportionately skewed towards the younger age brackets and correspondingly such migrants are far scarcer in the upper age brackets. Looking comparatively across all the figures we can see that Japan has by far the youngest immigrant population (two-thirds of all migrants under the age of 40 and four-fifths under 40 from South Asia). Following from our earlier discussion, we can see that Australia and New Zealand have by far the oldest immigrant populations (less than two-fifths of all immigrants under the age of 40 and less than half of all South Asians under 40), and an investigation of the South Asian migrant stocks over time reveals that this is the result of migrant selection as opposed to the bulk of these migrations occurring in the past.

An examination of the educational composition of migrants to various destinations reveals strong patterns of migrant selection (Figure 5.20). Broadly, Australia and New Zealand attract the most highly skilled South Asians, followed by the United States, Canada, Japan, and Korea. However, a higher proportion of highly skilled Indians migrate to North America. The countries of the Persian Gulf, other countries in South Asia, and the United Kingdom host the smallest fractions of highly skilled South Asians. The most highly skilled group across all our origins and destinations is Bangladeshis in Australia and New Zealand, while the least skilled are Bangladeshis in the United Kingdom and Nepalese in India. Taking simple averages across the origin countries reveals that Indians are the most highly skilled emigrants.

Figures 5.21a and 5.21b show the annual remittance inflows to our six major origin nations in the region. India is plotted separately since its remittances statistically dominate the remittances to the other countries in the region. Unsurprisingly, given the numbers involved, remittance inflows to India are greater than the sum of remittance flows to all of the other countries in South Asia combined. Interestingly, Pakistan's remittance inflows were on a downward trajectory from 1983 until 2002, soon after which (2005) Bangladesh overtook Pakistan in terms of the amount received at home despite having a marginally smaller population. Without bilateral remittance figures, however, we are not in a position to speculate on the relationship between destination or skill level and the amount of remittances sent home.

POLICY IMPLICATIONS

The current demographic patterns across the globe present important social and economic challenges. One of the key observations is the

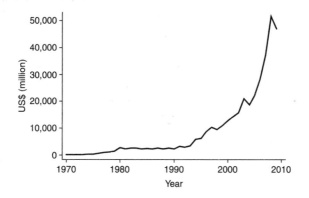

FIGURE 5.21a   Remittance Inflows to India, 1970–2009

Source: Mohapatra et al. (2010).

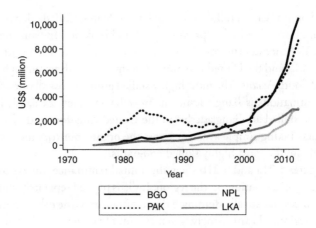

FIGURES 5.21b   Remittance Inflows to South Asian Countries, 1975–2009

Source: Mohapatra et al. (2010).

opposing patterns, especially between the many OECD countries and the South Asian countries (along with Sub-Saharan Africa to a certain extent). Western Europe and Japan and Korea are experiencing rapid aging and declining fertility levels. On the other hand, working-age populations are swiftly growing in South Asia and Sub-Saharan Africa with labour markets finding it difficult to digest these new entrants.

These divergent labour market and demographic trends in the two regions actually present the answers to each other's challenges. The solution is one of the oldest and simplest ideas in economics; in the presence of supply and demand imbalances, free mobility of products and/or inputs will lead to a more efficient outcome. In this context, excess labour that is unabsorbed by the labour markets needs to move from South Asia to the OECD countries which are experiencing rapidly growing shortages and imbalances. In other words, large cohorts of working-age people in South Asia who are not being efficiently employed at home can fill the vacancies created in the labour markets of the West.

Unfortunately, the window of opportunity is quite narrow. If the experiences of other developing regions (such as Latin America, Eastern Europe, and North Africa) are anything to go by, it will not be too long before the remaining South Asian countries complete their demographic transitions. Their fertility and population growths will start declining and the excess labour force will soon disappear. Thus it is important to act now and implement mechanisms that would allow the movement of working-age people from South Asia to the OECD countries within the next two decades.

A critical constraint in taking advantage of this 'arbitrage' opportunity in demographic trajectories is the political and public opposition to migration in OECD countries which became especially strong in the shadow of the current economic crisis. A possible solution involves temporary migration schemes which have built-in mechanisms that guarantee return migration. Such mechanisms involve both carrots and sticks, that is incentives to encourage return after a contract period is completed and punishment for those migrants who fail to honour their promises to return. Many incentive mechanisms provide benefits that the migrants enjoy during their stay in the destination country and after they return home but are lost if the temporary migrants overstay their visas. Among these are: (i) certain legal, economic, and social rights on healthcare, education, and access to legal services, (ii) portable pensions and social security benefits that are maintained via bilateral agreements, (iii) financial incentives where certain portions of the wages are paid after return, and (iv) training and human capital acquisition programmes for which migrants become eligible while they adhere to their contracts. In addition, firms and employers who hire overstaying migrant workers are punished, which tends to lower the attractiveness of overstaying in the first place.

In short, the world is going through an unprecedented demographic transition but there is still time to implement certain policies that would mitigate the negative effects for many parties involved. There is a unique opportunity for South Asian and OECD countries to jointly design temporary migration programmes and it is hoped that economic rationality and foresight do not fall victim to myopic political visions.

REFERENCES

Docquier, F., C. Ozden, A. Marfouk, and C.R. Parsons. 2010. 'Geographic, Gender and Skill Structure of International Migration', Working Paper, Catholic University of Louvain (UCL), Louvain-la-Neuve, Belgium.

Mohapatra, S. and C. Ozden. 2010. 'Migration and Remittances in South Asia', in E. Ghani (ed.), *The Service Revolution in South Asia*. New Delhi: Oxford University Press.

Mohapatra, S., D. Ratha, and A. Silwall. 2010. *Migration and Development Brief 13*. Washington, DC: World Bank.

Organisation for Economic Co-operation and Development. 2008. *A Profile of Immigrant Populations in the 21st Century: Data from OECD Countries.* Paris: OECD.

Ozden, C., C.R. Parsons, M. Schiff, and T.L. Walmsley. 2011. '"Where on Earth is Everyone?" The Evolution of Global Bilateral Migration, 1960–2000', *World Bank Economic Review,* 25 (1): 12–56.

Ratha, D. and S. Mohapatra. 2009. 'Remittances Expected to Fall by 5 to 8 percent in 2009', *Migration and Development Brief 9,* World Bank, Washington, DC.

United Nations, Department of Economic and Social Affairs, Population Division. 2009. 'World Population Prospects: The 2008 Revision, Highlights', Working Paper No. ESA/P/WP.210, United Nations, New York.

II

Challenges Ahead

6

Avoiding Lopsided Spatial Transformation

Arvind Panagariya

During the first several decades of their independence, countries in South Asia grew less than 2 per cent annually in per capita terms. Overall, annual GDP growth in the region as a whole in the 1970s was only 3 per cent (Table 6.1). Allowing for 2 per cent population growth, this would translate into just 1 per cent annual growth in per capita income in the 1970s. Such slow growth naturally meant virtually no change in people's lives over an entire decade. Because the starting level of income itself was extremely low, the governments in the region also failed to generate significant volumes of resources to finance the anti-poverty programmes that they were eager to pursue. In India, where the National Sample Survey Organisation (NSSO) has conducted regular expenditure surveys since the early 1950s, data exhibit no reduction in the trend poverty headcount ratio during 1951–80.

TABLE 6.1 GDP Growth Rates in South Asia

Country	1971–80	1981–90	1991–2000	2001–8
Bangladesh	1.0	3.7	4.8	5.8
India	3.1	5.6	5.5	7.5
Nepal	2.1	4.8	5.0	3.6
Pakistan	4.7	6.3	4.0	4.9
Sri Lanka	4.4	4.2	5.2	5.1
South Asia	3.0	5.4	5.2	7.0

Source: Author's calculations using data from the World Development Indicators online (accessed on 9 September 2010).

However, at least some of the countries in the region have at last begun to turn the corner. India, by far the largest country in the region, grew at an average rate of 7.5 per cent during 2001–8 compared with just 3.1 per cent in the 1970s. Bangladesh, another populous country in the region, appears similarly poised to take off, though at 5.8 per cent during the 2000s, its growth has been significantly below that of India. Growth has been steady in Sri Lanka during the four decades beginning with the 1970s with some upward shift in the 1990s and 2000s. But this growth is still well below the country's true potential, no doubt in part due to the insurgency that preoccupied the country until recently. Nepal also picked up some momentum during the 1980s and 1990s relative to the 1970s but experienced a setback recently as it transitioned from monarchy to democracy. Finally, matters have turned decidedly for the worse in Pakistan relative to the 1980s when it grew at an impressive annual rate of 6.3 per cent. Unlike in Sri Lanka and Nepal, prospects in Pakistan seem bleak in the short-run. Internal conflicts, which show no sign of abating, have made investments in the country highly risky (Table 6.1).

Beginning with 2003–4, the growth rate in India has shifted to the miracle levels that countries, such as Korea and the Taiwan Province of China experienced during the 1960s and 1970s. Prior to the recent financial crisis, the country averaged growth at 8.8 per cent for five years, which fell to only 6.7 and 7.4 per cent in 2008–9 and 2009–10 respectively. Therefore, the average growth rate during the last seven fiscal years has been 8.3 per cent. During the first quarter of the current fiscal year, 2010–11, growth has already hit 8.8 per cent with manufacturing growing at an unprecedented 12.4 per cent. Because the real value of the rupee in terms of the dollar has been steadily rising due to higher inflation rates in India than in the United States without equivalent devaluation of the rupee in nominal terms, the rate of growth in real dollars has been between 11 and 12 per cent in the seven years ending 31 March 2010.

The shift in the growth rate in the region, especially in Bangladesh and India, has also broken the long-standing trend of unchanging levels of poverty. Even by a conservative count, India alone lifted at least 200 million people out of poverty during its high-growth period. Based on the national poverty line, the headcount ratio fell from 51 per cent in 1996 to 40 per cent in 2005 in Bangladesh, from 36 per cent in 1993–4 to 27 per cent in 2004–5 in India, and from 41.8 per cent in 1996 to 30.9 per cent in 2004 in Nepal. Trends in Pakistan and Sri Lanka have been mixed, reflecting less robust growth on a sustained basis as also internal strife.

While the gains in poverty alleviation in India and Bangladesh are very welcome, they do not fare so impressively on a comparative basis: the process of poverty reduction has been much slower than in countries, such as South Korea and Taiwan during their high-growth periods of the 1960s and 1970s. In these countries, increasing shares of industry in the GDP and employment and declining shares of agriculture accompanied rapid growth. This can be gleaned from Table 6. 2 in the case of South Korea. In 1965, agriculture accounted for 36.9 per cent of GDP and 58.6 per cent of the labour force. By 1980, these shares had dropped to 15.1 and 34 per cent respectively. Correspondingly, the share of manufacturing in GDP rose from 17.7 to 30.6 per cent and that in employment from 9.4 to 21.6 per cent. This transformation also took place against the background of an average annual rise of 10 per cent in

TABLE 6.2   Sectoral Shares in the GDP and Employment in South Korea

Year	Agriculture, Forestry, and Fisheries	Mining	Manufacturing	Other
A. GDP by sector (as per cent of GDP)				
1960	36.9	2.1	13.6	47.4
1965	38.7	1.8	17.7	41.8
1970	25.8	1.3	21	51.9
1975	24.9	1.4	26.6	47.1
1980	15.1	1.4	30.6	52.9
1985	13.9	1.5	29.2	55.3
1990	9.1	0.5	29.2	61.2
B. Employment by sector (as per cent of total employment)				
1960	68.3	0.3	1.5	29.9
1965	58.6	0.9	9.4	31.1
1970	50.4	1.1	13.1	35.4
1975	45.7	0.5	18.6	35.2
1980	34	0.9	21.6	43.5
1985	24.9	1	23.4	50.7
1990	18.3	0.4	26.9	54.4

Source: Economic Planning Board, Major Statistics of Korean Economy, various issues and Bank of Korea, Economic Statistics Yearbook 1962 (as cited in Yoo 1997: Table 2, from which this table is taken).

real wages and a virtual elimination of abject poverty. Within a matter of 15 years, South Korea was transformed from a primarily agrarian economy to an industrial one.

This same rapid transformation has failed to materialize in South Asia. Despite the miracle levels of growth during the last seven years and approximately 6 per cent growth in the preceding 15 years, the countryside remains home to a majority of workers and people in India. The pace of migration from agriculture to industry and rural to urban regions has been painfully slow. Correspondingly, the decline in poverty has also been far slower than in the countries of East Asia and in China.

Looking to the future, therefore, we must ask where the existing trends and policies would take South Asia in the coming decades and what policy corrections are desirable to reshape these trends. The following discussion suggests that without policy correction the region, especially India, is heading towards a highly lopsided structure such that while the output share of agriculture will decline to a minuscule level, its employment share will remain disproportionately large. Concomitantly, an extremely large part of India will remain traditional and rural while the rest turns urban and modern, fully linked to the global economy. In other words, the current dualistic nature of the economy will persist with differences further sharpened rather than narrowed. Therefore, the need for corrective policy actions can be hardly overstated. This is the spirit in which I approach the remainder of the chapter.[1]

THE TRANSFORMATION PROBLEM

At least in India, the problem of transformation of the economy from a traditional, agrarian, and rural one to a modern, non-agrarian, and urban one has been manifested in three different forms. These manifestations are discussed in this section. In the next section, the immediate causes of why the course of India's economy has been different from that of other fast-growing economies in the past is probed. In the section that follows, the policy reforms necessary to achieve the desired transformation are discussed.

Persistently Large Employment Share of Agriculture

One unmistakable feature of growth in South Asia, as in virtually all other countries, has been the steadily shrinking share of agriculture. Table 6.3 shows this for the period from 1981 to 2008. In India, Nepal, and Sri Lanka, this share approximately halved during these 27 years.

---

[1] See also Dasgupta et al. (2010) in this context.

Table 6.3   Share of Agriculture in GDP

Country	1981	1991	2001	2008
Bangladesh	31.7	30.4	24.1	19.0
India	34.4	29.6	23.2	17.5
Nepal	60.9	47.2	39.5	33.7
Pakistan	30.8	25.8	24.1	20.4
Sri Lanka	27.7	26.8	20.1	13.4

Source: World Bank, WDI online (accessed on 9 September 2010).

In the remaining two countries, Bangladesh and Pakistan, the decline was one-third.

But whereas growth in other labour-abundant economies at low levels of income has also been accompanied by a rapid shift of the workforce out of agriculture, the same has not happened in the countries in the region, especially in India. Table 6.4 illustrates this point. During 11 years, from 1993–4 to 2004–5, employment in agriculture in India fell from 61.7 to 54 per cent of total employment. The change was sufficiently small for employment in agriculture in absolute terms to increase from

Table 6.4 Employment in Major Sectors of the Indian Economy

Sector	1993–4	1999–2000	2004–5
	Total (million workers)		
Agriculture	206	214.8	225
Industry	40.5	44.1	55.2
Services	87.5	107.9	136.3
Memo: Manufacturing	36.6	40.9	51.6
Total	334	366.8	416.5
	Per cent of Total		
Agriculture	61.7	58.6	54.0
Industry	12.1	12.0	13.3
Services	26.2	29.4	32.7
Memo: Manufacturing	11.0	11.2	12.4
Total	100.0	100.0	100.0

Source: Various NSSO Employment and Unemployment Survey reports, Government of India, and author's calculations.
Note: Industry includes manufacturing, mining and quarrying, and electricity and water but not construction.

206 million to 225 million. This meant that the labour–land ratio marginally increased over this period. A further observation is that only a very small part of the (small) decline in the share of agriculture in total employment was accounted for by an increased share of manufacturing, which increased from 11 to just 12.2 per cent over the 11-year period. Almost the entire decline in the employment share of agriculture was accounted for by services, which increased their employment share from 26.2 to 32.7 per cent.

One way to dramatize the transformation problem is that in 1993–4, agriculture employed 61.7 per cent of the workforce and contributed 30 per cent of the GDP. In 2004–5, the last year for which reliable employment data are available, the two shares fell to 54 and 20.2 per cent respectively. That is to say, the output per worker in agriculture was not only much smaller than in industry and services, the gap between the two outputs per worker is progressively increasing.

The Persistent Dominance of Informal Employment

One further worrisome feature of the current economic structure is the exceptionally large employment share of the informal sector and a large and increasing share of informal employment within the relatively small formal sector. A recent report by the National Commission for Enterprises in the Unorganized Sector (Government of India 2007) provides the necessary data to support the existence of this feature of the economy. The report defines the informal sector as consisting of all unincorporated enterprises owned by individuals or households engaged in the production and sale of goods and services operated on a proprietary or partnership basis and employing less than 10 workers. It also defines informal employment as employment in the informal sector excluding regular workers with social security benefits and employment in the formal sector without any employment or social security benefits provided by the employer.[2]

Table 6.5 shows the pattern of formal-informal employment across formal–informal sectors in 1999–2000 and 2004–5. Perhaps the most striking feature of the table is the low and declining proportion of formal employment in total employment. During the five years covered by the table, the share of formal employment in total employment declined

---

[2] The formal sector is to be distinguished here from the organized sector commonly defined in India as consisting of all firms with 10 or more workers using power and those with 20 or more workers even if not using power.

TABLE 6.5   Percentage Distribution of Employment in
Formal–Informal Categories and across Formal–Informal Sectors

Sector/Worker	Informal Employment	Formal Employment	Total
1999–2000			
Informal sector	99.6	0.4	86.4
Formal sector	37.8	62.2	13.6
Total	**91.2**	**8.8**	**100**
2004–5			
Informal sector	99.6	0.4	86.3
Formal sector	46.6	53.4	13.7
Total	**92.4**	**7.6**	**100**

Source: Excerpted from Table 1.1 of the 'Report on Conditions of Work
and Promotion of Livelihoods in the Unorganized Sector' (August 2007),
by the National Commission for Enterprises in the Unorganized Sector,
Government of India.

to 7.6 per cent in 2004–5 from the already low level of 8.8 per cent
in 1999–2000. Employment in the formal sector remained virtually
unchanged with the share of formal employment in it declining from
62.2 per cent in 1999–2000 to 53.4 per cent in 2004–5. There is clearly
increasing reluctance to provide formal employment even within the
relatively small formal sector.

Relying on two NSSO surveys conducted in 2001–2 and 2006–7,
a recent paper by Dehejia and Panagariya (2010) analyses in detail the
output and employment patterns in the major services sectors (excluding
public enterprises, wholesale and retail trade, and the financial sector).
They find that while almost four-fifths of the output in these services
is concentrated in establishment enterprises, almost three-fifths of the
employment is concentrated in own-account enterprises.[3] In other words,
a large proportion of the services labour force is in low-productivity own-
account enterprises. They summarize the pattern in these terms:

Perhaps the most important conclusion that follows from Table 4 is that a very
large proportion of the labor force in services remains employed in enterprises
with very low average productivity. The transformation problem India faces

[3] Own-account enterprises are defined as enterprises with no workers employed on a
regular basis. Enterprises that employ one or more workers on a regular basis are classified
as establishment enterprises. Many of the establishment enterprises are thus informal-
sector enterprises on the basis of the definition provided in footnote 2.

with respect to the movement of the vast workforce out of agriculture into more productive non-agricultural activities is also present within services. A majority of the workforce within services is in small, informal enterprises with relatively low output per worker. (Dehejia and Panagariya 2010: 19)

Observe that establishment enterprises include all enterprises employing one or more workers on a regular basis. As such, many of the establishment enterprises themselves belong to the informal sector. One way to convey how dramatically the output and employment relationship alters as we move towards larger enterprises is to note that according to the 2006–7 survey, the largest 626 enterprises accounted for as much as 38 per cent of output but only 2 per cent of employment in the sectors covered.

The Slow Pace of Urbanization

A final disappointing characteristic of the evolution of South Asia's economic structure has been the low level of and generally piecemeal increase in the share of urban population in total population. All the countries share low and gradual rates of urbanization in broad terms. Figure 6.1 plots urban population as a per cent of total population in the five major countries of the region from 1960 to 2008.

Among the countries shown, only Pakistan shows a rate of urbanization exceeding 30 per cent. Growth in the rate of urbanization has been highly piecemeal in all countries, including in Pakistan. It began with 25.1 per cent of its population in urban areas in 1971 and reached 36.2 per cent in 2008. On average, these figures imply less than 3 percentage points per decade of gain in urbanization. In India, the pace has been even slower: based on the census conducted once every decade, this proportion increased from 17.3 per cent in 1951 to 18 per cent in 1961, 19.9 per cent in 1971, 23.3 per cent in 1981, 25.7 per cent in 1991, and 27.8 per cent in 2001. On average, the shift in the composition of the population has been just 2 percentage points per decade. The estimated rate of urbanization in India was 29.5 per cent in 2008. Nepal and Bangladesh started with a very low urban base, which initially grew rapidly but has slowed down since the 1980s, especially in Nepal. Both countries had lower urban-total population ratios compared to India and Pakistan. The story of Sri Lanka has been the most disconcerting from this perspective: its rate of urbanization has actually seen a gradual decline since 1971, falling from 19.5 per cent in that year to 15.1 per cent in 2008.

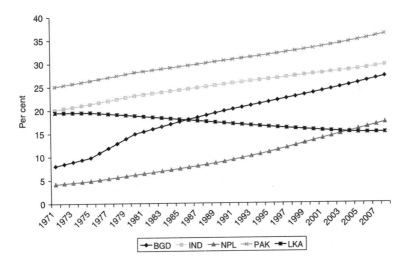

FIGURE 6.1   Urban Population as per cent of Total Population in
South Asia

Source: Author's construction using data from World Bank, WDI online (accessed
on 9 September 2010).

SOME KEY FEATURES RELATED TO THE
SLOW TRANSFORMATION

While the countries in the region broadly share the characteristics
discussed here, albeit with some variations, the factors giving rise to
those shared characteristics are likely to vary across countries. I would
hypothesize that in countries other than India, a key reason for the slow
transformation remains slow growth. In Bangladesh, a policy framework
conducive to rapid growth needs to be strengthened. In Pakistan,
Nepal, and Sri Lanka, internal strife leading to general lack of safety
of investments has added to policy failure. In India, the story is more
complicated involving a policy framework that has inhibited the rapid
growth of labour-intensive industry.

The key characteristic on which I wish to focus next relates to the
slow movement of workers from agriculture into industry and services
relative to other similarly fast-growing economies such as South Korea
and Taiwan in the past. In the Indian case, we can point to several
structural features of the economy that are themselves the result of the
economic policies introduced following independence, and especially
in the 1970s.

A Low and Stagnant Share of Manufacturing in the GDP

As noted earlier, a common feature observed in most labour-abundant economies as they grow from relatively low levels of per capita income is the rapidly expanding share of manufactures in both output and employment. This was the case, for example, in South Korea and Taiwan in the 1960s and 1970s. This was also the pattern observed in China during the 1980s and 1990s. Going back into history, today's industrial economies exhibited the same pattern when they started their ascent from poverty to prosperity some 150 to 200 years ago.

Surprisingly, however, this pattern has failed to decisively reproduce itself in almost any of the larger countries in South Asia except, arguably, Bangladesh. As Table 6.6 shows the share has been entirely stagnant in India over the 27-year period covered by the data. In the other countries, there is at best a mildly increasing trend with a just 2 to 5 percentage point increase over a period of 27 years with the share staying below 20 per cent in every single case.

Slow growth in manufacturing in the face of rapid GDP growth need not by itself worry us provided it is not in the way of growth in employment opportunities for unskilled and low-skilled workers at decent wages in industry and services so that these sectors still manage to rapidly pull the underemployed workers in agriculture into gainful employment. This can happen through a variety of channels in a rapidly growing economy. First, in fast-growing economies, growth in industry and services is almost always faster than in agriculture so that the former may pull some of the workers out of the latter even if manufacturing is growing at approximately the same rate as the GDP as a whole. Second, the composition of output within manufacturing may shift towards unskilled or low-skilled labour-intensive products. This would help raise the overall labour intensity of manufacturing and generate rising numbers of well-paid jobs even when manufacturing

TABLE 6.6   The Share of Manufactures in GDP

Country	1981	1991	2001	2008
Bangladesh	13.7	13.4	15.6	17.8
India	16.8	15.7	15.0	15.8
Nepal	4.1	6.7	9.3	7.4
Pakistan	15.1	17.1	15.5	19.7
Sri Lanka	16.2	14.8	16.0	18.0

Source: World Bank, WDI online (accessed on 9 September 2010).

grows more slowly than services. Third, even with an unchanged composition of output, technology may progressively shift towards increased unskilled or low-skilled workers. Finally, the non-manufacturing sectors, mainly services, that drive the rapid growth may themselves increasingly absorb unskilled and low-skilled workers. For example, increasing incomes may expand the demand for domestic servants; car mechanics; plumbers and electricians; car, truck, and taxi drivers; repairmen for household appliances; gardeners; beauticians; and caterers.

However, data suggest that so far only the first and the last mechanisms have facilitated some movement of workers out of agriculture into non-agricultural activities. The remaining two mechanisms have actually worked in the opposite direction. The result has been a relatively slow transition from an agrarian and rural to a non-agrarian and urban structure of the economy. This is seen in the slow pace of movement of workers from agriculture to industry and services and of population from rural to urban regions. Despite rapid growth that dramatically produced some 69 billionaires in dollar terms in 2010 in India, the broad character of the country remains agrarian and rural.[4]

Low and Stagnant Share of Labour-intensive Products in Manufacturing

Unfortunately, the share of labour-intensive products in manufacturing has been low in India and it has shown little signs of increasing with accelerated growth. In a recent paper, Das et al. (2009) assemble output and input usage data on 96 four-digit organized manufacturing industries from 1990–1 to 2003–4. Measuring labour intensity by the ratio of workers to gross fixed capital stock, they define industries exhibiting higher labour intensity than is the average in manufacturing as labour intensive. This criterion leads to the identification of 31 four-digit industries, such as food and beverages, apparel, textiles manufactures, and manufacture of furniture as labour intensive. Surprisingly, gross value added (GVA) in these 31 industries between 1990–1 and 2003–4 turns out to average only 13.8 per cent of the total organized sector manufacturing value-added (Das et al. 2009: 5).

Therefore, to begin with, India has not specialized in the labour-intensive sectors within manufacturing. Calculations by Das et al.

[4] For the list of billionaires, see http://en.wikipedia.org/wiki/List of Indians by net worth (accessed on 11 September 2010). Of the 57 billionaires on this list, three are Indians with non-Indian citizenships.

(2009: 8) also show that during the first 13 years of economic reforms ending in 2003–4, there was no perceptible movement towards labour-intensive sectors within manufacturing: the share of labour-intensive manufactures in total manufactures GVA increased from 12.94 per cent in 1990–1 to 15.90 per cent in 2000–1 but fell back to 12.91 per cent in 2003–4.

While I do not have the necessary data to demonstrate this, a plausible hypothesis is that during the high-growth period (2003–4 to 2009–10), the overall production structure of the economy (rather than just manufactures) moved further away from labour-intensive activities. Some of the fastest-growing sectors during the last seven years have been automobiles, two- and three-wheeler vehicles, auto parts, software, telecommunications, petroleum refining, pharmaceuticals, and finance. None of these is a major producer of employment opportunities for unskilled and low-skilled workers.

Some indirect evidence in favour of the hypothesis that the overall production structure has moved towards capital and skilled labour-intensive sectors can be gleaned from the changes in the composition of India's exports. India's commodity exports show a very high and increasing bias in favour of capital-intensive products. Figure 6.2 captures this phenomenon.

In 1990–1, engineering goods, chemicals and related products, gems and jewellery, petroleum products, and textile products other than readymade garments, which are either capital-intensive or semi-skilled labour-intensive, accounted for 43 per cent of the total commodity exports. By 2007–8, these products came to account for 71 per cent of the total commodity exports. Readymade garments, the most unskilled or low-skilled labour-intensive product, fell in share from 12 to just 6 per cent. Engineering goods and petroleum products, both highly capital-intensive, showed the largest expansion.

High and Rising Capital–Labour Ratio in Manufacturing Production

In addition to specialization in capital and skilled labour-intensive rather than unskilled labour-intensive products, India also employs a very high capital–labour ratio (or very low labour–capital ratio) in the production of any given product relative to its factor endowment ratio and the level of development. Moreover, the capital–labour ratio has shown a rising trend over time. A recent paper by Hasan et al. (2010) shows that labour intensities in the vast majority of manufacturing industries in India are

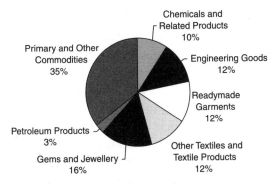

Total Commodity Exports (1990-1): $8.1 Billion

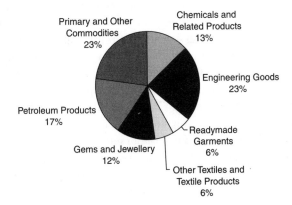

Total Exports (2007–8): $163.1 Billion

FIGURE 6.2   India: Shift in Exports in Favour of
Capital-intensive Products

Source: Author's construction using the statistics from Directorate General of Commercial Intelligence and Statistics (DGCI&S).

lower than in other countries at its level of development and with similar factor endowments. More dramatically, Hasan et al. (2010: 14) report the following comparison between India and China:

Figure 2 (a) presents capital stock per labor in thousands of 1995 Chinese Yuan per labor adjusted for PPP for India and China from 1989 through 2004 in 19 manufacturing industries. Capital stock per labor in Indian manufacturing is consistently above capital stock per labor in China. Even though both countries were comparable in many ways in 1980 with similar income and development indicators, also reflected in the similar levels of capital stock per labor in 1980, from 1980 through 2000, India's growth in capital stock per labor was higher than that of China with significant divergence from 1990 through 2000. Figure 2 (b) presents employment in these 19 industries in India and China in thousands of standardized workers. While Chinese manufacturing shows steady growth during the period, except for a slump in the late 1990s and early 2000s, India's manufacturing employment shows very little growth.

Hasan et al. (2010) also compare the actual capital–labour ratio in 13 broad industry groups in India to the corresponding ratio that would prevail in the United States had the wages there been the same as in India. They find that the actual capital–labour ratio in India is higher than that predicted for the United States at Indian wages in every single industry group. When the authors disaggregate data into 22 sectors, the same result still obtains in 18 of them. The evidence that India employs extra-high capital–labour ratio in production in relation to its factor endowments is highly compelling.

In addition to the capital–labour ratio being uniformly high relative to that in comparable countries, there has also been a rising trend in this ratio. Rani and Unni (2004) calculate the capital–labour ratios in both the organized and unorganized manufacturing sectors and find them to exhibit sharply rising trends. Chaudhuri (2002) studied the trend in labour–capital ratio in three-digit organized manufacturing sectors from 1990–1 to 1997–8 and found that labour intensity progressively declines. Finally, Das et al. (2009) calculate the average labour–capital ratio in 31 labour-intensive organized manufacturing industries and find a sharply declining trend between 1990–1 and 2003–4.

In principle, the increasing trend in capital–labour ratio can be a perfectly rational response to changing economic conditions. For example, the ratio may rise in response to a rise in wages relative to the cost of capital.[5] Likewise, for given factor prices, technological change may have led to a shift away from the use of labour as has surely been happening with the spread of information technology. Another explanation may be a shift towards more capital-intensive products within each broader product category analysed. While the observed trend may seem unsurprising for these possible reasons, what makes it worrisome is the presence of high capital–labour ratios in Indian manufacturing relative to the country's factor endowment ratio to begin with and the

---

[5] At least on the basis of the average real wage increases in the labour-intensive sectors of 2.73 per cent per annum between 1990–1 and 2003–4 reported by Das et al. (2009), this factor would seem to have limited explanatory power.

total absence of a structural shift towards more labour-intensive products that would aid faster movement of workers away from agriculture and into industry and services.

Missing Large-scale Firms in Labour-intensive Sectors

In India, truly large-scale firms are generally absent from labour-intensive sectors. Firms that employ tens of thousands of workers exist but they are in capital-intensive sectors, such as automobiles and engineering goods. This is in contrast to China and, to some degree even Bangladesh and Sri Lanka, where very large firms in sectors such as apparel can be found.

Because small firms naturally look for markets in their immediate vicinity, India's export performance has been greatly impacted by this size difference. India has relatively limited or sometimes no presence in many light consumer goods in world markets. For example, Indian toys are nearly absent from world markets. A more telling example is that of clothing and accessories (category SITC 84), which have a vast world market and which formed China's leading export in the 1980s and 1990s. Indeed, despite the emergence of electronic products as its leading export, China still dominates the market for clothing and accessories. In contrast, exports from India in this category are barely able to match those from Bangladesh.

Table 6.7, which shows India's exports of clothing and accessories as per cent of those by Bangladesh and China, illustrates this point.

TABLE 6.7 **Exports of Clothing and Accessories (SITC 84) by India as a Percentage of Exports by Bangladesh and China**

	Bangladesh		China	
Year	USA	World	USA	World
2001	85.9	134.6	33.4	15.0
2002	95.0	143.0	32.1	14.1
2003	100.8	124.6	25.7	12.1
2004	98.8	110.0	23.9	11.2
2005	117.4	126.5	20.2	11.8
2006	107.4	115.0	18.5	10.0
2007	96.4	105.7	15.4	8.6
2008			15.3	9.1
2009			13.8	11.2

Source: Author's calculations based on the United Nations commodity trade data.

Between 2001 and 2007, exports from India to the United States were approximately the same as those by the much smaller Bangladesh. In the world market as a whole, India had a more than 40 per cent lead over Bangladesh in 2002. This lead steadily eroded in the following years, dropping to just 5.7 per cent in 2007. In comparison with China, India's presence was much smaller in both the United States and the world markets in 2001. And even as electronic products have emerged as the largest export from China, its lead in clothing and accessories over India has considerably widened.

TOWARDS POSSIBLE SOLUTIONS

Dehejia and Panagariya (2010) find that even own-account enterprises (which do not hire workers on a regular basis) and establishment enterprises (which do hire workers on a regular basis) with less than five workers that can be thought of as belonging entirely to the informal sector experienced some growth between 2001–2 and 2006–7. This finding is consistent with the hypothesis that pro-market reforms, which stimulated growth in the formal sectors of the economy, increased incomes of certain sections of society and therefore their demand for the services in the informal sector. For example, increased incomes would be associated with increased expenditures on weddings, religious ceremonies, conferences, and other events. They would also lead to expanded travel and transportation needs which would in turn increase the demand for automobile drivers, mechanics, and workers at ports, airports, and railway stations. Increased incomes also increase the demand for domestic help creating well-paid jobs in the household sector. It is probable that it is this increase in the demand for informal-sector workers that led to the observed decline in both rural and urban poverty despite limited decline in the employment share of agriculture and an outright decline in formal employment in the formal sector.[6]

In principle, a continuation of this process, complemented by income transfers to the poor made possible by increased government revenues following accelerated growth, can be counted on to eventually eradicate poverty. But this process is bound to be slow as has been the case to date. Growth has delivered less poverty reduction in India than would have been the case if the leading sectors had been unskilled labour-intensive rather than capital and skilled labour-intensive. Likewise, future growth

[6] Rural poverty fell from 37.3 to 28.3 per cent and urban poverty from 32.4 to 25.7 per cent between 1993–4 and 2004–5.

will lead to less poverty reduction and greater inequality if it relies on the existing process. It will also leave a disproportionately large workforce in the rural and agricultural sector, impeding urbanization and modernization. For instance, at the current growth of 2 percentage points per decade in urbanization, it will be another 50 years before urbanization reaches even 40 per cent. India will remain dualistic in the decades to come.

If the process of poverty alleviation and modernization is to be accelerated, a series of reforms that create a large volume of well-paid jobs for unskilled workers is needed. India is a labour-abundant country and must, accordingly, reorient itself toward specialization in labour-intensive industries. It is striking that while the reforms in China beginning in the late 1970s led it to quickly move into labour-intensive sectors and turned it into a large exporter of labour-intensive products, the same has not happened in India. The end to investment licensing, removal of restrictions on investments by big business houses outside the so-called 'core' sectors, elimination of reservations for small-scale industries, and import liberalization that were expected to stimulate labour-intensive industries have so far failed to do so. The likely reason is that there still remain binding restrictions on the expansion of labour-intensive sectors that must be addressed. In the remainder of this section, I list a series of measures aimed at achieving this objective.[7]

A More Flexible Labour Market Regime

India needs to modernize its labour market laws. In the formal, organized sector, the current laws give disproportionately large amount of power to workers. The result has been a flight of entrepreneurs away from workers and towards capital. As the evidence presented in the previous section shows, entrepreneurs have generally avoided labour-intensive sectors and technologies. In the labour-intensive sectors, they have also shied away from large-scale operations and therefore chosen to forego the economies of scale that could potentially allow them to challenge the dominance of China in light manufacturing industries in world markets. For example, one of the provisions of the Industrial Disputes Act 1947, makes it extremely difficult for establishments with 50 or more workers to reassign the latter from one task to another. Another provision effectively prohibits manufacturing firms with 100 workers or more from laying-off

---

[7] The remainder of the discussion in this section extensively draws on Panagariya (2008a, 2010).

workers under any circumstances. Even if a specific operation of the firm becomes unprofitable and requires closing down, the firm must pay the workers out of profits from other operations. While it may be possible to remain competitive under these onerous conditions for large-scale firms in capital-intensive manufacturing industries, such as automobiles where labour costs are a small proportion of the total cost, the same is not true for unskilled labour-intensive industries where labour costs are 80 per cent or more of the total costs.

At a broader level, the entire labour law regime in India requires an overhaul. The number of labour laws in India easily exceeds 100 and many of them are mutually inconsistent: a wit has even remarked that you cannot implement 100 per cent of the labour laws in India without violating 20 per cent of them. Laws relating to unions, strikes, definition of a workman, contract labour, and employment of women all need reforms.

A Transparent Bankruptcy Law

India also needs a modern bankruptcy law along the lines of Chapter 11 of the US bankruptcy law. Under the current laws, firms are often denied permission to liquidate and asked to restructure even though they are insolvent. In cases where a decision in favour of liquidation is made, the process takes a very long time. The government-appointed Eradi Committee, which submitted its report in 2000, noted that as of December 1999, 48 per cent of the cases under liquidation had been in process for 15 or more years and 15 per cent of the cases had been in the works for 25 years or longer. The onerous and long-drawn process has detrimental effects on entry. When firms realize that exit is very costly, they hesitate to enter. In cases when workers have to be paid their dues out of the assets of an exiting firm, bankruptcy hurts their interests as well.

Land Acquisition Laws

India also needs to reform the Land Acquisition Act 1894, which is antiquated and has proved to be a major barrier to the entry of large-scale firms even in capital-intensive sectors. In recent years, entering firms that need large pieces of land have found it very difficult to acquire it. In many cases state governments have tried to acquire land on their behalf using their powers under the Land Acquisition Act 1894, only to be forced to retreat in the face of widespread discontent among and demonstrations by landowners.

The key problem has been that state governments have tried to acquire land at prices well below market prices to provide it cheaply to industrialists. This was the case, for example, with the West Bengal government that tried to acquire 997 acres of land for Tata Motor's Nano car project. The government agreed to give land to Tata on a 90-year lease at a throwaway annual rent of just Rs 10 million (Rs 15,380 per acre) for the first five years, with modest increases allowed subsequently. At the other end, it tried to acquire land by force at the prevailing registered price, which is well known to be far below the market price to evade hefty transfer taxes. A popular movement by farmers ultimately forced the government's hand, which was unable to deliver on its contract with Tata. In turn, the latter had to move the manufacturing site of Nano out of West Bengal to Gujarat.[8]

The current law must be replaced by one that provides for investors to privately negotiate land transactions in most cases and requires government intermediation only under exceptional circumstances. In the rare cases that the government does get involved, the law must require the payment of actual market price to landowners rather than the price officially registered in the sales records in the immediately preceding years. Buyers and sellers in India register land transactions at well below actual prices to evade hefty transfer taxes. Therefore, forced acquisition of land by the government at prices reflected in the registered prices falls well short of fully compensating landowners for the true value of their land.

Education

While primary education is receiving its deserved share of attention from policymakers and more than 95 per cent of the children below 14 years of age are now in schools, higher education in India is in urgent need of reform. Without such reform, shortages of skilled workers are bound to arrest the growth of Indian manufacturing and service sectors. The quality of education inside the classroom also remains low. The only reason why Indian universities and other institutions of higher education continue to produce world class graduates is that they get to select from a very large pool of highly talented students, thanks to the excellent school education in grades 9 through 12. A large number of private schools in India fiercely compete against one another and many of them impart very high quality education. This gives the universities well-prepared students who often master the curriculum on their own

---

[8] For further details, see Panagariya (2008b).

knowing well that scoring high marks in university examinations will mean a ticket to a good job in a burgeoning economy or, better still, to further education abroad.

There are no quick fixes for the Indian higher education system. But the starting point has to be genuine entry to both domestic and foreign private universities with no strings attached either to tuition fees or employee salaries. Only then will a few high-quality universities have the chance to emerge and bring about the necessary competitive pressure for improvements in public universities. Of course, private entry will also help expand higher education faster; it is no secret that the government lacks the resources for the expansion of university education at the required pace.

The existing higher education system is highly centralized with virtually all the power residing in the University Grants Commission (UGC). The government simply needs to abolish the UGC and free universities and colleges from its yoke. After more than 50 years of operating under the current highly centralized system, universities and colleges have matured enough to make their own decisions. There is no body like the UGC in the United States, the country that currently imparts by far the best higher education. Universities and colleges also have to be permitted to charge significant amounts of tuition fees to alleviate the severe resource constraints that they face. Higher education imparts enough private gain to the students to justify such fees.

Modernizing Social Safety Nets

India needs to evolve a modern system of social safety nets. Regressive subsidies, such as those on water, electricity, fertilizer, and food procurement, which are all captured by large farmers, must be ended. The Mahatma Gandhi National Rural Employment Guarantee Scheme (NREGS), which has reached a relatively limited segment of the poor population must be replaced by a system of cash transfers and medical insurance to cover hospitalization on at least a limited scale for those below the poverty line.[9] Abolition of other subsidies can free up ample resources for medical insurance and other social programmes.

Perhaps the worst example of a vast and regressive food subsidy is provided by India's public distribution system (PDS) and the associated

[9] See Panagariya (2009) for details on why employment guarantee to all rural households is an inappropriate instrument for placing purchasing power in the hands of the poor.

costs of food storage, food procurement, and public employment. The Food Corporation of India (FCI), the agency entrusted with overseeing PDS, maintains a workforce of 400,000 individuals. It procures foodgrains at above-market prices from mostly rich farmers, with few marginal farmers able to access its high price. It also maintains vast stocks of food—60 million tonnes at the time of writing—without proper storage facilities. The result is that a significant part of its stocks is washed away by rains, eaten by rats, or rendered unusable by pests. The government could release vast resources to finance social safety nets for the poor by grossly downsizing the FCI. The Unique Identification (UID) project, popularly known by its name in Hindi, Adhar, and currently under implementation, would make it a relatively straightforward matter to make cash transfers to the poor. The poor could then buy foodgrains from the open market like the non-poor. The FCI would then need to maintain its operations only in areas where the private market might not reach and therefore could be greatly downsized.

Conceptually, it is important to understand that the current social programmes create a strong incentive against migration out of rural to urban areas. Workers receive employment under the MGNREGA only if they offer themselves for work in rural public works programmes. Likewise, water and fertilizer subsidies accrue to those engaged in cultivation. In contrast, cash transfers made available to the poor regardless of their location will leave the workers free to seek employment in the most productive alternatives whether they are in rural or urban areas.

Agricultural Reforms

Speeding migration out of agriculture also requires reforms within that sector. Enhanced productivity in agriculture will help release workers from land to move into other activities. Currently, farms in India are predominantly tiny and discourage the use of machinery. High procurement prices for specific crops also discourage farmers from moving into other commercial crops. Reforms are required with respect to land sales as well as land leasing and above-market procurement prices need to end.

India also needs to experiment more aggressively with genetically modified crops to raise productivity. Giving farmers proper ownership titles to land will allow them to lease their piece of land without fear of losing it and this will permit consolidation. Any ceilings on rent of leased land must be lifted as well. Steps necessary to facilitate contract farming must be taken. Where feasible, commercial farming must be given a chance. The adoption of some of the best and most productive techniques in agriculture will require the entry of the corporate sector in farming. Any barriers to the development of food processing must be removed as well.

Infrastructure

More rapid transformation will also require improved performance in building infrastructure. At least three points need to be mentioned in this context. First, apparel exports, the labour-intensive product with the greatest export potential, requires just-in-time delivery. Each new season opens with new fashions in clothing and a manufacturer unable to deliver clothes accordingly at the exact time stands to lose the market. This outcome can only be achieved if the factories are well connected to the ports by world-class roads and turnaround time at the ports is low. Second, producers of labour-intensive products must have access to continuous supply of electricity at reasonable prices. Electricity costs are the major non-wage costs for these manufacturers so that high electricity tariffs can quickly price them out of world markets. Finally, all-weather roads must connect villages to the nearest cities and electricity provided to all villages to help modernize and urbanize the villages themselves.

Within infrastructure, perhaps the most important area in need of reform is electricity. The Electricity Act 2003 provides an excellent framework for this reform but its implementation has been slow. It is crucial to end the culture of power subsidies to the farm sector and of cross-subsidy from industry to households and restore the financial health of various distribution companies. The entry of private players in generation crucially depends on the ability of distribution companies to credibly sign long-term purchase contracts. If the distribution companies are ill, they lack the credibility to deliver on for such contracts.

Trade Liberalization

Finally, it needs reminding that continued trade liberalization including in agriculture is an essential part of the policy package aimed at achieving the transition to a modern economy. Following the recent global economic crisis and frequent condemnation of China for its contribution to global financial imbalances, there has been a tendency on the part of some analysts to assert that the era of reliance on outward-oriented policies is now over. Such assertions reflect very poor understanding of both facts and the role of outward-oriented policies. The key point is that outward orientation is not equivalent to current account surpluses. Most developing countries that achieved miracle-level growth in the presence of outward-oriented policies have actually run current account deficits. This was true, for example, of South Korea and Taiwan during the 1960s and 1970s and, indeed, even of China until the end of the 1990s. Shift in India's own trade policy regime since 1991 towards outward orientation has been accompanied by continued current account deficits in all but three or four years.

Gradual liberalization in agriculture is also required to improve its efficiency. Advocates of continued high protection argue that liberalization will hurt India's subsistence farmers. This defence of protection is reminiscent of the advocacy of continued protection in manufacturing prior to the 1991 reform. It was argued then that liberalization would lead to the destruction of domestic industry. The actual outcome was the opposite. Increased trade only led to a restructuring of the industry with exports and imports both expanding. There is no reason to expect any different outcome in agriculture. India could emerge as a major exporter of agriculture as a consequence of liberalization. And marginal farmers and landless workers would be served much better by increased productivity in agriculture and improved prospects of well-paid jobs in labour-intensive industry. With the wages of unskilled and semi-skilled workers steadily rising in China, India has a unique opportunity to gradually replace it as the exporter of labour-intensive products.

CONCLUSION

I began this chapter by documenting the low pace of urbanization and modernization in the countries of South Asia. In particular, while the share of agriculture in the GDP has steadily declined in almost all countries in the region, the movement of workers out of the countryside as reflected in the pace of urbanization has been slow. Recognizing that the reasons for this phenomenon are likely to differ across countries, I focus on the largest country in the region, India, when seeking explanations for it. I demonstrate that the slow transformation is rooted in a persistently low share of labour-intensive products in manufactures and high and rising capital–labour ratios in various manufactures.

In the last section of the chapter, I discuss the reforms needed to speed up the transformation. My list of reforms is unabashedly long. I do not subscribe to the view that one or two key reforms should suffice to achieve the desired goal. It would surely be nice if development and poverty alleviation were a matter of relaxing one or two binding constraints. But India's own experience shows that a multiplicity of reforms is required to reach where India stands today. Reforms are politically difficult but they must be introduced whenever the opportunity arises. Having a diversified agenda has the advantage that if progress is politically difficult in one area, it may not be so in another. For instance, progress was illusive in India in the area of higher education under the previous two regimes. But it has become possible under the current regime. It must also be remembered that hardly any reform can be accomplished in one stroke. Even the far-reaching trade reform of 1991 had to leave import licensing on consumer goods in place with its abolition becoming possible only ten years later in 2001. This constraint also favours having a diversified agenda that can be gradually advanced on various fronts.

A final point is that in a parliamentary democracy such as India, the determination of the leadership at the top to carry out reforms is of utmost importance. Given the executive serves only because it holds a majority in parliament, it has the power to change the laws as necessary to advance the reforms. Often it is argued that coalition politics can impair the ability to bring about policy changes. But in the end most coalition members also want to enjoy the power that comes with membership of the government.

REFERENCES

Chaudhuri, Sudip. 2002. 'Economic Reforms and Industrial Structure in India', *Economic and Political Weekly*, 37 (2): 155–62.

Das, Deb Kusum, Deepika Wadhwa, and Gunajit Kalita. 2009. 'The Employment Potential of Labor Intensive Industries in India's Organized Manufacturing', ICRIER Working Paper 236, June.

Dasgupta, Dipak, Ejaz Ghani, and Ernesto May. 2010. 'Economic Policy Challenges for South Asia', in O. Canuto and M. Gingale (eds), *The Day After Tomorrow—The Future of Economic Policy in the Developing World*. Washington, DC: World Bank.

Dehejia, Rajeev and Arvind Panagariya. 2010. 'Services Growth in India: A Look Inside the Black Box', Working Paper 2010–4, Columbia Program on Indian Economic Policies, Columbia University.

Government of India. 2007. *Report on the Conditions of Work and Promotion of Livelihood in the Unorganized Sector*. New Delhi: National Commission for Enterprises in the Unorganized Sector.

Hasan, Rana, Devashish Mitra, and Asha Sundaram. 2010. 'The Determinants of Capital Intensity in Manufacturing: The Role of Factor Endowments and Factor Market Imperfections', Syracuse University, mimeo.

Panagariya, Arvind. 2008a. *India: The Emerging Giant*. New York: Oxford University Press.

————. 2008b. 'El Nano: A Perfect Storm', *The Economic Times*, 25 September, op-ed page.

————. 2009. 'More Bang for the Buck', *The Times of India*, 19 September.

————. 2010. 'Building a Modern India', Chapter 1 in the Business Standard's *India 2010*.

Rani, Uma and Jeemol Unni. 2004. 'Unorganized and Organized Manufacturing in India: Potential for Employment Generating Growth', *Economic and Political Weekly*, 39 (41): 4568–80.

World Bank. 2010. *World Development Indicators*. Available at http: //data. worldbank.org/data-catalog/world-development-indicators/wdi-2010

Yoo, Jungho. 1997. 'Neoclassical Versus Revisionist View of Korean Economic Growth', Development Discussion Paper No. 588, Harvard Institute for International Development, Harvard University, Cambridge, Mass.

7

Promoting Entrepreneurship, Growth, and Job Creation

Ejaz Ghani, William R. Kerr, and Stephen O'Connell

WHY IS ENTREPRENEURSHIP IMPORTANT TO SOUTH ASIA'S FUTURE?

This volume discusses many aspects of how South Asia will look in 2025. Entrepreneurship is one dimension in which, as Figure 7.1 shows, South Asian countries have underperformed in both absolute and relative terms. Entrepreneurship, however, is a central factor in economic growth and development. It helps allocate resources efficiently, strengthens competition among firms, supports innovation and new product designs, and promotes trade growth through product variety. To achieve the strong economic growth and job creation essential for development, South Asia must harness and promote entrepreneurship.

Despite the importance of entrepreneurship, our understanding of its role in regional development is in its infancy. We have yet to answer even the most basic questions: How should one measure entrepreneurship? Are the appropriate measures different from those used in advanced economies? What is the degree of spatial variation for entrepreneurship? What factors determine the locations of entrepreneurs? How does regional entrepreneurship relate to regional growth? Do these patterns resemble or differ from those in advanced economies?

While recognizing that we can only scratch the surface of these important issues for South Asia's future, this chapter provides a first analysis using the manufacturing sector in India. It provides an overview of various entrepreneurship metrics and relates them to regional growth.

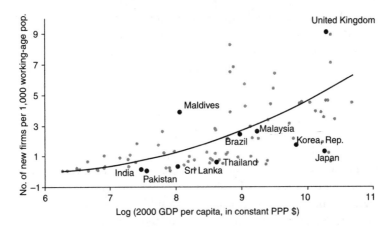

FIGURE 7.1   New Business Registration Density and GDP per Capita
by Country, 2008

Source: World Bank Group Entrepreneurship Survey (2010); World Development
Indicators (2010).

The link is quite strong and robust across many specification variants. We
also compare our results throughout the study with work on the United
States. Many of the conclusions regarding the regional link between
employment growth andentrepreneurship found for the United States
also hold for South Asia, which is encouraging for the international
portability of research findings. These conclusions are a foundation for
future research on these important questions, and they provide initial
guidance for policymakers.

Moreover, entrepreneurship and job creation have strong links to
the other aspects of growth in South Asia discussed in this volume.
Earlier chapters focus on the demographic dividend for South Asia
and the rise of the middle class. Entrepreneurship is a central force for
employing and expanding the economic opportunities for this growing
population of South Asia. Globalization and the future of migration are
also discussed. In this period of rapid development for South Asia, the
capacity of regions to respond to new economic opportunities and build
employment in emerging industries will shape the flows of people and
businesses, domestically and internationally (witness only the spectacular
rise of Bangalore). Finally, looking ahead to the challenges documented
in the second half of this book, movements from the informal sector
into the formal will depend in large part on the capacity of local and

regional economies to scale up their economies formally. Fernandes and Pakes (2010) observe that India's manufacturing sector is underdeveloped relative to economies of similar size, and it is important to identify how formal jobs in this sector can be created to aid economic transitions and growth. Entrepreneurship will play a fundamental role in future urban economics for South Asia.

While focusing on entrepreneurship in this chapter, we clearly recognize that large firms also play an important role in regional development. The giant firms of South Asia are becoming globally powerful and growing in efficiency, which is to be applauded. They too will shape employment opportunities in the decades ahead. However, the history of regional development shows that big firms are not sufficient. An entrepreneurial foundation that provides for local growth and regeneration is essential for long-term success and prosperity. This is evident in the current struggles of Detroit, Michigan, and its car manufacturers. Jane Jacobs (1970) highlights how Manchester, England, and its giant textile mills in the 1800s were a model of short-term efficiency and power but also ultimately insufficient for long-term regional growth. Likewise, the very dynamic times ahead for South Asia require that entrepreneurship be embraced and supported.

The next section of this chapter briefly reviews some theoretical and empirical linkages between entrepreneurship and growth. The section that follows discusses the measurement of entrepreneurship and our data. The next section analyses the link between entrepreneurship and region-industry growth in India. The section that follows considers whether entrepreneurial returns or cost factors are behind the spatial distribution of entrepreneurship. The final section gives a conclusion and provides some initial policy implications from this work.

ENTREPRENEURSHIP AND GROWTH: THEORETICAL AND EMPIRICAL UNDERPINNINGS

This section reviews theoretical and empirical foundations for studying entrepreneurship and growth. We keep this discussion short and non-technical, but interested readers can consult Parker (2009) for a more detailed overview of prior literature.

Theoretical Underpinnings

The concept of entrepreneurship has a rich intellectual tradition dating back to the foundations of economics as a discipline. Cantillon (1730) first described entrepreneurship as self-employment of any sort, with entrepreneurs buying at certain prices in the present and selling at uncertain prices in the future. Knight (1921) further developed the unique role that entrepreneurs can play by emphasizing how entrepreneurs predict and act upon fundamental market changes: recognizing opportunity, bearing uncertainty, and directing new ventures. In a related vein, Kirzner (1972, 1979) emphasized how entrepreneurs drive markets toward equilibrium. Schumpeter (1942) was perhaps the first to link entrepreneurship and growth by emphasizing how entrepreneurs convert new ideas into successful innovations, generating 'creative destruction' by simultaneously creating new products and eliminating others. While these conceptualizations lack formal mathematical models, they remain at the heart of our view of entrepreneurship today.

Formal models of economic growth have meanwhile been developed over the past several decades, culminating in the endogenous growth theory. Classics among these include Solow (1956), Romer (1986, 1990), and Aghion and Howitt (1992). Barro and Sala-i-Martin (1995) and Acemoglu (2009) provide comprehensive reviews. These models mostly emphasize innovation as a central driver of economic growth. The accumulation of physical capital and complementary investments in worker education and skills are important, but long-run economic growth depends on innovations and technological developments that increase our productivity from a given set of resources. As innovation is the central focus of this work, these models can be formulated to include entrepreneurship, but this is not necessary. One can set up textbook endogenous growth models so that innovations are developed by entering entrepreneurial firms pursuing profit incentives, but the models can also be formulated around incumbent firms.

Recent theoretical work provides more explicit links between entrepreneurship and growth. Continuing first with the endogenous growth framework, Akcigit and Kerr (2010) developed a model of an economy with complete firm size distribution, firm entry and exit behaviour, and choices by firms to pursue exploration versus exploitation innovations. Exploration innovations seek to develop new technologies to capture product lines a firm does not already have, while exploitation innovations seek to enhance the product lines that a firm currently serves. Akcigit and Kerr (2010) show that new entrants and young firms invest comparatively more in exploration investments, while larger firms naturally invest more in exploitation efforts given their many existing product lines. The model devises simple tests which highlight that growth spillover effects are stronger for exploration innovations, showing that entrepreneurship explicitly matters for economic growth.

Another mechanism through which this relationship becomes apparent is that of occupational choice. Baumol (1990) and Murphy et al. (1991) emphasized the importance of how the best talent in the economy is allocated across activities. Talent can either be placed in entrepreneurial efforts, which generates growth spillover effects through innovations and productivity enhancements that are shared in the economy, or go into professions that mostly seek to govern how output is distributed across the economy (for example, lawyers and bureaucracies). The types of technologies that exist, the relative sizes of markets, and similar factors govern how talent allocates itself across sectors. Economies where the most talented individuals enter entrepreneurship grow faster through this occupational choice mechanism. Banerjee and Newman (1993) also describe how these choices relate to income and wealth distribution in an economy.

Theoretical and conceptual models have also emphasized increased risk-taking (Khilstrom and Laffont 1979), benefits due to diversity (Jacobs 1970), and enhanced labour flows and industrial organization for technology (Fallick et al. 2006) as the means through which entrepreneurship impacts growth. There are thus multiple channels through which entrepreneurship can matter for economic growth and development.

Empirical Underpinnings

Strong empirical research on the role of entrepreneurship in economic growth has been slower to develop than the theory. This sluggishness has been primarily due to data constraints rather than lack of interest, as only in the last two decades have micro-level data become available that allow us to accurately measure entry rates at the disaggregated levels (for example, cities and industries) required to test the relationship. Prior to this, while we could see clear correlations between entrepreneurship and development/growth in business cycle dynamics or in cross-sectional relationships for regions or countries (Klapper et al. 2010; Acs and Armington 2006; Audretsch et al. 2006; Acs and Audretsch 1993), it was impossible to assess entrepreneurship's specific role versus general economic conditions in greater detail.

Much existing evidence focuses on the experience of the US, which was among the first countries to develop the necessary data detail, and on the manufacturing sector in particular. Dunne et al. (1989a, 1989b) and

Davis et al. (1996) provide among the first detailed accounts of the high firm entry and exit rates that exist in industries using manufacturing data from the US Census Bureau. Building on this tradition, Haltiwanger et al. (2010) provide very systematic documentation of the important role of start-ups and young firms in the employment growth process. This strong empirical link at the aggregate level is perhaps even more striking when examining urban or regional data in the United States (Glaeser et al. 2010). Cities in the United States with more entrepreneurship in the late 1970s have consistently grown faster in the three decades since then. This continues to hold at the industry level within cities.

These studies mostly provide a decomposition of entrepreneurship's role, and causal identification of the elasticity between entrepreneurship and growth for the economy as a whole remains elusive so far (for understandable reasons given the strong endogenous relationship between growth and entrepreneurship). There has been greater progress, however, with respect to the impact of high-growth start-ups, especially those backed by venture capital investors. Kortum and Lerner (2000) and Samila and Sorenson (2011) link the development of risk capital financing to growth-spillover effects for industries and cities respectively. These settings are attractive as identification frameworks are feasible within this sub-sector of the economy (for example, endowment shocks that impact the volume of available venture capital financing).

MEASUREMENT OF ENTREPRENEURSHIP FOR SOUTH ASIAN COUNTRIES

This section describes the measurement of entrepreneurship. We begin with a general overview, owing mostly to Glaeser and Kerr (2009), that also highlights issues particular to South Asia. We then describe our manufacturing data for India in detail.

Definitions of Entrepreneurship

Defining entrepreneurship is hard and controversial even in advanced countries.[1] One approach, dating back to Cantillion (1730), is to describe entrepreneurship as the number of people leading independent businesses. Evans and Jovanovic (1989), Blanchflower and Oswald (1998), and many others have accordingly used self-employment rates as

---

[1] See, for example, the work of the OECD Entrepreneurship Indicators Programme in 2008 and 2009.

their metric of entrepreneurship. This choice has also been encouraged by the fact that self-employment questions have typically been included in censuses of families or households. Thus data on self- employment rates became available much earlier than any other potential measure.

However, recent studies note the challenges that come with using self-employment metrics to describe the entrepreneurship necessary for economic growth and job creation. Due to the much larger raw count of self-employed workers, self-employment indices accord much more weight to small-scale, independent businesses and hobby entrepreneurship than entrepreneurship that can lead to substantial job creation for others. The vast majority of self-employment businesses as captured in labour and census surveys will not generate employment opportunities for other workers, and they may even be the products of a lack of employment opportunities for the business owner (Astebro et al. 2010; Schoar 2009). This latter factor is particularly acute in South Asia. Should each self-employed taxi driver be accorded the same weight as a new start-up company that is hoping to grow to employ hundreds of workers?

These criticisms are evident in some simple examples. Silicon Valley is the exemplar of US regional entrepreneurship and the world's largest venture capital market. Yet San Jose, CA, ranks last among America's 300+ metropolitan areas in terms of self-employment, with West Palm Beach, FL, instead being crowned as America's most entrepreneurial city. This questionable pattern is also evident in country rankings. Southern European countries (for example Portugal and Greece) rank much higher than Scandinavian countries in terms of self-employment within Europe, but much lower in terms of most growth entrepreneurship indicators like venture capital markets (Bozkaya and Kerr 2010). Klapper et al. (2010) document the negative correlation between self-employment levels and economic development across a broad cross-section of countries, and we shall see later in this chapter that self-employment metrics for India perform poorly for describing job growth compared to better-specified alternatives.

Hence, most recent studies of entrepreneurship and growth instead focus exclusively on formal firms that employ paid workers. These thresholds—being incorporated, paying payroll taxes—are in some sense arbitrary, but they are natural given our fundamental interest in describing regional job creation. Their relevance is even greater for South Asia given the need to pull members of the informal economy into the formal sector. Here too, however, there are substantial disagreements as to what should be measured. A vast, earlier literature develops estimates of the number or share of small businesses in a region. A similar metric is average firm size (Glaeser 2007).

These measures of small businesses overcome some of the problems of the earlier self-employment measures, but they still weight small businesses that are not attempting to grow substantially (for example a small, family-run business that has employed the same number of workers for many years) very heavily. In other words, they do not capture the important dynamic aspects of entrepreneurship for economic growth. These metrics may also be additionally skewed in the Indian context given the well-known problem of the 'missing middle' in the firm-size distribution, which is often associated with rigid employment laws. A large count of small firms may not represent an entrepreneurial cluster as much as an environment where these laws are particularly binding (Besley and Burgess 2004).

Understandably, many researchers are instead drawn to metrics that are more tightly connected to the dynamic nature of entrepreneurship. The more recent micro-data have both enabled these measurements and stressed their better performance relative to small business counts (Haltiwanger et al. 2010). One approach focuses on start-ups within a single industry so that finer characterizations and case studies can be made (Feldman 2003; Saxenian 1994). Others look at new product introductions (Audretsch and Feldman 1996), venture capital placement (Samila and Sorenson 2011), or the founding of new firms (Rosenthal and Strange 2010; Kerr and Nanda 2009). These dynamic measures of entrepreneurship are less available than self-employment rates or small business statistics, but are more tightly connected to entrepreneurship that can generate job growth.

We follow this emerging strand and principally define entrepreneurship as the presence of young manufacturing establishments (but we will test all three variants). Haltiwanger et al. (2010) emphasize how in the US experience, young firms are more tightly associated with employment growth than small firms (conditioning on age). While we would also like to employ measures of entering establishments in their first year (Glaeser and Kerr 2009), our data are only every few years in frequency. Thus the young establishment definition—less than three years old—is the most refined measure feasible for India at this time. We will separately test using all young establishments, which combines both stand-alone young firms and young establishments of multi-unit firms, and measures that focus exclusively on young firms.

Thus our study of entrepreneurship falls between two more common types of studies, thereby hitting on a key element of South Asia's future. On the one hand, we purposely steer clear of self-employment measures and the informal sector except as robustness checks or to contrast our results. Even for the United States, self-employment is a second-best link for measuring entrepreneurship for job creation. These methodological challenges for low return or subsistence efforts are compounded in South Asia where the informal sector employs 90 per cent of workers (Schoar 2009). To realize long-term employment growth, it is necessary to distinguish transformative entrepreneurship from subsistence entrepreneurship.

On the other hand, we also do not study the development of very high-growth entrepreneurship or venture capital markets in South Asia (except to the extent that they are a part of our official statistics). This is not because these entrepreneurs are not important for South Asia; quite the opposite and many recent studies focus on software's emergence, returnee entrepreneurs, diasporas, and similar exciting developments (Nanda and Khanna 2010; Kerr 2008; Arora and Gambardella 2005). Yet these specialized sectors are still an extremely small part of the Indian economy, and we focus on identifying measures of entrepreneurship that apply more broadly across the entire manufacturing sector.

Indian Entrepreneurship and Growth Data in Manufacturing

We now describe our data on Indian manufacturing. Fernandes and Pakes (2010) also describe the Indian manufacturing sector and its firm-size distribution in detail. Our primary sources are repeated cross-sections of the Indian manufacturing sector based on Government of India industrial survey data. Separate industrial surveys of both the organized and unorganized manufacturing sectors were carried out in fiscal years 1989–1990, 1994–5, 2000–1, and 2005–6. This dataset links the organized and unorganized sector survey data for these years, providing four snapshots of the entire Indian manufacturing industry back to 1989. Nataraj (2009) and Kathuria et al. (2010) provide detailed overviews of similarly constructed databases.

Typically, manufacturing establishments with more than 10 workers are required to register under the India Factories Act of 1948. The organized sector is surveyed by the Central Statistical Organisation every year through the Annual Survey of Industries (ASI). Some large establishments are surveyed every year as part of a census frame, while approximately one-third of the smaller establishments are surveyed with state and industry stratification. We use sample weights provided with the data to create population-level estimates of total establishments, output, and employment by region and three-digit National Industry Classification (NIC). Establishments below the employment threshold for the organized sector are not required to register under the Factories Act. This unorganized sector is surveyed by the National Sample Survey Organisation (NSSO), with a sampling universe of all manufacturing establishments that are not registered under the Factories Act. Unorganized establishments are unregistered, do not pay taxes, and are generally outside the purview of the state. For this reason, we use the organized–unorganized sector distinction readily available in our data to roughly distinguish between the formal and informal sectors. As with the ASI data, sampling weights supplied by the NSSO are used to expand the sample to be representative of the entire population.

The final dataset contains many of the elements common to both ASI and NSSO surveys. This includes information on location, NIC industry, legal status and ownership structure, as well as detailed balance sheet and income statement accounts. An element of age—specifically whether the establishment is less than three years old—is also included. Data on employment, fixed assets, wages, revenues, output, and raw material expenses are also available. We convert nominal values to constant 2005 US dollars at purchasing power parity (PPP). We also update earlier NIC classifications to the current (NIC 2004) classification using concordances provided with ASI data.

Descriptive Statistics on Indian Entrepreneurship in Manufacturing

Tables 7.1a and 7.1b provide some basic descriptive statistics relating to our sample. Table 7.1a gives various metrics of entrepreneurship that we will relate to job growth across Indian regions. The first two rows are measures of the prevalence of young and small firms respectively on a per worker basis. The third and fourth rows give the employment share in these establishments. The fifth row is the self-employment share. For each metric, we provide three data cuts: the formal sector only, the informal sector only, and the two sectors combined. In all cases, we adjust the metrics so that they are comparable. For example, the denominator for the first row changes from per 1,000 formal workers, to per 1,000 informal workers, and finally to per 1,000 formal + informal workers.

TABLE 7.1a   Description Statistics on Entrepreneurship in Indian
Manufacturing

	Formal Sector Only	Informal Sector Only	Combining Formal and Informal
Count of young establishments per 1,000 workers (<3 years old), 1989	2.2	105.6	84.6
Count of small establishments per 1,000 workers (<20 employees), 1989	6.4	513.5	410.8
Share of workers in young establishments, 1989	9.6%	19.8%	17.7%
Share of workers in small establishments, 1989	7.3%	99.9%	81.2%
Self-employment share, 1989	0.0%	18.0%	14.3%
Count of young establishments per 1,000 workers (<3 years old):			
1989	2.2	105.6	84.6
1994	2.1	73.4	58.0
2000	2.2	42.0	34.9
2005	2.1	59.9	48.3
Count of young establishments per 1,000 workers (<3 years old):			
Andhra Pradesh	2.3	124.9	98.5
Goa	3.3	138.3	75.5
Gujarat	2.4	143.7	87.8
Haryana	1.8	152.7	89.9
Karnataka	1.6	110.9	87.2
Kerala	1.9	158.6	135.6
Madhya Pradesh	1.3	64.8	50.4
Maharashtra	1.6	100.7	60.8
Orissa	1.6	40.8	38.9
Punjab	2.5	159.9	94.5
Tamil Nadu	2.8	172.3	131.9
Uttar Pradesh	3.6	129.9	110.7
West Bengal	0.7	55.5	51.6

Source: Annual Survey of Industries; National Sample Survey, various rounds (1989–2005).
Notes: Descriptive statistics taken from Annual Survey of Industries and National Sample Statistics for years 1989, 1994, 2001, and 2005. 'Young' establishments are less than three years old at the time of the survey, 'small' establishments have fewer than 20 permanent employees.

The differences across the measurements and columns are to be expected. Counts of young establishments in the formal sector are low in India relative to advanced economies, much as Figure 7.1 suggests. Small establishments are somewhat more common, but have a smaller employment share than young establishments. Self-employment is virtually non-existent in the formal manufacturing sector in India, but it should be noted that this is in some sense a result of the de facto definition arising from India's registration laws. The informal sector has much higher levels of small establishments and self-employment, but young establishments are under-represented. The bottom two panels of Table 7.1a provide additional details on our primary metric of entrepreneurship: young establishments per 1,000 workers in the formal sector. This measure shows a slight upward trend over time and significant heterogeneity across Indian regions. The highest levels of young establishments are in Uttar Pradesh, Andhra Pradesh, and Orissa, while the lowest are in Haryana (including Delhi) and West Bengal.

To provide a rough comparison, Schmitt and Lane (2009) report that self-employment rates outside of agriculture among 16 Organisation for Economic Cooperation and Development (OECD) economies ranged from about 7 per cent (Norway and United States) to 25–30 per cent (Greece and Italy) in 2000. India appears at the upper end of this distribution after including the informal sector. Schmitt and Lane (2009) also report that manufacturing employment in enterprises with fewer than 20 employees ranged from 9–11 per cent (Luxembourg, Ireland, and United States) to 30–35 per cent (Greece, Italy, and Portugal) in 2006. Davis et al. (1996) report that about 5 per cent of US manufacturing employment for 1973–88 was in establishments with fewer than 20 employees. Our Indian data are not as comparable on these latter dimensions—as these external statistics define the formal manufacturing sector in ways that are difficult for us to replicate with our two separate datasets—but India again appears to be at the upper end of the range.

Fernandes and Pakes (2010) similarly conclude that Indian manufacturing firms are disproportionately represented in the small end of the size distribution. Thus India has a relatively high share of small establishments and self-employment in manufacturing, and also a relatively low share of young establishments or new firm start-ups. Schoar (2007) concludes that India has too many entrepreneurs, in the sense of having high rates of self-employment and small businesses, but too little entrepreneurial growth. Finally, Ardagna and Lusardi (2008) analysed harmonized micro-data on entrepreneurship collected by the Global Entrepreneurship Monitor, finding that India has entry rates comparable to those of its peers. They also estimated that the subsistence rate of entrepreneurship in India is high in absolute terms and comparable to that of its peers. These patterns likely reflect both push and pull factors.

Table 7.1b describes the correlation between the young establishments per worker measure and the other metrics across states or industries. There is a modest degree of correlation within the formal group, which is comparable to the 0.4–0.6 correlations that Glaeser and Kerr (2009) observed across US cities for entrepreneurship metrics. The link across metrics is much weaker in the informal sector, especially in regional variation. Unreported correlation matrices show that the correlation

TABLE 7.1b   Correlation between Measures of Entrepreneurship in Indian Manufacturing

	Correlation with Log of Young Establishments per Worker, 1989		
	Formal sector only	Informal sector only	Combining formal and informal
	Correlation across regions		
Count of small establishments per 1,000 workers (<20 employees), 1989	0.20	0.10	0.15
Share of workers in young establishments, 1989	0.64*	0.91*	0.78*
Share of workers in small establishments, 1989	0.23	−0.04	−0.07
Self-employment share, 1989	0.45	0.34	0.49*
	Correlation across industries		
Count of small establishments per 1,000 workers (<20 employees), 1989	0.68*	0.39*	0.52*
Share of workers in young establishments, 1989	0.66*	0.77*	0.80*
Share of workers in small establishments, 1989	0.71*	0.04	0.66*
Self-employment share, 1989	0.22	0.49*	0.18

Notes: See Table 7.1a

*significant at 10% level.

between formal and informal sector measures is much weaker. For example, the correlation between young establishments per worker in the formal sector and the self-employment rate in the informal sector is about 0.1. There is likewise a much weaker correlation between small establishment metrics and self-employment metrics.

ENTREPRENEURSHIP AND EMPLOYMENT GROWTH ACROSS SOUTH ASIA

We now turn to an empirical analysis of employment growth and entrepreneurship across regions. We first provide very simple graphs and correlations that test relationships using our full range of metrics. We then undertake an extended region–industry analysis using our primary metric of young establishments per worker. We close this section with some sample decomposition tests to begin uncovering region and industry traits that govern the relationships.

General Relationship between Entrepreneurship and Growth

Figure 7.2a provides the simplest representation. The vertical axis is the log of employment growth in the region from 1989 to 2005, while the horizontal axis is the log of the count of young firms per worker in 1989. There is a strong upward slope to the trend line, similar to that found across cities in the United States (Glaeser et al. 2010), and it is clear that the relationship does not overly depend upon any one region. Figure 7.2b provides a comparable picture using region–industry employment growth and initial entrepreneurship levels. The pattern looks even more powerful and robust at this level of detail. It is important to note that these correlations are not between contemporaneous entry rates and employment growth, which can potentially have a mechanical relationship, but instead between initial entry rates and subsequent region–industry employment growth.

Table 7.2 provides a systematic comparison of our entrepreneurship metrics using the region–industry variation. The sample includes 575 region–industry pairs that have positive employment in 1989, and we exclude nine extreme observations from Figure 7.2b. These exclusions make our estimations more conservative. Panel A presents an unconditional estimation, while Panel B conditions on log initial employment (Glaeser et al. 2010; Delgado et al. 2008). Column headers indicate the entrepreneurship metric employed. The coefficient in the first column of Panel A is akin to the slope of the trend line in Figure 7.2b. Regressions are unweighted and report robust standard errors.

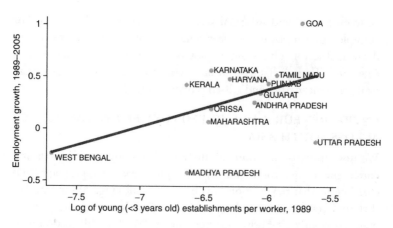

FIGURE 7.2a   Entrepreneurship and Growth in Indian Manufacturing
by State, 1989–2005

Source: Annual Survey of Industries (1989–2005).

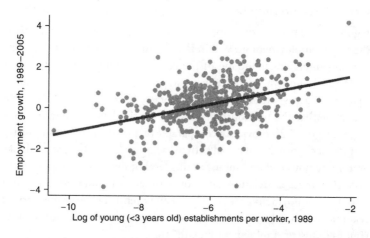

FIGURE 7.2b   Entrepreneurship and Growth in Indian Manufacturing
by State and 3-digit Industry, 1989–2005

Source: Annual Survey of Industries (1989–2005).

Elasticities over the first four columns in Panel A range from 0.18 to
0.33 at the region–industry level. These elasticities are quite comparable
to those estimated in the United States using a similar design (Glaeser and
Kerr 2010). All estimates are statistically significant. Unreported regressions
find that these elasticities range from 0.22 to 0.35 when including the nine
omitted observations or from 0.29 to 0.52 when estimated at the region

TABLE 7.2 Region–Industry Employment Growth in Formal Manufacturing and Various Entrepreneurial Metrics

	Count of Young Establishments per Worker	Count of Small Establishments per Worker	Share of Workers in Young Establishments	Share of Workers in Small Establishments	Self-employment Share in Formal Sector	Self-employment Share in Informal Sector
	(1)	(2)	(3)	(4)	(5)	(6)
A. Dependent variable: Region–industry employment growth in formal manufacturing, 1989–2005						
Entrepreneurship level in region–industry in 1989	0.334 (0.040)***	0.255 (0.040)***	0.178 (0.046)***	0.269 (0.040)***	0.051 (0.028)*	0.072 (0.037)**
Adjusted R-squared	0.108	0.087	0.038	0.090	0.002	0.006
B. Panel A, controlling for initial employment						
Entrepreneurship level in region–industry in 1989	0.258 (0.049)***	0.163 (0.040)***	0.101 (0.045)**	0.176 (0.041)***	0.017 (0.027)	0.040 (0.038)
Employment level in region–industry in 1989	−0.097 (0.030)***	−0.137 (0.027)***	−0.149 (0.027)***	−0.135 (0.027)***	−0.161 (0.024)***	−0.191 (0.026)***
Adjusted R-squared	0.125	0.126	0.087	0.129	0.079	0.104

Notes: Estimations quantify the relationship between region–industry employment growth in the formal manufacturing sector over 1989–2005 and initial entrepreneurship conditions in 1989. Column headers indicate entrepreneurship metric employed. All variables are in logs. Estimations report robust standard errors, are unweighted, and have 575 observations.

*significant at 10% level, **significant at 5% level, ***significant at 1% level.

level. In strong contrast, there is a much weaker link from self-employment metrics, in either the formal or informal sector, to subsequent job growth. This stresses the importance of how entrepreneurship is measured for estimating its link to local job growth.

We find similar results in Panel B after controlling for initial employment levels in region–industries. Coefficients tend to be a quarter to a third smaller, but they remain economically and statistically significant. High levels of initial employment are correlated with lower job growth to 2005, indicative of convergence in the economic growth process. We noted earlier that our sample includes all region–industry pairs that had positive employment in 1989. Some region–industry cells have zero young businesses, which does not define an initial entrepreneurship metric. To maintain a consistent sample size across specification variants, we recode these cases to have one young establishment, creating an unreported indicator variable that specifies these cases in the regressions. We obtain very similar results if instead we simply drop these cases.

Extended Analysis at Region–Industry Level

The estimates discussed provide simple and transparent evidence, but it is natural to worry about omitted factors that could influence both employment growth and firm ages. Tables 7.3a and 7.3b provide a more formal set of growth regressions using young establishments in a region-industry context. We begin in the first column by simply including the explanatory variables of initial entrepreneurship and employment levels at both region and region–industry levels. This starting point is interesting in that it highlights that entrepreneurship at both the levels is important for growth in the focal region–industry. Similar patterns are evident in the United States, and we return in the next section to a more formal analysis of entrepreneurial returns and the Chinitz effect to trace why this might be so.

The second column further incorporates a vector of industry fixed effects. These fixed effects capture the general growth of industries in India between 1989 and 2005 and the levels of entrepreneurship that existed in 1989. Whereas the simplest correlations could have reflected, for example, general differences between textile and chemical industries, these fixed effects require that the estimates only exploit variations across regions after controlling for general industry differences. These fixed effects also account for other fixed industry factors like capital intensity and export behaviour. Elasticities are similar in this estimation, although the region–industry entrepreneurship variable loses about half of its strength. This suggests that general industry differences—some sectors being very entrepreneurial and fast growing across all Indian regions—partly explain the strong effects in Table 7.2. Nevertheless, region–industry entrepreneurship remains important economically and is precisely estimated in the conditional regression.

The third column goes a step further and includes a vector of region fixed effects. Like industry fixed effects, the regional fixed effects remove general differences across locations, for example the lower average entry in West Bengal or the higher average entry in Uttar Pradesh. They also remove traits and policies that influence all industries equally, for example aggregate regional growth that increases demand for all manufacturing goods. The estimation now requires that higher employment growth at the region–industry level be linked to higher rates of young establishments after removing any systematic industry and region effects. The importance of region–industry entrepreneurship is very robust for this specification choice.

This estimate of 0.138 (0.055) is our preferred specification. In words, it finds that a 10 per cent increase in initial entrepreneurship in a region–industry in 1989 was associated with a 1.3 per cent higher rate of employment growth to 2005. We get this estimate after removing effects of initial employment levels and systematic growth effects by regions and industries. While India has historically been weaker in terms of growth-oriented entrepreneurship overall, industries and regions that have embraced entrepreneurship have grown faster. Given the potential for the manufacturing sector to expand in South Asia, this is very encouraging for future growth prospects.

Columns 4–6 provide additional robustness checks on this conditional specification. We first test for outliers by weighting the regression by initial employment in the region–industry, finding very similar effects. Column 5 further controls for average age of establishments in the region–industry to verify that the observed young establishment relationship is not due to broader product cycles and industry evolution (Faberman 2007; Jovanovic and MacDonald 1994; and Klepper and Graddy 1990). This broader age regressor does little to explain the relationship between job growth and young establishments.

The first five columns of Table 7.3a use young establishments per worker regardless of whether they are independent firms or part of larger enterprises. We make this more encompassing measure our baseline to allow comparability to the World Bank reports and surveys that key off this

TABLE 7.3a Region–Industry Growth Estimations for Formal Manufacturing Employment

	Base Estimation with Young Establishments	Including Industry Fixed Effects	Including Industry and Region Effects	Weighting by Initial Region–Industry Size	Controlling for Age Structure of Region–Industry	Using Only Stand-alone Establishments
	(1)	(2)	(3)	(4)	(5)	(6)
	Dependent variable: Region–industry employment growth in formal manufacturing, 1989–2005					
Entrepreneurship level in region–industry in 1989	0.215 (0.050)***	0.113 (0.054)**	0.138 (0.056)**	0.164 (0.054)***	0.148 (0.060)**	0.090 (0.044)**
Employment level in region–industry in 1989	−0.124 (0.034)***	−0.226 (0.049)***	−0.236 (0.049)***	−0.228 (0.047)***	−0.236 (0.049)***	−0.265 (0.046)***
Entrepreneurship level in region in 1989	0.244 (0.110)**	0.308 (0.102)***				
Employment level in region in 1989	0.0831 (0.058)	0.196 (0.068)***				
Average establishment age in region–industry in 1989					0.071 (0.146)	
Adjusted R-squared	0.133	0.300	0.328	0.344	0.327	0.325
Industry fixed effects		Yes	Yes	Yes	Yes	Yes
Region fixed effects			Yes	Yes	Yes	Yes

Notes: Estimations quantify the relationship between region–industry employment growth in the formal manufacturing sector over 1989–2005 and initial entrepreneurship conditions. Entrepreneurship conditions are described through young establishments per worker. Estimations report robust standard errors, are unweighted excepting Column 4, and have 575 observations.
*significant at 10% level,** significant at 5% level, ***significant at 1% level.

concept. This choice also has the conceptual underpinning that encouraging entrepreneurship may involve the initial expansion and replication of highly productive enterprises to offer formal jobs to subsistence workers. Finally, a practical issue is that our data do not truly identify firm ownership structures of establishments; we only have self-reported data on whether the respondent is part of a larger firm. We thus cannot assess whether a young establishment is part of a young multi-unit firm or an older multi-unit firm. Column 6 shows that we obtain very similar outcomes when using just young, stand-alone establishments that state that they are not part of a larger firm. The elasticity is somewhat smaller, which may be due to a weaker economic effect or due to greater measurement error in the single-unit metrics, but the general effect is very persistent.

Finally, Table 7.3b includes the informal sector. Growth and entrepreneurship in the informal sector, which accounts for approximately 90 per cent of Indian manufacturing, were excluded in Table 7.3a. The dependent variable in Table 7.3b across all four columns is the log growth of manufacturing employment by region–industry in the combined formal and informal sectors. Likewise, the initial employment level across all four columns combines both sectors. Comparing the coefficients on this control variable to Table 7.3a, regions and industries with very high informal employment in 1989 experienced disproportionately slow subsequent job growth.

The first column shows that our basic finding holds when our entrepreneurship measure combines young businesses from both the sectors. The elasticity declines by about a third, and columns 2–4 investigate why. High rates of entrepreneurship in the informal sector do little to promote job growth in manufacturing. On the other hand, high rates of entrepreneurship in the formal sector robustly increase employment growth. The coefficient for combined job growth in the formal and informal sectors is lower than that for the formal sector alone (Table 7.3a), which is to be expected. The remainder of this chapter focuses on just formal-sector definitions, but the importance that we place on formal entrepreneurship is robust to a wider focus.

Sample Composition

To close this section, Tables 7.4a and 7.4b provide a variety of sample decomposition exercises by region and industry respectively. In each exercise, we split the sample at the median value of each trait and estimate our core regression with region and industry fixed effects (Column 3 of Table 7.3a) in both halves. Our choices of dimensions on which

TABLE 7.3b Region–Industry Growth Estimations for Formal and Informal Manufacturing Employment

	Combined Formal and Informal Sector Entrepreneurship	Informal Sector Entrepreneurship Only	Formal Sector Entrepreneurship Only	Separate Formal and Informal Sector Entrepreneurship
	(1)	(2)	(3)	(4)
	Dependent variable: Region–industry employment growth in formal + informal manufacturing, 1989–2005			
Entrepreneurship level in region–industry in 1989, combined	0.097 (0.043)**			
Entrepreneurship level in region–industry in 1989, informal		0.036 (0.041)		0.043 (0.042)
Entrepreneurship level in region–industry in 1989, formal			0.084 (0.050)*	0.089 (0.051)*
Employment level in region–industry in 1989	−0.369 (0.058)***	−0.397 (0.059)***	−0.365 (0.065)***	−0.358 (0.066)***
Adjusted R-squared	0.414	0.406	0.408	0.408
Industry fixed effects	Yes	Yes	Yes	Yes
Region fixed effects	Yes	Yes	Yes	Yes

Notes: See Table 7.3a. Estimation contrast formal and informal entrepreneurship for total employment growth in the manufacturing sector. Estimates have 592 observations.

*significant at 10% level, **significant at 5% level, ***significant at 1% level.

to partition the sample are motivated by factors that the economic growth/development and entrepreneurship literature have found to be important.

These decompositions are not meant to systematically test the importance of each factor, but instead to provide some suggestive evidence of the best places for future researchers to examine. It is important to understand that by splitting the sample we allow lots of flexibility in how the differences emerge. The coefficients on the unreported region and industry fixed effects, for example, are not constrained to be equal to each other. Some relationships may look different in more structured specification tests.

Before discussing each partition, the broad and most important observation from Tables 7.4a and 7.4b is the remarkable stability of the findings. In both halves of each decomposition, we find a positive effect of entrepreneurship for job growth that exceeds 0.095 (compared to the sample average of 0.138 in Table 7.3a). Moreover, while some estimates are not statistically significant after cutting the sample size in half, the t-statistics are all greater than 1.2 in value. This general economic and statistical power across many different divisions of the data is very encouraging for our baseline result.

Table 7.4a finds that job growth effects from entrepreneurship are stronger in economically lagging regions. This may suggest that entrepreneurship is particularly important in helping initial job growth and informal to formal sector transitions. Unreported specifications find that while the leading region effect is lower using region–industry data, as in Table 7.4a, it is higher when using just the regional variation. This may reflect the fact that other region-level factors are central for the economic progress of leading regions, or may perhaps reflect more subtle differences in the industrial traits of leading and lagging areas. We hope that future research can refine this assessment.

Columns 3 and 4 examine differences across states in labour regulations (Ahsan and Pages 2007). Several studies link labour regulations in the Indian states to economic progress (Aghion et al. 2008; Besley and Burgess 2004), and one might hypothesize that entrepreneurial job creation would be similarly affected by these policies. However, we do not find that the job growth effects of entrepreneurship depend systematically upon these regulations. But it is interesting to note that this is the only place where our results depend meaningfully on the excluded, extreme region–industry cases. In examining the full sample, there is a positive gap between states with lower labour regulations and those with higher regulations. Future research on this topic would be particularly useful for clarifying these issues.

TABLE 7.4a Sample Composition Exercises for Region–Industry Growth Estimations—Region Traits

	Region Development Status		Region Labour Regulations		Region Education Levels		Region Financial Development	
	Leading	Lagging	High	Low	High	Low	High	Low
	(1)	(2)	(3)	(4)	(5)	(6)	(7)	(8)
Entrepreneurship level in region–industry in 1989	0.103 (0.069)	0.229 (0.097)**	0.165 (0.076)**	0.158 (0.083)*	0.203 (0.078)***	0.132 (0.086)	0.120 (0.076)	0.111 (0.071)
Employment level in region–industry in 1989	−0.209 (0.064)***	−0.294 (0.076)***	−0.377 (0.065)***	−0.160 (0.068)**	−0.208 (0.072)***	−0.233 (0.065)***	−0.290 (0.073)***	−0.159 (0.059)***
Adjusted R-squared	0.265	0.400	0.493	0.244	0.255	0.408	0.356	0.302
Observations	356	219	268	307	305	270	306	269
Industry fixed effects	Yes	Yes	Yes	Yes	Yes	Yes	Yes	Yes
Region fixed effects	Yes	Yes	Yes	Yes	Yes	Yes	Yes	Yes

Notes: See Table 7.3a. Region divisions are determined through the median value of the indicated metric. Development status follows the classification methodology used by Honarati and Mengistae (2007). They use a two-way classification, which follows Purifield (2006) but uses more recent data. States are designated as having high or low labour regulations based on the state's cumulative labour adjustment index from Ahsan and Pages (2007) in 1989. Education levels are those states with above-average literacy rates. Financial development is based on a weighted measure of total loans/output.

*significant at 10% level, **significant at 5% level, ***significant at 1% level.

Columns 5 and 6 show a higher elasticity among regions with stronger educational attainment (as measured through literacy rates). On the other hand, Columns 7 and 8 show that financial development (as measured through loans to output ratios) appears to matter less. We hope to examine more closely the financial dependence among industry sectors using a Rajan and Zingales (1998) approach in future research.

Table 7.4b turns to industry traits. We define four traits directly from our industrial dataset: (i) labour intensity (total wage bill over output), (ii) average wage, (iii) financial dependence (value of bank loans over output), and (iv) trade intensity (value of exports over output). These measures are calculated at the industry level after aggregating all establishments. We divide the sample based upon the median industry value observed for each ratio.

The effects are very comparable in industries with high and low labour intensity. This initial cut is promising in that the division separates textiles from chemicals, which are two of India's largest industries and account for a majority of the manufacturing employment. Columns 3–8 find that entrepreneurship's effects are somewhat stronger in industries with lower wages, while industry financial dependence or export intensity appears to matter less. But, looking across the columns the bigger message is simply that job creation effects are reasonably comparable in all cases despite the different divisions of the sample. Regional traits appear to matter more than industry traits in determining these responses.

ENTREPRENEURIAL RETURNS AND THE CHINITZ EFFECT

Our main goals in this chapter are to spark further research on the role of entrepreneurship in South Asia's future and to identify a platform from which to proceed. There are many potential follow-up studies that are worth pursuing. For example, each of the basic breakdowns in Tables 7.4a and 7.4b could be more closely examined to provide a causal assessment of their role for India's regional development, with entrepreneurship as a channel or mechanism. And there are many other regularities and features of entrepreneurship in advanced economies that are not discussed in this chapter but would be interesting to test in South Asia (for example, the role of innovation centres documented by Duranton 2007 and Kerr 2010 for urban industry evolution).

We end this chapter by examining in greater detail whether heightened entrepreneurial returns and/or the Chinitz effect (which relates to cost factors) appear to be the first-order determinants for regional placements.

TABLE 7.4b Sample Composition Exercises for Region–Industry Growth Estimations—Industry Traits

	Industry Labour Intensity		Industry Average Wages		Industry Financial Dependency		Industry Trade Intensity	
	High	Low	High	Low	High	Low	High	Low
	(1)	(2)	(3)	(4)	(5)	(6)	(7)	(8)
Entrepreneurship level in region–industry in 1989	0.147 (0.071)**	0.143 (0.085)*	0.095 (0.079)	0.155 (0.079)**	0.156 (0.087)*	0.130 (0.074)*	0.146 (0.075)*	0.110 (0.080)
Employment level in region–industry in 1989	−0.268 (0.065)***	−0.194 (0.081)**	−0.250 (0.068)***	−0.247 (0.073)***	−0.232 (0.087)***	−0.243 (0.061)***	−0.155 (0.076)**	−0.336 (0.065)***
Adjusted R-squared	0.481	0.136	0.391	0.265	0.422	0.240	0.267	0.403
Observations	297	278	283	292	247	328	315	260
Industry fixed effects	Yes	Yes	Yes	Yes	Yes	Yes	Yes	Yes
Region fixed effects	Yes	Yes	Yes	Yes	Yes	Yes	Yes	Yes

Notes: See Table 7.3a. Industry divisions are determined through the median value of the indicated metric. Labour intensity is based on the ratio of wages to output. Financial dependence is based on the ratio of total loans to output. Trade intensity is based on the ratio of export value to output. Metrics are calculated by 2-digit National Industrial Classification (NIC) industries for 1989.

*significant at 10% level, **significant at 5% level, ***significant at 1% level.

Both of these effects operate at the region–industry level, in contrast to the general region and industry traits studied in Tables 7.4a and 7.4b. Glaeser et al. (2010) provide a model that jointly considers these two effects, and they find empirical evidence that the Chinitz relationship is more important than heightened entrepreneurial returns for determining the spatial distribution of entrepreneurship in the United States. We extend these tests to India in Tables 7.5 and 7.6 using the variation across regions and industries.

Table 7.5 tests the entrepreneurial returns hypothesis. From Indian manufacturing data we calculate the dollar value of shipments per worker in 2005 in each region–industry separately for single-unit and multi-unit establishments. We use this shipments per employee metric as a proxy for future profitability and therefore the returns to entrepreneurship. This proxy is subject to including industry fixed effects that control for industry-level production techniques.

We do not find a strong relationship between the heightened presence of young establishments in 1989 and the subsequent value per worker in the region–industry. This weak explanatory power is for both economic magnitude and statistical significance. Similar to the United States, these patterns suggest that anticipation of abnormal returns is not the driving force behind the observed relationships for job creation.

Table 7.6 tests the Chinitz argument, which relates to lower costs for entrepreneurs. A number of studies list the many factors that bring about industry agglomeration (Ellison et al. 2010; Rosenthal and Strange

TABLE 7.5   Estimations of Localized Entrepreneurial Returns

	Average Labour Returns for Single-units in 2005	Average Labour Returns for Multi-units in 2005
	(1)	(2)
Entrepreneurship level in region–industry in 1989	0.024 (0.105)	−0.090 (0.225)
Employment level in region–industry in 1989	−0.015 (0.079)	0.033 (0.039)
Adjusted R-squared	0.273	0.145
Observations	607	346
Industry fixed effects	Yes	Yes
Region fixed effects	Yes	Yes

Notes: See Table 7.3a.

*significant at 10% level, ** significant at 5% level, ***significant at 1% level.

2001, 2003; Marshall 1920). Chinitz (1961) goes further to describe factors that specifically affect the entry rates of new firms. He particularly emphasizes the role of input suppliers: new ventures have many needs that must be met by the local economy, in contrast to larger incumbents that may source internally or from greater distances. Chinitz emphasizes that greater competition and smaller establishment sizes for suppliers help new ventures source specialized inputs and avoid hold-up problems.

In a famous comparison, Chinitz argues that the large, integrated steel firms of Pittsburgh depressed external supplier development; moreover, existing suppliers had limited interest in providing inputs to small businesses. By contrast, New York City's much smaller firms, organized around a more decentralized garment industry, were better suppliers to new firms. Jacobs (1970) also holds this view, and empirical evidence for the United States is documented by Drucker and Feser (2007), Rosenthal and Strange (2010), Glaeser and Kerr (2009), and Glaeser et al. (2010).

Table 7.6 tests the Chinitz effect through an additional regressor that calculates the average establishment size in each region c that typically supplies a given industry i,

TABLE 7.6   Estimations of the Chinitz Effect

	Young Establishment Employment by Region–Industry, 1994–2005	Employment Growth by Region–Industry, 1989–2005
	(1)	(2)
Entrepreneurship level in region–industry in 1989	0.203 (0.093)**	0.126 (0.057)**
Employment level in region–industry in 1989	0.651 (0.094)***	−0.261 (0.055)***
Chinitz index in supplier industries in 1989	0.311 (0.205)	0.145 (0.129)
Adjusted R-squared	0.672	0.328
Observations	575	575
Industry fixed effects	Yes	Yes
Region fixed effects	Yes	Yes

Notes: See Table 7.3a. Chinitz index is a weighted average measure of establishments per worker across supplier industries based on input–output flows.

*significant at 10% level, **significant at 5% level, ***significant at 1% level.

$$Chinitz_{ci} = v \sum_{k=1,...,I} \frac{Firms_{kc}}{E_{kc}} \frac{E_{kc}}{E_c} Input_{i \leftarrow k} = \sum_{k=1,...,I} \frac{Firms_{kc}}{E_c} Input_{i \leftarrow k}$$

where $Firms_{kc}$ is the count of firms. Higher values of this index indicate that greater numbers of firms are typically providing input needs of new entrants, weighted by the importance of the inputs in question. If the Chinitz effect holds, we will find a positive elasticity for subsequent entry and potentially realized employment growth for the region–industry.

The results in Table 7.6 suggest that the Chinitz effect may operate in India. The first column finds strong elasticity of the Chinitz regressor to the development of future entrepreneurship specifically in region-industry pairs. The coefficient is, in fact, larger in economic magnitude than our main effect and of borderline statistical significance (t-stat of 1.52). This is quite remarkable given that we are only able to identify local supplier conditions at the regional level rather than at the city level that is typical for these studies. Favourable local industrial conditions and cost factors thus appear to be associated with greater subsequent entry. The second column shows that this Chinitz factor might also be related to subsequent employment growth. While a positive elasticity is observed, our results do not have sufficient precision for definitive conclusions. We hope that future work can tackle these effects at the city level, where we anticipate that the employment growth effects will emerge clearly.

These patterns are similar to the United States, with cost factors more influential than spatial variations in entrepreneurial returns; moreover, the importance of initial entrepreneurial conditions persists even after controlling for local industrial conditions. Glaeser et al. (2010) conclude from a similar pattern that the supply side of entrepreneurship must be a factor for the US spatial distribution of entry. This echoes studies on the local bias of entrepreneurship in multiple countries (Michelacci and Silva 2007; Figueiredo et al. 2002). Entrepreneurs are more likely to be located in their home regions than wage workers; moreover, on average, home-town entrepreneurs tend to be more successful than migrating entrepreneurs. We have not examined these factors for South Asia, but more evidence in this regard is needed, and South Asia would be an attractive laboratory in this period of high migration and rapid emergence. Comparisons between manufacturing and services (Ghani 2010) would also be very illuminating.

POLICY IMPLICATIONS

This chapter has covered a lot of ground, describing first why entrepreneurship is important for South Asia to reach its potential for 2025. We then discussed how we should measure entrepreneurship, recommending that the prevalence of young, new establishments is the most appropriate metric. We have further shown that entrepreneurship rates in 1989 are strong systematic predictors of employment growth in India's manufacturing sector over the 1989–2005 period. The elasticities between initial entrepreneurship levels and subsequent growth across region–industry observations are comparable to those observed in the United States across cities. Finally, we gave some initial indications about traits of regions and industries that are good candidates for explaining the spatial patterns that we observe. We hope that future research continues to refine these estimates and better identifies the policy levers that can promote entrepreneurship.

Overall, our message is quite positive. It is well-known that manufacturing is under-developed in India relative to its economic size, and while India has a disproportionately high rate of self-employment and many small manufacturing firms, this has not translated as readily into as many young, entrepreneurial firms as could be hoped. Yet there is no question that entrepreneurship works in India! Formal economic job growth—which is what India needs to build a robust path to prosperity—has been the strongest in regions and industries that have exhibited high rates of entrepreneurship and dynamic economies.

Looking ahead, if India and South Asia continue to undertake some basic policy steps to help entrepreneurs—lowering entry costs, reducing regulatory burdens, and further developing financial access—they have the potential to unleash entrepreneurship and job growth that will strongly expand the formal manufacturing sector. Improving infrastructure, especially electricity and roads, is very important. The entrepreneurial potential of the region is very large (Khanna 2008). Most policy steps are not unique to South Asia, but are encouraged worldwide (Klapper and Love 2010; Acs et al. 2008). These simple steps will both strongly help South Asia realize its growth potential discussed in the first half of the book, and overcome the challenges discussed in the second half of the book.

India has experienced record growth over the past decade. Imagine if entrepreneurship in India were to move from its position in Figure 7.1 to the trend line or above. Given our link between entry, young firms, and job growth, how fast would its growth then be?

REFERENCES

Acemoglu, Daron. 2009. *Introduction to Modern Economic Growth.* Princeton, NJ: Princeton University Press.

Acs, Zoltan and Catherine Armington. 2006. *Entrepreneurship, Geography and American Economic Growth.* New York: Cambridge University Press.

Acs, Zoltan and David Audretsch. 1993. *Small Firms and Entrepreneurship: An East-West Perspective.* Cambridge, UK: Cambridge University Press.

Acs, Zoltan, Edward Glaeser, Robert Litan, Lee Fleming, Stephan Goetz, William Kerr, Steven Klepper, Stuart Rosenthal, Olav Sorenson, and William Strange. 2008. 'Entrepreneurship and Urban Success: Toward a Policy Consensus', Kauffman Foundation Report.

Aghion, Philippe and Peter Howitt. 1992. 'A Model of Growth through Creative Destruction', *Econometrica*, 110: 323–51.

Aghion, Philippe, Robin Burgess, Stephen Redding, and Fabrizio Zilibotti. 2008. 'The Unequal Effects of Liberalization: Evidence from Dismantling the License Raj in India', *American Economic Review*, 98 (4): 1397–412.

Ahsan, Ahmed and Carmen Pages. 2007. 'Are All Labor Regulations Equal? Assessing the Effects of Job Security, Labor Dispute and Contract Labor Laws in India', World Bank Policy Research Working Paper 4259, Washington, DC.

Akcigit, Ufuk and William Kerr. 2010. 'Growth through Heterogeneous Innovations', NBER Working Paper 16443, National Bureau of Economic Research, Cambridge, MA.

Ardagna, Silvia and Annamaria Lusardi. 2008. 'Explaining International Differences in Entrepreneurship: The Role of Individual Characteristics and Regulatory Constraints', NBER Working Paper 14012, National Bureau of Economic Research, Cambridge, MA.

Arora, Ashish and Alfonso Gambardella (eds). 2005. *From Underdogs to Tigers? The Rise and Growth of the Software Industry in Brazil, China, India, Ireland, and Israel.* Oxford, UK: Oxford University Press.

Astebro, Thomas, Jing Chen, and Peter Thompson. 2010. 'Stars and Misfits: Self-Employment and Labor Market Frictions', Working Paper 1003, Florida International University, Department of Economics.

Audretsch, David and Maryann Feldman. 1996. 'R&D Spillovers and the Geography of Innovation and Production', *American Economic Review*, 86: 630–40.

Audretsch, David, M. Keilbach, and E. Leimann. 2006. *Entrepreneurship and Economic Growth.* Oxford, UK: Oxford University Press.

Banerjee, Abhijit and Andrew Newman. 1993. 'Occupational Choice and the Process of Development', *Journal of Political Economy*, 101 (2): 274–98.

Barro, Robert and Xavier Sala-i-Martin. 1995. *Economic Growth.* Cambridge: MIT Press.

Baumol, William. 1990. 'Entrepreneurship: Productive, Unproductive, and Destructive', *Journal of Political Economy*, 98: 893–921.

Besley, Timothy and Robin Burgess. 2004. 'Can Labor Regulation Hinder Economic Performance? Evidence from India', *Quarterly Journal of Economics*, 119 (1): 91–134.

Blanchflower, David and Andrew Oswald. 1998. 'What Makes an Entrepreneur?', *Journal of Labor Economics*, 16 (1): 26–60.

Bozkaya, Ant and William Kerr. 2010. 'Labor Regulations and European Private Equity', NBER Working Paper 15627, National Bureau of Economic Research, Cambridge, MA.

Cantillion, Richard. 1730. Essai sur la Nature du Commerce en Général (An Essay on Economic Theory). Translated by Chantal Saucier, edited by Mark Thornton. Auburn, Alabama: Ludwig Von Mises Institute.

Chinitz, Benjamin. 1961. 'Contrasts in Agglomeration: New York and Pittsburgh', *American Economic Review*, 51 (2): 279–89.

Davis, Steven, John Haltiwanger, and Scott Schuh. 1996. *Job Creation and Destruction*. Cambridge, MA: MIT Press.

Delgado, Mercedes, Michael Porter, and Scott Stern. 2008. 'Convergence, Clusters and Economic Performance', Working Paper.

Drucker, Joshua and Edward Feser. 2007. 'Regional Industrial Dominance, Agglomeration Economies, and Manufacturing Plant Productivity', US Census Bureau Center for Economic Studies Paper No. CES–07–31.

Dunne, Timothy, Mark Roberts, and Larry Samuelson. 1989a. 'Patterns of Firm Entry and Exit in U.S. Manufacturing Industries', *RAND Journal of Economics*, 19: 495–515.

———. 1989b. 'Plant Turnover and Gross Employment Flows in the U.S. Manufacturing Sector', *Journal of Labor Economics*, 7: 48–71.

Duranton, Gilles. 2007. 'Urban Evolutions: The Fast, the Slow, and the Still', *American Economic Review*, 97 (1): 197–221.

Ellison, Glenn, Edward Glaeser, and William Kerr. 2010. 'What Causes Industry Agglomeration? Evidence from Coagglomeration Patterns', *American Economic Review*, 100: 1195–213.

Evans, David and Boyan Jovanovic. 1989. 'An Estimated Model of Entrepreneurial Choice under Liquidity Constraints', *Journal of Political Economy*, 97 (4): 808–27.

Faberman, Jason. 2007. 'The Relationship between the Establishment Age Distribution and Urban Growth', Working Paper No. 07-18, Research Department, Federal Reserve Bank of Philadelphia.

Fallick, Bruce, Charles Fleischman, and James Rebitzer. 2006. 'Job-Hopping in Silicon Valley: Some Evidence Concerning the Microfoundations of a High-Technology Cluster', *Review of Economics and Statistics*, 88 (3): 472–81.

Feldman, Maryann. 2003. 'The Locational Dynamics of the US Biotech Industry: Knowledge Externalities and the Anchor Hypothesis', *Industry and Innovation*, 10 (3): 311–28.

Fernandes, Ana and Ariel Pakes. 2010. 'Factor Utilization in Indian Manufacturing: A Look at the World Bank Investment Climate Survey Data', NBER Working Paper 14178 (2008).

Figueiredo, Octávio, Paulo Guimaraes, and Douglas Woodward. 2002. 'Home-Field Advantage: Location Decisions of Portuguese Entrepreneurs', *Journal of Urban Economics*, 52 (2): 341–61.

Ghani, Ejaz (ed.). 2010. *The Service Revolution in South Asia*. New Delhi: Oxford University Press.

Glaeser, Edward. 2007. 'Entrepreneurship and the City', NBER Working Paper 13551, National Bureau of Economic Research, Cambridge, MA.

Glaeser, Edward and William Kerr. 2010. 'Entrepreneurship, Mines, and Urban Growth', Working Paper.

———. 2009. 'Local Industrial Conditions and Entrepreneurship: How Much of the Spatial Distribution Can We Explain?', *Journal of Economics and Management Strategy*, 18 (3): 623–63.

Glaeser, Edward, William Kerr, and Giacomo Ponzetto. 2010. 'Clusters of Entrepreneurship', *Journal of Urban Economics*, 67 (1): 150–68.

Haltiwanger, John, Ron Jarmin, and Javier Miranda. 2010. 'Who Creates Jobs? Small vs. Large vs. Young', NBER Working Paper 16300, National Bureau of Economic Research, Cambridge, MA.

Honorati, Maddelena and Taye Mengistae. 2007. 'Corruption, the Business Environment, and Small Business Growth in India', World Bank Policy Research Working Paper 4338.

Jacobs, Jane. 1970. *The Economy of Cities*. New York: Vintage Books.

Jovanovic, Boyan and Glenn MacDonald. 1994. 'The Life Cycle of Competitive Industry', *Journal of Political Economy*, 102 (2): 322–47.

Kathuria, Vinish, Seethamma Natarajan, Rajesh Raj, and Kunal Sen. 2010. 'Organized versus Unorganized Manufacturing Performance in India in the Post-reform Period', MPRA Working Paper No. 20317.

Kerr, William. 2010. 'Breakthrough Inventions and Migrating Clusters of Innovation', *Journal of Urban Economics*, 67: 46–60.

———. 2008. 'Ethnic Scientific Communities and International Technology Diffusion', *Review of Economics and Statistics*, 90: 518–37.

Kerr, William and Ramana Nanda. 2009. 'Democratizing Entry: Banking Deregulations, Financing Constraints, and Entrepreneurship', *Journal of Financial Economics*, 94: 124–49.

Khanna, Tarun. 2008. *Billions of Entrepreneurs: How China and India Are Reshaping Their Futures—and Yours*. Boston, MA: Harvard University Press.

Khilstrom, Richard and Jean-Jacques Laffont. 1979. 'A General Equilibrium Entrepreneurial Theory of Firm Formation Based on Risk Aversion', *Journal of Political Economy*, 87: 719–48.

Kirzner, Israel. 1979. *Perception, Opportunity, and Profit: Studies in the Theory of Entrepreneurship*. Chicago, IL: University of Chicago Press.

————. 1972. *Competition and Entrepreneurship*. Chicago, IL: University of Chicago Press.

Klapper, Leora, Raphael Amit, and Mauro F. Guillén. 2010. 'Entrepreneurship and Firm Formation across Countries', in Josh Lerner and Antoinette Schoar (eds), *International Differences in Entrepreneurship*. Chicago, IL: University of Chicago Press, pp. 129–58.

Klapper, Leora and Inessa Love. 2010. 'New Firm Creation', *The World Bank Group Viewpoint*, 324: 1–4.

Klepper, Steven and Elizabeth Graddy. 1990. 'The Evolution of New Industries and the Determinants of Market Structure', *RAND Journal of Economics*, 21 (1): 27–44.

Knight, Frank. 1921. *Risk, Uncertainty, and Profit*. Boston, MA: Houghton Mifflin.

Kortum, Samuel and Josh Lerner. 2000. 'Assessing the Contribution of Venture Capital to Innovation', *RAND Journal of Economics*, 31 (4): 674–92.

Marshall, Alfred. 1920. *Principles of Economics*. London: MacMillan and Co.

Michelacci, Claudio and Olmo Silva. 2007. 'Why So Many Local Entrepreneurs?', *Review of Economics and Statistics*, 89 (4): 615–33.

Murphy, Kevin, Andrei Shleifer, and Robert Vishny. 1991. 'The Allocation of Talent: Implications for Growth', *Quarterly Journal of Economics*, 106: 503–30.

Nanda, Ramana and Tarun Khanna. 2010. 'Diasporas and Domestic Entrepreneurs: Evidence from the Indian Software Industry', *Journal of Economics and Management Strategy*, 19 (4): 991–1012.

Nataraj, Shanthi. 2009. 'The Impact of Trade Liberalization on Productivity and Firm Size: Evidence from India's Formal and Informal Manufacturing Sectors', Working Paper.

Parker, Simon. 2009. *The Economics of Entrepreneurship*. Cambridge, UK: Cambridge University Press.

Purfield, Catriona. 2006. 'Is Economic Growth in India Leaving Some States Behind?', IMF Working Papers WP/06/103.

Rajan, Raghuram and Luigi Zingales. 1998. 'Financial Dependence and Growth', *American Economic Review*, 88 (3): 559–86.

Romer, Paul. 1990. 'Endogenous Technological Change', *Journal of Political Economy*, 98 (5): S71–S102.

————. 1986. 'Increasing Returns and Long-Run Growth', *Journal of Political Economy*, 94 (5): 1002–37.

Rosenthal, Stuart and William Strange. 2010. 'Small Establishments/Big Effects: Agglomeration, Industrial Organization and Entrepreneurship', in Edward Glaeser (ed.), *Agglomeration Economics*. Chicago, IL: University of Chicago Press, pp. 227–302.

————. 2003. 'Geography, Industrial Organization, and Agglomeration', *Review of Economics and Statistics*, 85 (2): 377–93.

————. 2001. 'The Determinants of Agglomeration', *Journal of Urban Economics*, 50: 191–229.

Samila, Sampsa and Olav Sorenson. 2011. 'Venture Capital, Entrepreneurship and Economic Growth', *Review of Economics and Statistics*, 93 (1): 338–49.

Saxenian, Anna Lee. 1994. *Regional Advantage: Culture and Competition in Silicon Valley and Route 128*. Cambridge, MA: Harvard University Press.

Schmitt, John and Nathan Lane. 2009. 'An International Comparison of Small Business Employment', Center for Economic and Policy Research, Washington, DC.

Schoar, Antoinette. 2009. 'The Divide Between Subsistence and Transformational Entrepreneurship', in Josh Lerner and Scott Stern (eds), *Innovation Policy and the Economy*, Vol. 10, pp. 57–71.

————. 2007. 'Entrepreneurial Firms in an Emerging Market', 8th Annual NBER–NCAER Neemrana Conference Presentation.

Schumpeter, Joseph. 1942. *Capitalism, Socialism, and Democracy*. New York: Harper Brothers.

Solow, Robert. 1956. 'A Contribution to the Theory of Economic Growth', *Quarterly Journal of Economics*, 70: 65–94.

8

Managing Capital Flows

Barry Eichengreen

The disjuncture between interest rates in advanced economies and emerging markets has created severe discomfort for monetary policymakers in the second set of countries. Low rates are appropriate for the conditions of slow growth, economic slack, and financial weakness currently characterizing the advanced economies. Higher rates are appropriate for the conditions of strong growth, incipient inflation, and potential overheating prevailing in emerging markets. But the two together provide an incentive for the carry trade—for capital to flow from where the cost of borrowing is low to where the return on investment is high.[1] These financial inflows feed the boom conditions that motivated the adoption of high interest rates by central banks in emerging markets in the first place. They frustrate efforts to put in place policies of restraint.[2]

Monetary policymakers have no easy solution to this problem. They may be tempted to increase rates further to counter the inflationary effects of the additional spending induced by capital inflows. But doing so only increases the interest differential providing the incentive for the carry trade, attracting additional inflows. It creates a tendency for

[1] The interest differential fully captures that cost/return differential and the incentive for capital movements when the exchange rate is not expected to change. When the currency used in the destination markets is expected to appreciate, as tends to be the case at the moment, the associated financial flows will be even larger.

[2] This problem of not being able to maintain an independent monetary stance in an environment of open capital markets when the authorities also care about the level of the exchange rate is popularly known as the 'trilemma' after the inability to simultaneously have an independent monetary policy, a pegged exchange rate, and perfect capital mobility.

the exchange rate to appreciate, which is uncomfortable for domestic producers. Alternatively, central banks may be tempted to cut rates to make the carry trade less attractive and discourage inflows. But by doing so, they only encourage additional borrowing and spending, aggravating overheating risks. It is not surprising that central bankers often seem frozen, like deer in the headlights, in the face of this problem.

What is true in general is true of South Asia, the focus of this chapter, which saw a significant rise in capital inflows up through 2007 and again more recently (Figure 8.1). India specifically has been experiencing uncomfortably large inflows. In 2007–8 net inflows rose to an unprecedented US$108 billion, or 9 per cent of the gross domestic product (GDP), more than double the levels of 2006–7 and triple those of 2005–6. Debt inflows, which are of particular concern to those responsible for financial stability, increased strongly, with both external commercial borrowings (ECBs) and short-term borrowing by Indian banks and corporations increasing year over year. Short-term borrowing, the form of foreign borrowing of greatest concern to policymakers,

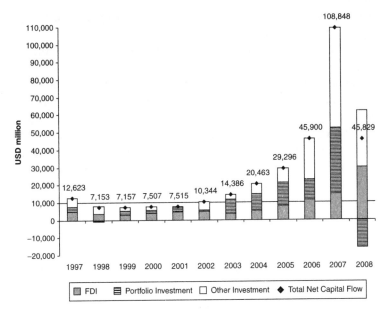

FIGURE 8.1   Net Capital Flows to South Asia

Source: *International Financial Statistics.*
Note: South Asia defined to include Bangladesh, India, Nepal, Pakistan, and Sri Lanka.

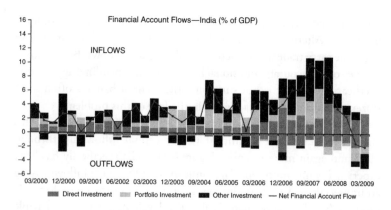

FIGURE 8.2   Inflows into India

Source: IMF, *International Financial Statistics*; Reserve Bank of India; and CEIC Database.

tripled in net terms between 2005–6 and 2008–9.[3] Although inflows fell off with deleveraging and flight to quality in the crisis of 2008–9 (see Figures, 8.2 and 8.3 and Table 8.1), this did not pose a dire threat to financial stability, unlike the situation in other emerging markets. This is something that requires explaining.[4]

As the global credit crisis receded, capital inflows into India recovered. Recent estimates put net incapital flows in financial year 2009–10 at $50 billion (nearly 4 per cent of GDP) (see Arora and Rathinam 2010). Meanwhile, Indian corporations have become increasingly active in international mergers and acquisitions, increasing capital outflows, and opening an additional channel for international transmission. On balance, inflows have exceeded outflows, putting a sharp upward pressure on the real exchange rate, which increased by 18 per cent between March 2009 and March 2010, leading observers such as Acharya (2010) to warn that the development of Indian industry is being set back as a result.

In the other countries in South Asia, portfolio capital inflows have been more limited, reflecting lower levels of financial development, tighter restrictions on capital account transactions, and less confidence in the political environment. Figure 8.4 places overall capital flows to different

[3] According to the estimates of the Reserve Bank of India as compiled by Mohan and Kapur (2009).

[4] As Kumar and Vashisht (2009) describe it, commercial credit on global markets raised by Indian companies fell by 41 per cent between 2007–8 and 2008–9. The concurrent fall in foreign direct investment (FDI) inflows was a relatively modest 2 per cent.

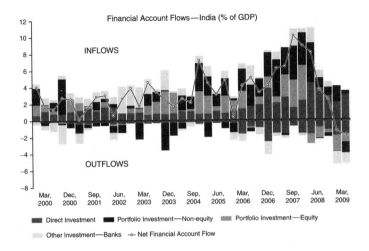

Financial Account Flows—India (% of GDP)

INFLOWS

OUTFLOWS

| | | | | | | | | | | | | |
Mar, Dec, Sep, Jun, Mar, Dec, Sep, Jun, Mar, Dec, Sep, Jun, Mar,
2000 2000 2001 2002 2003 2003 2004 2005 2006 2006 2007 2008 2009

▇ Direct Investment   ▇ Portfolio Investment—Non-equity   ▇ Portfolio Investment—Equity

▨ Other Investment—Banks   -○- Net Financial Account Flow

FIGURE 8.3   Inflows into India: Bank, Government, and Others
Compared

Sources: IMF, *International Financial Statistics*; Reserve Bank of India; and CIEC
Database.

South Asian countries in a comparative perspective, while Appendix A8.1 provides more details. Only in Pakistan have these started approaching Indian levels in recent years, reflecting mainly inward FDI (which has fallen off recently in response to political uncertainty).

But if capital inflows have been limited, remittances have surged. As Gopalan and Rajan (2010) show, remittances as a share of GDP approached 22 per cent in Nepal, 11 per cent in Bangladesh, 7 per cent in Sri Lanka, and 4 per cent in Pakistan in 2008 and rose further in 2009.[5] In India they have added to the pressure created by financial capital inflows (see Figure 8.5). Remittances have had effects analogous to those of financial capital inflows—they have eased credit conditions and increased real estate and other asset prices—posing similar challenges for monetary policy.[6] They have put upward pressure on

[5] Data for 2008 are from the World Bank's *World Development Indicators* (WDI). The WDI does not provide data for 2009, but Ratha et al. (2009) estimate that remittances increased strongly in Bangladesh, Nepal, and Pakistan (but not in Sri Lanka). Almekindes et al. (2009) forecast further strong growth in Bangladesh based on the estimated stock of foreign workers.

[6] The main difference being that remittances are less strongly pro-cyclical than other forms of external financing. See Gopalan and Rajan (2010) as well as Almekindes et al. (2009) and Singer (2010).

TABLE 8.1 Capital Flows, Major Components (per cent to GDP)

| | Non-debt Flows | | | | Debt Flows | | | |
| Year | Inward FDI, Net | Outward FDI, Net | Inward Portfolio, Net | External Assistance, Net | ECB, Net | ECB Disbursements | Short-term Borrowings, Net | Non-resident Deposits, Net |
1	2	3	4	5	6	7	8	9
1990–1	0.0	0.0	0.0	0.7	0.7	1.3	0.3	0.5
1991–2	0.0	0.0	0.0	1.1	0.5	1.2	-0.2	0.1
1992–3	0.1	0.0	0.1	0.8	-0.1	0.5	-0.4	0.8
1993–4	0.2	0.0	1.3	0.7	0.2	1.1	-0.3	0.4
1994–5	0.4	0.0	1.1	0.5	0.3	1.3	0.1	0.1
1995–6	0.6	0.1	0.7	0.2	0.4	1.2	0.0	0.3
1996–7	0.7	0.0	0.9	0.3	0.7	1.9	0.2	0.9
1997–8	0.9	0.0	0.4	0.2	1.0	1.8	0.0	0.3
1998–9	0.6	0.0	0.0	0.2	1.0	1.7	-0.2	0.2
1999–2000	0.5	0.0	0.7	0.2	0.1	0.7	0.1	0.3
2000–1	0.9	0.2	0.6	0.1	0.9	2.1	0.1	0.5
2001–2	1.3	0.3	0.4	0.3	-0.3	0.6	-0.2	0.6
2002–3	1.0	0.4	0.2	-0.6	-0.3	0.7	0.2	0.6
2003–4	0.7	0.3	1.9	-0.5	-0.5	0.9	0.2	0.6

2004–5	0.9	0.3	1.3	0.3	0.8	1.3	0.5	−0.1
2005–6	1.1	0.7	1.5	0.2	0.3	1.8	0.5	0.3
					(1.0)	(2.5)		
2006–7	2.5	1.6	0.8	0.2	1.8	2.2	0.7	0.5
2007–8	2.9	1.6	2.5	0.2	1.9	2.5	1.5	0.0
2008–9	3.0	1.5	−1.2	0.2	0.6	1.2	−0.5	0.4

Source: Mohan and Kapur (2009).

Note: Figures in parentheses in columns 5 and 6 are after excluding the impact of issuances (2001–2) and redemptions (2005–6) under India Millennium Deposits (IMDs).

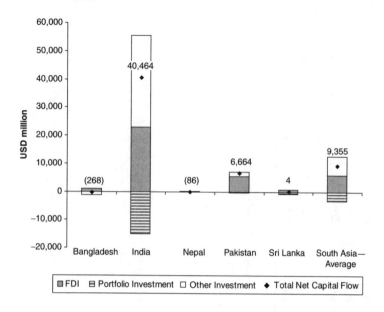

FIGURE 8.4   Net Capital Flows to South Asia, 2008

Source: *International Financial Statistics.*

exchange rates and created a Dutch-disease-type dilemma for South Asian policymakers.[7]

Since much has been written about these problems and how South Asia has dealt with them, I simply attempt to present the received wisdom in a somewhat different way in this chapter. I use insights from the post-financial crisis literature on the conduct of monetary policy to reframe the question of how central banks should address the capital-inflows problem. Inspired by the analogy between capital-flow volatility and financial volatility more generally, I make the following points.

1. In a first-best world where there are multiple policy authorities with multiple instruments, the central bank can concentrate on setting interest rates in a manner consistent with the standard inflation-targeting framework, capital inflows or not. That is, it can continue to concentrate on the deviation of inflation from target and the output gap. Insofar as capital inflows raise additional concerns, these can be addressed by financial regulators and fiscal authorities. There is an

---

[7] The Dutch-disease impact of remittances is emphasized in IMF (2005). This also suggests that schemes like the one Pakistan has introduced subsidizing remittance service providers for a portion of their expenses may be a mixed blessing.

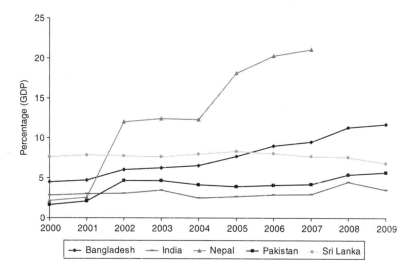

FIGURE 8.5   Workers' Remittances, Compensation of Employees, and
Migration Transfers, Credit

Sources: World Bank staff estimates based on the IMF's *Balance of Payments Statistics
Yearbook 2008* and *International Financial Statistics*.

analogy with the new post-crisis conventional wisdom regarding the
pursuit of both price stability and financial stability in the advanced
economies: in a first-best world, price stability is pursued by the central
bank, while financial stability is pursued by other authorities.

2.   But in the real world, as opposed to the first-best world, other
policymakers have additional objectives and constraints. Inside and
outside lags and political pressure may make it impossible to adjust
fiscal policy to the extent and with the speed needed to address the
challenges created by capital inflows. Capture and/or inadequate
resources may prevent regulators from fully discharging their
responsibility for financial stability. The central bank will then be
forced to balance multiple objectives. This in turn means that it will be
important for the monetary authorities to develop and utilize multiple
policy instruments, not just the standard instruments of monetary
control, such as interest rates but also non-standard instruments,
such as direct regulation of the volume of bank lending.

3.   Finally, in the absence of additional instruments, central banks will
need to adjust interest rates in response to capital flows, independent
of their implications for inflation, insofar as those capital flows
pose a danger to financial stability. *How* they adjust interest rates

should depend on the exact nature of the problem posed by capital flows. For example, if inflows associated with the carry trade pose a threat because of the possibility that they may reverse erratically, precipitating a capital account crisis, then the appropriate response is to *cut* interest rates in order to discourage inflows. On the other hand, if inflows are a danger because they feed housing and other asset bubbles that may cause serious financial dislocations when they burst, then the appropriate response is to *raise* interest rates in order to fight the bubble—the bubble rather than the capital flow that may be further encouraged being the fundamental problem in this case. Thus the appropriate policy response in this third-best world depends on the precise nature of the threat to financial stability. An appropriate policy response therefore requires, first and foremost, identifying the nature of the threat.

The rest of this chapter elaborates on these points. The next section summarizes the conventional, if not wholly satisfactory, wisdom about how emerging markets should deal with capital inflows. The section that follows presents more details about the nature of the capital inflows problem and its implications for the conduct of monetary policy, using India as a case study. It suggests that the approach taken by the Reserve Bank of India (RBI)—using multiple instruments to pursue multiple targets and adopting a flexible response suitable for dealing with changing shocks—exemplifies the approach that will increasingly be elaborated upon not just by other South Asian central banks but by emerging and, indeed, advanced-country central banks seeking to balance price stability and financial stability objectives. The last section returns to the implications for the conduct of monetary policy.

MANAGING CAPITAL INFLOWS

While it is a bit of an exaggeration to say that there is broad-based consensus on how central banks should deal with capital flows, such exaggerations are the raison d'tre for this kind of chapter.[8] One element of the consensus, such as it is, is that capital flows cannot be treated with benign neglect. They cannot be seen as relevant only insofar as they

---

[8] How to manage capital-flow volatility in open economies is not a new question. My own take (Eichengreen 2000) dates back more than a decade. It is tempting to remark on how little has changed since that time, other than the fact that once radical ideas now represent the policy mainstream. Other than this footnote, I will resist.

have implications for future inflation. Rather, they may have first-order implications for the allocation of resources and financial stability that should be considered along with their implications for inflation. Another element is that no single policy is appropriate for addressing those further implications. Rather, policymakers need to pursue a range of policies in response to inflows, depending on their sources and effects and on the market structures through which they impact the economy.

Central banks being the 'first responders' to financial problems, it is frequently suggested that monetary policy should react to capital inflows and outflows. Unfortunately, there is no agreement on how it should react. Loosening and tightening are both problematic (ADB 2010; IMF 2010a). Loosening to discourage carry trade motivated inflows threatens to aggravate the problems of inflation and overheating that may have prompted the adoption of high interest rates in the first place. Reducing the cost of funding from the central bank may only further inflate an incipient stock market and real estate bubbles. But tightening will widen the interest differential and encourage additional carry-trade-related inflows. It may only encourage additional remittances by workers abroad chasing after higher returns.[9] It may put uncomfortable upward pressure on the exchange rate. If the adverse impact on the competitiveness of the tradables sector persists even after the appreciation is reversed, the authorities may be reluctant to pursue this course.[10]

Alternatively, the central bank may attempt to sterilize the impact of capital inflows. But sterilized intervention—selling domestic bonds to mop up the monetary effects of capital inflows—has limits. The limited size of bond markets may mean that the central bank has limited instruments with which to sterilize inflows. The smaller the domestic bond market and the less elastic the demands of investors, the higher will be the cost of issuing additional debt. This constraint can be relaxed by developing domestic securities markets, at national as well as regional levels, but relaxing it will take time (see also Box 8.1). More generally, in an emerging market setting where domestic interest rates exceed foreign rates, sterilized intervention will have a quasi-fiscal cost: the central bank will earn less on the foreign bonds it buys than the domestic bonds

---

[9] Ratha et al. (2009) argue that interest differentials have been important for stimulating remittance inflows into India, for example.

[10] Thus the governor of the RBI expressed reservations about the 'Dutch-disease effects' of inflow-induced appreciation at a conference organized by IMF and the Swiss National Bank in May 2010. See Subbarao (2010).

Box 8.1 Building Securities Markets at the Regional Level

Building deep and liquid local currency bond markets is one way of insulating an economy from the effects of capital-flow and exchange rate volatility. The deeper the markets, the less the extent to which prices will be perturbed by capital inflows and outflows. When assets and liabilities are denominated in the local currency, balance sheet dislocations from exchange rate fluctuations will be less. And deep and liquid markets are a convenient venue for intervention by central banks seeking to manage financial conditions. These are lessons that the East Asian countries took from their experience with the financial crisis of the late 1990s.

The East Asian countries also learned that bond markets do not develop spontaneously: they need the support of a robust financial infrastructure of a sort that can only be provided by government policy. To this end, these countries launched an Asian Bond Market Initiative to encourage participation in local bond markets by a wide range of potential issuers. In addition, there was awareness that markets become liquid only when they achieve a certain minimum efficient scale, which in turn makes it hard to build liquid markets at the national level, especially in smaller economies. Hence the East Asian countries launched an Asian Bond Fund in an effort to build a regionally integrated local currency bond market.

The South Asian countries could usefully follow this example. Starting first with government securities, they could harmonize their auction calendars for public debt issuance. They could develop compatible benchmark yield curves. They could establish compatible negotiated dealing systems like that launched by India in 2005 to facilitate anonymous electronic-order matching and settlement.

Creating deep, liquid, and vibrant corporate bond markets is a more daunting task, given that information on corporate finances often remains hard to obtain and there are only a handful of corporates with the scale and credit ratings required to publicly place debt securities. Even India, with the largest number of potential issuers, has made only limited progress in developing corporate bond markets: corporate bond market capitalization remains little more than 1 per cent of GDP. Corporations issue barely 1 per cent of domestic debt securities outstanding (with the balance split into three relatively even parts between the central bank, the public sector, and financial institutions). Market participants ascribe this to inadequate development of the institutional investor base (which is dominated by a few mutual funds and provident funds), regulatory constraints on the participation of those institutional investors in the corporate bond market, restrictive issuance procedures, poor price transparency (most trading taking place over the counter), the deduction of interest income at source, and regulatory overlap (which fosters the perception of inconsistencies and undermines confidence in the market).[1]

These complaints in turn suggest an agenda for policy reform and market development. Coordinating such efforts across countries would expedite the process by facilitating information exchange and learning by doing. With neighbouring countries moving down the same path towards the same destination—and encountering many of the same obstacles—solutions that worked in one national context could be shared with other nations.[2]

Finally, regional cooperation in building and integrating financial markets might encourage regional cooperation in other issues and areas.

One worry about the regional approach is that it would require full capital account liberalization, exposing the South Asian countries to new dangers. Fortunately, the East Asian experience suggests that market development can proceed with only partial capital account liberalization (the policy approach of important Asian Bond Fund participants such as China) and with the retention of price-based disincentives for short-term foreign funding (like those put in place by South Korea in 2010). Developing bond markets at the regional level may require some further relaxation of capital account restrictions, to be sure, but 'some further relaxation' is not the same as full capital account liberalization.

Another worry is that efforts to build a bond market at the regional level will favour the first mover, India, leading to the migration of transactions to Mumbai. Again, the East Asian experience is not consistent with this scenario. Gehrig (2000) suggests that transactions in informationally sensitive securities is likely to become increasingly concentrated in a single financial centre as the costs of transacting across borders decline, since it is in a single centre where information can be most efficiently aggregated and communicated. In contrast, this tendency will be less powerful in the case of standardized securities, where the convenience value of transacting locally may continue to dominate the advantages in terms of information aggregation and communication of greater centralization.[3] Indeed, some of Gehrig's analysis suggests that

---

[1] High Level Expert Committee on Corporate Bonds and Securitization (2005) and IMF (2008) document these problems.

[2] This is argued by Ma and Remolona (2006).

[3] Then there are the challenges that India faces in transforming Mumbai into an international financial centre. On these, see High Powered Expert Committee (2007).

transactions in standardized securities may become more decentralized as market frictions decline. Overall, then, integration of securities markets within South Asia may lead to both greater concentration of transactions in certain securities in a single dominant financial centre and greater volume of decentralized transactions in other securities.

it sells.[11] This is another face of the familiar phenomenon of reserve accumulation in emerging markets, something that can have quasi-fiscal costs.[12] (On reserve accumulation in South Asia, see Figure 8.6.)

Sterilization may also elicit further inflows because it does nothing to eliminate the gap between domestic and foreign interest rates. It may also encourage borrowers to look to offshore sources of funding (IMF 2010a).

The central bank may also seek to discourage inflows and outflows motivated by the perception of one-way bets and by the assumption of carry traders that the prospect of short-term exchange rate changes can be ignored by allowing greater exchange rate variability. Looking specifically at India, the IMF reports that greater exchange rate volatility tends to reduce both external commercial borrowings and portfolio equity inflows (IMF 2010b: 27). More generally, it finds that the impact of external financial conditions on asset valuations is smaller in countries with more flexible exchange rates (see IMF 2010a). But the authorities may hesitate to allow a significant increase in exchange rate volatility on the grounds that this makes life more difficult for exporters. Hedging exchange risk is costly. And a highly volatile exchange rate may raise questions about the conduct of the monetary policy itself.

---

[11] IMF (2010a) observes that the interest differential on the relevant instruments was as much as 4–8 per cent in the second half of 2009, suggesting substantial costs of emerging market central banks engaging in intervention.

[12] See Rodrik (2006). One sometimes hears South Asian policymakers bemoan reserve accumulation on different grounds, namely, that resources that might better be used for infrastructure investment are instead tied up in low-yielding foreign treasury bonds. The low yield may be a problem (as noted in the text), but the point of reserve accumulation through sterilized intervention in periods of surging capital inflows is precisely to prevent additional spending (including infrastructure spending) from resulting in real overvaluation, inflation, and overheating. The best way of thinking about reserves in this context is that they should be accumulated in good times, when private demand requires little public support, and de-accumulated in bad times, when additional infrastructure spending will have the greatest macroeconomic bang for the buck.

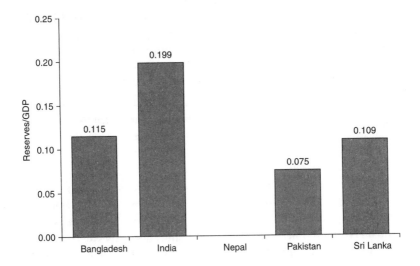

FIGURE 8.6   South Asia: Reserves/GDP, 2009

Sources: IMF's *International Financial Statisitics.*

Fiscal policy is another obvious policy lever to adjust in response to capital flows. But its use is constrained by political factors, and it is subject to both inside and outside lags.[13] ADB (2010) suggests that this problem might be solved by adopting fiscal rules that mandate taking away the fiscal punchbowl when the party heats up. But the record of governments' adherence to self-imposed fiscal rules is, at best, mixed.

Regulation of the banking and financial system can also be strengthened to limit the impact of capital inflows on the economy and on the financial system. Numerical ceilings can be placed on the level or rate of increase of bank lending. Banks can be required to hold additional reserves. Those funding themselves offshore, with risky short-term foreign-currency-denominated credit in particular, can be made subject to more stringent liquidity requirements.[14] Not only will such measures moderate the impact of foreign capital on the economy, but they will strengthen the banking system that is typically revealed as the weak link in the financial chain when capital flows reverse direction. The downside

[13] That is, lags between recognition of the need for a policy response and implementation of that response, and lags between implementation and impact on the economy.

[14] It would also be necessary to maintain strict limits on banks' positions in derivatives, as these could otherwise be used to circumvent administrative measures.

of this response is that it will raise the cost of intermediation.[15] It will slow the development of the banking system. It will encourage funds to flow instead through informal non-bank channels, frustrating policy and the efforts to strengthen prudential supervision generally.

There is no consensus on whether the responsibility for implementing these prudential measures should be assigned to the central bank or a separate regulatory agency. The traditional argument against assigning it to the central bank is the possibility of conflict between the central bank's price stability mandate and its responsibility as the supervisor of the health and stability of financial institutions. When inflation targeting was in ascendancy, this argument for separate regulatory agencies tended to hold sway. Since 2008, with growing concern over financial stability issues, the pendulum has swung in the other direction. Episodes like the run on Northern Rock suggest that communication problems between a financial services authority and the central bank can be serious. Observers question whether responsibility for macro-prudential stability (which belongs, in part, to the central bank) and micro-prudential stability can be segregated in practice. The convention in India and elsewhere in South Asia is to assign the central bank significant responsibility for prudential supervision, including that related to international capital flows. Recent events suggest that this is a sensible arrangement.

If normal prudential measures do not suffice, the authorities may contemplate supplementing them with direct controls on capital flows. Figure 8.7 has evidence on the extent of such controls in South Asia. India, it is evident, has gone furthest in the direction of capital account liberalization, although Bangladesh and Sri Lanka, it turns out, are not that far behind.

The debate over the effects and effectiveness of controls is less than conclusive. One reading is that they have relatively little impact on the overall volume of capital inflows and outflows but that they can be effective in altering the composition of flows towards less volatile FDI and away from portfolio flows.[16] They can limit banks' recourse to short-term, foreign currency denominated non-core funding, thereby

---

[15] Of course, to the extent that foreign-capital-funded intermediation throws off negative externalities in the form of systemic risk, this is precisely what policy should aim to do. On the other hand, in developing countries where other pre-existing distortions have already elevated the cost of intermediation, additional costs may be especially burdensome.

[16] For a review of literature, see Ostry et al. (2010).

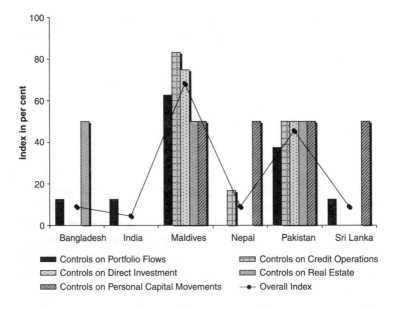

FIGURE 8.7   Index of Capital Account Liberalization in South Asia
(as of 31 December 2008)

Source: IMF Annual Report on Exchange Arrangements and Exchange Restrictions
(2009).

addressing one important source of stability risks. But there are other, conflicting readings of the literature as well.

Not surprisingly, the evidence on whether countries with capital controls in place prior to the 2008–9 crisis suffered smaller output declines is inconclusive. IMF (2010a) suggests a positive answer; Eichengreen (2010) is more sceptical. IMF (2010a) finds that countries with larger ratios of external debt to GDP suffered larger growth declines in the 2008–9 crisis, as did countries with more inward FDI in the financial sector. In contrast, countries with more non-financial FDI did better. This suggests that it is not only the portfolio capital/FDI mix that matters for economic and financial stability but also the composition of FDI.

While controls are often seen as a second-best form of prudential supervision where supervisors lack the capacity to efficiently deploy first-best tools, limited administrative capacity may similarly circumscribe the effectiveness of direct controls. A variety of studies have found that capital controls are more effective in countries with greater institutional/ administrative capacity (ADB 2010).

Although the focus in recent years has been on inflow controls, some commentators point to the possibility of liberalizing controls on outflows as a way of limiting the pressure on domestic financial markets and the exchange rate. The problem is that liberalizing outflows may also encourage further inflows insofar as it increases confidence on the part of investors that they can get out (ADB 2010).

Perhaps the most fundamental problem with using capital controls to deal with capital flows is that the latter come in surges and cycles. Effectively dealing with them therefore requires policies that can be adjusted in response to current financial conditions. And (much as in the case of fiscal policy) it is hard to adjust capital account regulation in response to current financial conditions. Slapping on and removing controls repeatedly will not enhance investor confidence or cultivate the impression of a stable and predictable policy regime. Investors interested in investing in local property and stock markets and knowing that the authorities may be inclined to tighten capital account restrictions as a result have an incentive to anticipate the authorities' response and get their investments in under the wire, which will only make the problem worse.

WHAT INDIA HAS DONE

India has been the main recipient of portfolio capital inflows in South Asia. This section looks in detail at how its policymakers have responded.[17]

In liberalizing international financial flows India has consistently favoured FDI over portfolio flows and equity flows over debt flows.[18] It continues to restrict institutional portfolio flows by limiting the share of a company's capitalization that can be held by foreign institutional investors. Individual foreign institutional investors are prohibited from holding more than 10 per cent of an Indian company's paid up capital. Prior regulation also limited the share of a company that foreign investors could hold collectively, although most of these provisions have now been relaxed or removed.

The access of the non-financial corporate sector to external debt continues to be subject to regulations related to purpose, interest rates

---

[17] In a previous paper also written for the World Bank (Eichengreen 2010), I considered how policymakers in other South Asian countries have managed capital account flows. Readers are referred there for details. See also subsequent notes of this chapter for comparisons of policy in other South Asian countries.

[18] This is described by Mohan and Kapur (2009), from which this section draws.

spreads, and volumes of borrowing. Portfolio investment in domestic corporate and government debt by non-residents is similarly subject to overall quantitative limits. For example, regulation limits foreign investment in government securities to just US$5 billion. It is argued that domestic funding of the government debt has protected the debt market against volatility when foreign investors deleverage.[19]

All inflows by non-residents are freely repatriable; there are no holding-period taxes or requirements, and no other restrictions on non-resident outflows. Resident non-financial companies are now permitted to invest abroad relatively freely. Individuals, however, can only invest abroad subject to specified quantitative limits. Individuals are still prohibited from borrowing abroad.

Notwithstanding this cautious and calibrated approach to capital account liberalization, capital flows are large and volatile. While India favours equity over debt flows on the presumption that the former are likely to be less volatile, IMF (2010b) finds no evidence of this; on the contrary, it finds that equity investment inflows are especially sensitive to global risk aversion as proxied by the VIX (Chicago Board Options Exchange Volatility Index). Consistent with this, Ahya (2010) argues that trends in capital inflows into India are influenced even more strongly by external factors (such as global risk appetite) than by growth opportunities in India itself.

In turn, there is evidence that capital formation and hence economic growth are highly sensitive to these equity flows. Not only were capital inflows the equivalent of more than a third of total capital expenditure in the 12 months ending in March 2010, but they appear to have been targeted at high-risk projects that would not have been funded otherwise.[20] Moreover, the domestic stock market, the other main source of risk capital, is highly correlated with the developed world equity markets. Foreign investors own 17 per cent of Indian equity-market capitalization. Their purchases and sales of domestic equity are thought to

---

[19] See Mohan and Kapur (2009). The same argument is made to explain the contrast between Italy on the one hand and other southern European countries on the other: the fact that the vast majority of Italian government debt is held domestically explains why Italy did not suffer equally severe sovereign debt problems in 2010. Time will tell (Italy will provide a test) whether this argument is correct.

[20] See Ahya (2010). He reports that in the 12 months ending March 2010 capital inflows were 4.5 per cent of GDP, compared with private corporate capex of about 12.5 per cent of GDP.

have a very large price impact. This makes domestic risk capital allocation behaviour highly correlated with global markets and capital flows.

The RBI has responded actively to the rise and fall of capital flows.[21] It raised its main policy rate (base rate) in steps during the period of capital inflows, from 6¼ per cent in 2003 to 7¾ per cent in 2007. During the period of strongest inflows in the first half of 2008, it boosted rates from 7¾ to 9 per cent, and then cut them sharply when capital flows reversed direction following the Lehman Brothers failure. Once capital inflows resumed, it began raising its base rate once more.

In its role as regulator, the RBI implemented measures limiting the exposure of the banking system to sensitive sectors and requiring banks to repeatedly rebalance the risk weights of different assets. Thus the RBI effectively did the opposite of US and European regulators who, relying on banks' internal models and credit ratings to gauge risk, allowed them to reduce risk weights on broad classes of assets during the pre-crisis boom. Instead it increased risk weights and provisioning requirements on certain classes of assets during the expansionary phase of the business and credit cycle. It further raised reserve requirements to limit the amplitude of the lending boom.[22]

---

[21] In analysing how the RBI has responded to these problems, we can start by describing the general framework for monetary policy. Prior to 1998, the RBI targeted monetary aggregates. At that point it switched to a 'multiple indicator approach' where, when formulating policy, it looked at a collection of variables, not just those consistent with the standard inflation targeting framework (interest rates, inflation rates, and the output gap) but also a range of other macroeconomic and financial indicators, including money supply, credit extended by banks and financial institutions, the fiscal balance, trade, capital flows, the exchange rate, and transactions on foreign exchange. This approach has been praised as eclectic and appropriate for the circumstances of a heavily regulated financial system in which policy operates through a number of different channels, making it important to consider a number of different indicators. Other South Asian central banks follow similarly eclectic strategies. Bangladesh Bank, for example, describes itself as aiming to hit both inflation and monetary aggregate targets set in light of a range of macroeconomic and financial indicators (Bangladesh Bank 2010). In Pakistan the central bank has been using M2 as an intermediate target for monetary policy as well as targeting inflation directly (see Qayyam 2008). The RBI has been criticized for being inadequately transparent and for inadequately anchoring expectations. Nonetheless, as Singh (2010) shows, RBI interest rate setting in recent years is fairly approximated by the flexible inflation-targeting framework embodied in the Taylor rule, which suggests more predictability than what some of the critics allege.

[22] The fact that the RBI acted pre-emptively is documented in its annual policy statement for 2007–8. See RBI (2007).

Vigorous regulation has also meant that Indian banks are less highly leveraged than their counterparts in the US and Europe. Leverage is notoriously difficult to calculate (there is no one measure, and comparisons across financial systems with very different structures are especially problematic), but one recent study defining leverage as banks' tangible assets relative to the book value of their capital net of intangibles put Indian commercial banks' leverage as of mid-2009 at 11.6 per cent, compared to 24.8 per cent in the US and 40.5 per cent in Europe.[23]

Importantly, and in contrast to other countries (South Korea for example), RBI limited the access of financial and non-financial firms to foreign funding, requiring prior approval and limiting such approval to a few sectors and purposes. The goal was to limit foreign currency exposures by linking external borrowing to export activity.[24] This had the ancillary benefit of limiting banks' recourse to non-core funding.

As a result, the banking system was not destabilized when foreign investors, caught in a liquidity squeeze, deleveraged violently.[25] Although inter-bank rates increased to 20 per cent in October 2008 and remained high for a month, no bank failures resulted. The rupee fell sharply when foreign investors deleveraged, but the banks' limited foreign currency exposures insulated them from the worst effects. This positive outcome also reflected the quick reaction of policy authorities. As noted earlier, RBI cut policy rates starting in October. Cash reserve ratios for the banks were brought down from 9 to 5 per cent, and the repo rate was cut by 425 basis points. The required liquidity ratio was reduced by 1 percentage

---

[23] See Nomura Securities (2009). Private banks happily saw their leverage ratios decline further in 2009–10, as it became easier to raise additional capital as the global credit crisis receded. Less happy was that leverage ratios rose in 2009–10 among the country's public banks. See Dey (2010). Leverage ratios of Indian investment banks are typically lower than those of commercial banks —the opposite of the situation in the US prior to the crisis. See Shah et al. (2008).

[24] Under the rules governing ECB, firms can only borrow in foreign currency with the approval of the Reserve Bank, which can approve or disapprove depending on maturity of the loan, the interest rate, and whether the firm is active in exporting. See Patnaik (2010).

[25] Financial stability also benefited from the fact that the RBI had targeted potential excesses in the property market. Kumar and Vashisht (2009) note how it imposed a temporary ban on the use of bank loans for land purchases when land prices were skyrocketing in 2006. More generally, it imposed higher provisioning requirements on commercial bank lending to the real estate sector. As a result, only one systemically significant private bank, ICICI, was considerably affected by the slump in the property market.

point. And a variety of special refinancing schemes were announced to provide liquidity to specific sectors. The result was a reduction in the prime lending rates of commercial banks by 150–175 basis points between October 2008 and January 2009.

The RBI also took steps to encourage capital inflows. The foreign institutional investor limit on corporate bonds was raised from US$ 6 billion to US$ 15 billion. Starting in October 2008, property developers and non-bank financial institutions dealing with infrastructure projects but finding it more difficult to obtain funding domestically were permitted to raise ECBs.

In sum, Indian policy proved capable of coping with the surge of capital inflows experienced in 2007–8 and then the sharp drop in 2008–9 because the authorities had at their disposal, and made active use of, a range of instruments, from interest rate policy and counter-cyclical capital and liquidity requirements to direct controls on bank lending and funding and caps on portfolio capital flows to limit the impact on the economy. Capital inflows in the first phase created pressure for inflation and rupee appreciation, but less than otherwise. The rupee appreciated against the dollar by roughly 7 per cent in the course of 2007, a substantial but not unmanageable amount. Privileging portfolio equity flows meant that when global financial conditions changed, the equity market and therefore corporate capital expenditure were hit hard. The SENSEX (the main Bombay Stock Exchange index) lost half its value in the course of 2008 and more than a third between September and December 2008 alone, and the economy experienced a sharp slowdown. But, in contrast to other countries, the banking system and the government bond market were largely insulated from the shock. Thus the usual pattern of capital inflows followed by a sudden reversal precipitating a banking and financial crisis did not occur in India. Growth was therefore relatively quick to recover.

In contrast to the monetary policy, which was adjusted actively in response to inflows in 2007–8, their reversal in 2008–9, and their resumption in 2010, the fiscal policy response was muted. The opening section of this chapter noted that part of the response to a surge of capital inflows should be fiscal tightening. This limits the increase in domestic demand and the upward pressure on the real exchange rate that otherwise threatens to create Dutch-disease-type problems and slow the expansion of manufactured exports. The problem, also noted in the opening section, is that sharp changes in fiscal policy are difficult politically. Fiscal policy is formulated on an annual cycle, making it hard to adjust quickly in response to capital-inflow fluctuations. Fiscal tightening in good times (when foreign capital inflows are abundant) is especially difficult for democratically elected governments.

Thus India had no trouble adopting a large fiscal stimulus in 2008–9, when export demand weakened significantly. Fiscal tightening in 2010 proved more difficult. The deficit for 2010–11 is projected to run at 7.8 per cent of GDP at the time of writing (including off-budget food, fuel, and fertilizer subsidies), down modestly from 9.6 per cent in 2009–10. But this has not cooled off domestic demand sufficiently to moderate interest rates and discourage carry-trade-related inflows. Most of the improvement in the budget is due to increased revenues as the economy continues to expand, more one-time privatization revenues, and one-time sale of G3 licences—and not from cuts in subsidies or other forms of spending, which are politically more difficult and more important for managing capital inflows. India has a large budget deficit and a relatively high public debt (more than 75 per cent of GDP). It should welcome the opportunity of moving faster with fiscal consolidation in periods when foreign capital is flooding in. That it has not done so is indicative of the difficulty of subordinating fiscal policy to the imperatives of capital-flow management.

IMPLICATIONS FOR THE CONDUCT OF MONETARY POLICY

What are the implications that follow for the conduct of monetary policy in the face of international capital flows from this review of general principles and the Indian experience?

The first implication is that a central bank engaged in flexible inflation targeting (either formally or informally) and therefore adjusting policy to expected inflation and the output gap can deal with the inflationary consequences of capital inflows using its standard instruments, typically the policy rate. There is no dilemma about whether to tighten or loosen, since the two arguments of the standard objective function (inflation and the output gap) both point in the same direction: inflation and growth both rise in response to inflows (and fall in response to outflows), other things being equal.[26] There may be some danger that tightening leading to higher interest rates attracts further inflows. But as it pushes up the exchange rate, there will come a point where the investors will see the currency as sufficiently strong that the possibility arises that it will

---

[26] This is the effect of a policy of monetary tightening in the classic Dornbusch (1976) model.

fall—which will be enough to discourage the carry trade and associated capital inflows.

However, the real appreciation associated with this response may be uncomfortable. It may undermine a development strategy of export-led growth seeking to promote the flow of resources into export-linked sectors that throw off positive externalities for the rest of the economy.[27] By discouraging exports and encouraging imports, it may enlarge the current account deficit, leaving the economy vulnerable to a sudden stop in the availability of financing.[28] Inflows may feed asset bubbles and encourage banks to rely more on non-core funding, on both counts heightening financial risks.[29]

In the wake of the subprime crisis in the US, it will be clear that these problems are universal. In the US context, they have given rise to a debate about whether the Federal Reserve should have tightened more quickly in 2003–4 as financial excesses became evident. The consensus answer is that the associated problems—asset bubbles, excessive leverage in the financial system, and over-reliance on foreign funding—are best addressed by other policy authorities. Fiscal tightening can reinforce the efforts of the monetary authorities to deal with potential overheating problems. Fiscal tightening will mean less domestic demand pressure causing the exchange rate to appreciate. It will mean lower domestic interest rates, other things being equal, providing less of an incentive for capital to flow in. Conversely, when capital flows out, governments with fiscal credibility will be in a position to loosen to offset the economic effects. This was, in fact, precisely the response of governments in a number of emerging Asian and Latin American countries in 2008–9.

Real estate and stock market bubbles fuelled by foreign capital inflows, for their part, can be addressed directly by raising down payment and margin requirements. Excessive growth of bank lending and excessive reliance by banks on non-core funding can be dealt with directly by financial supervisors, ideally through the use of market-friendly instruments like liquidity and capital requirements, if necessary, with directives. Assuming that there are as many independent policy instruments as there are objectives and that those instruments are utilized

---

[27] Two studies emphasizing the link between the real exchange rate and the positive externalities thrown off by the export sector on the one hand and growth prospects on the other are Eichengreen (2008) and Rodrik (2008).

[28] The classic study of current account reversals is Milesi-Ferretti and Razin (2000).

[29] On the non-core funding problem, see Shin (2010).

appropriately, there still is no dilemma for monetary policy even when one acknowledges that capital flows may have additional implications.

Those are strong assumptions, of course. The record of adjusting fiscal policy in response to capital flows is not encouraging, whether in India or generally. The volume and even direction of capital flows can change on a dime. Fiscal policy, in contrast, is generally made on an annual cycle. It is subject to inside and outside lags. Even when the annual cycle is disregarded, budgetary revisions can be painfully slow to emerge from the legislative process.[30] More time may have to pass before the impact of budgetary revisions on actual spending is felt. Above all, fiscal policy is political; fiscal policymakers are constrained by pressures not to increase taxes paid by politically pivotal interest groups or cut the expenditures from which they benefit. Monetary policy is political too, but less so insofar as it is delegated to a nominally independent central bank.

Similarly, the assumption that regulatory policy can be used to deal with real estate bubbles, stock market booms, lending surges, and pro-cyclical movements in leverage may be unrealistic. Regulators may fall asleep at the wheel. They may be prone to capture by the regulated. They may not have developed the expertise to detect risks to financial stability in real time, or they may lack the policy instruments necessary to address them.

It is at this point that it becomes appropriate to contemplate unremunerated deposit requirements for foreign investors and direct controls on capital flows. Controls can be thought of as a second-best form of prudential supervision and regulation, where the first-best alternative is unavailable (for one or another of the reasons described earlier).[31] As a second-best alternative, controls will tend to have undesirable side effects. If adopted to limit foreign capital fuelled real estate and stock market bubbles, they may also have the undesirable effect of limiting foreign finance for, inter alia, trade credit. But there may be circumstances where suffering these side effects is better than doing nothing. In particular, smaller countries, which are very small relative to global capital markets, are likely to find themselves and their conventional policy levers overwhelmed by capital flows and, as such, to have to resort to the unconventional policy instruments described

---

[30] Consider, for example, the pace of fiscal consolidation in southern Europe, taken in response to the 2009–10 reversal in the direction of capital flows.

[31] The analogy between capital controls and prudential supervision originates, if I am correct, with Eichengreen and Mussa (1998).

here. This suggests that controls, whether in the form of borrowing and investment restrictions or unremunerated deposit requirements, should play a more prominent role in the policy strategy of small countries like Nepal than in large countries like India, other things being equal.[32]

Where the side effects are deemed too costly or controls are too easily evaded, the problem will end up back in the lap of the central bank. In this case the monetary authorities will have no choice but to contemplate further adjustments in policy rates in response to additional risks. The direction of the adjustment should depend not simply on whether capital is flowing in or out but on the precise nature of the problem created by those flows. Again, consider the response to inflows. If the problem is asset bubbles or a dangerously rapid increase in bank lending, then the appropriate response is to raise policy rates. The direct negative effect on asset prices and bank lending will presumably dominate the influence of capital inflows. The effect in the short-run may also be to attract additional inflows, but the volume of inflows is not the issue—the behaviour of asset markets and bank lending is. Alternatively, if the problem is the risk of a capital-flow reversal, then the appropriate response is to lower policy rates. Reducing interest differentials and discouraging carry trade will reduce the volume of inflows and address the risk it poses to economic and financial stability. The point, again, is that when contemplating how to adjust policy rates in response to capital inflows, monetary policymakers should focus not on inflows per se but on the particular problem that those inflows create.

Capital inflows create very immediate problems in the region and, as such, require a very immediate response. But while addressing immediate problems, it is important for policymakers not to neglect longer-term strategies. In the long run, the best defence against dislocations due to capital flow surges is larger and more inclusive financial markets (see also Box 8.2.) Larger corporate debt markets will mean that foreign capital flows into and out of those markets will do less to move prices and distort firms' funding costs. Larger equity markets will mean that foreign inflows and outflows will similarly do less to move prices and wrong-foot domestic institutions. Developing domestic financial markets and corporate bond markets, in particular, is a long hard slog. In India it requires institutional and regulatory reforms to further strengthen transparency, contract enforcement, and market liquidity. In the smaller

[32] More so insofar as Nepal's maintenance of an exchange rate peg limits the scope for adjusting monetary policy in response to capital flows.

Box 8.2 Making Financial Markets Inclusive

An important dimension of building larger, more liquid, and more efficient financial markets is making those markets inclusive. Many potential borrowers in South Asia can access only informal financial markets, where credit availability is limited and the interest rates are high. India's Committee on Financial Sector Reforms (2008) found that nearly 70 per cent of loans obtained by those in the bottom quarter of income distribution were from the informal sector (moneylenders, friends, and relatives), while nearly half of the loans obtained by this market segment were at rates of interest exceeding 36 per cent. There is reason to think that the problem is equally, or more, serious in the other countries of South Asia. Integrating lower-income households and producers into formal financial markets is one way of developing market size and liquidity, but it is also a way of distributing the benefits of financial development among a larger share of the population. These benefits include not just access to credit but also production against risk afforded by insurance and instruments (for example, crop insurance, index insurance, disaster insurance, and health insurance).

Making financial markets inclusive requires a multifaceted effort. Where government policies are the obstacle—as with requirements that banks finance priority sectors—those policies should be modified or eliminated. Where previous efforts at fostering financial inclusion focused on largely excluded economic activities and sectors, agriculture being the notable example, future efforts should instead concentrate on largely excluded segments of the population: on low-income households and small producers in the service and industrial sectors, that is, irrespective of the activity or sector in which they are engaged.[1]

Traditional instruments for addressing the exclusion of low-income households and producers from foreign financial markets are government sponsored rural banks and credit cooperatives. These government sponsored institutions are not always driven by administrators with intimate local knowledge or do not always adequately monitor borrowers. Their costs are high and their market penetration is limited (as evidenced by the continuing dominance of the informal sector). Micro-finance institutions that borrow from banks and foreign sources and lend to individuals, households, and small producers on the basis of local knowledge and peer monitoring, often with relatively little overhead, have been more successful and provide an increasingly attractive alternative.

---

[1] With economic development and diversification, the traditional view that low-income households are concentrated in a particular sector, such as agriculture becomes less defensible, making policies targeting particular sectors less effective.

This suggests a strategy for more effectively fostering financial inclusion.[2] First, rather than establishing government sponsored banks with extensive branch networks, encourage the establishment of small rural banks located close to particular groups of potential clients. Such entities will be in a stronger position to monitor borrowers. Entry can be encouraged by adapting regulation and subsidizing shared (low-cost) technological platforms for back-office functions. Second, foster the establishment of an inter-bank market linking those small rural banks and non-bank micro-finance corporations to their larger urban counterparts through formal business-correspondent relationships; this would facilitate the flow of funding from market segments where it is relatively abundant—including foreign sources—to where it is scarce. Third, build non-financial networks (such as those possessed by the postal service and sellers of agricultural inputs and produce, and cell phones), as a way of providing financial services through existing outlets.[3]

Another priority should be bringing crop and weather insurance products to smaller producers (see Eichengreen 2009a). Subsistence farmers are especially at risk from fluctuations in temperature and precipitation. India, Pakistan, Bangladesh, and Sri Lanka all have large coastal, low-lying regions susceptible to flooding by monsoons, cyclones, and tsunamis whose frequency is affected by climate change. Meanwhile the markets and instruments that farmers, firms, and households in high-income countries use to insure against such risks are underdeveloped. Compared to other forms of micro-insurance, crop and disaster insurance are less widely available to poor households. Whereas roughly a third of the population of Bangladesh has health, life, and loan insurance, disaster and crop insurance are widely unavailable. One recent estimate is that only about 4 per cent of micro-insurance clients (1 per cent of the population) has disaster and crop insurance (Ahmed et al. 2005).

Crop insurance is subject to problems of moral hazard and adverse selection, since yields and losses depend also on farmer effort, which is observed only with difficulty.[4] Skees (2006) describes how

---

[2] For details, see Committee on Financial Sector Reforms (2008).

[3] For specific suggestions on how to utilize the postal service to provide savings accounts, micro-loans, and payments services to the poor, see Expert Committee (2010).

[4] The alternative is index insurance, where payouts are subject to non-manipulable, independently verifiable indices, such as temperature or rainfall. The problem here is basis risk, the risk that rainfall or wind speed in a given area corresponds poorly to the actual losses suffered by the policy holder. Recent advances in

a small micro-finance bank, BASIX, in southern India has provided cooperative insurance that relies on peer monitoring to limit moral hazard and adverse selection. Village committees decide on payouts. Half of the insurance premium paid by the participants is deposited in a village fund, a quarter goes to BASIX, and the remainder goes toward an inter-village fund that provides diversification. Another example from India is the Working Women's Forum which provides micro-insurance for health, life, accident, and property to its micro-credit clients. Disasters are insured in the property scheme: clients get Rs 1,000 for damages due to natural disasters in return for paying a small percentage of the micro-credit they obtain. The scheme works in part because, as in the micro-credit component, clients are organized into neighbourhood groups of eight to ten persons who engage in peer monitoring.

Making disaster insurance widely available to the poor is, if anything, an even more formidable challenge, given high covariate risks (flooding, for example, is widespread when it occurs). Covariate risks can be dealt with through reinsurance and issuing of catastrophe bonds. But both approaches face a high minimum efficient scale. One way of achieving the requisite scale and reducing the extent of covariate risks is for the South Asian countries to cooperate in contracting for and issuing the relevant instruments. In pursuing financial inclusiveness, just as in building regional securities markets (Box 8.1), there is a case for the South Asian countries working together.

---

technology, however, suggest that it is becoming easier to tailor the indices to local growing conditions.

countries in South Asia, which lack the scale to build bond markets at the national level but possess it if they are willing to work together with their neighbours, it also requires market integration and regulatory harmonization. Although both domestic market development and regional financial integration will take time, they are no less important for the fact. But they are rightly the subject of another paper (see Eichengreen 2009b).

APPENDIX A8.1

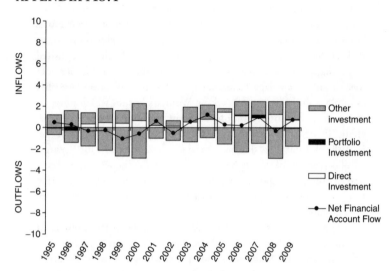

FIGURE A8.1.1 Financial Account Flows (% GDP), Bangladesh

Source: *International Financial Statistics.*

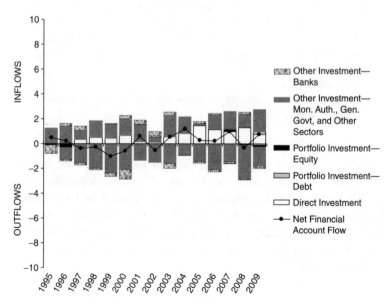

FIGURE A8.1.2   Financial Account Flows (% GDP), Bangladesh

Source: *International Financial Statistics.*

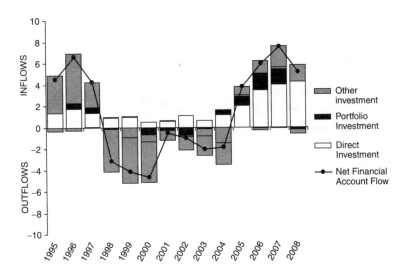

FIGURE A8.1.3   Financial Account Flows (% GDP), Pakistan

Source: International Financial Statistics.

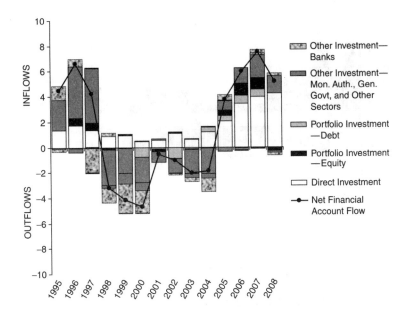

FIGURE A8.1.4   Financial Account Flows (% GDP), Pakistan

Source: International Financial Statistics.

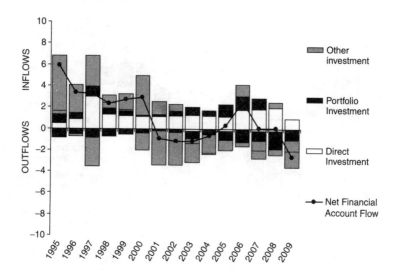

FIGURE A8.1.5   Financial Account Flows (% GDP), Sri Lanka

Source: International Financial Statistics.

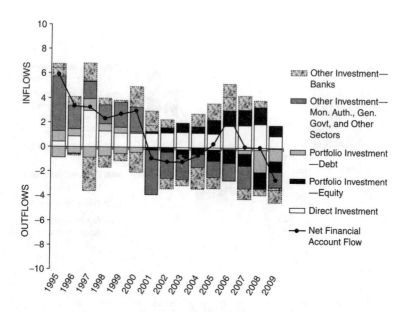

FIGURE A8.1.6   Financial Account Flows (% GDP), Sri Lanka

Source: International Financial Statistics.

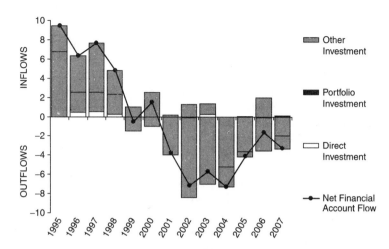

FIGURE A8.1.7   Financial Account Flows (% GDP), Nepal
Source: *International Financial Statistics.*

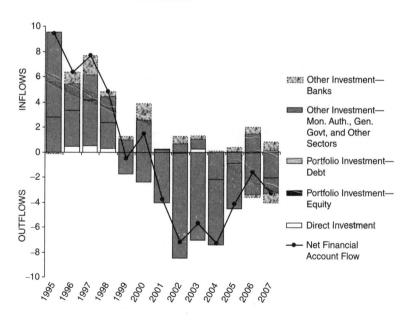

FIGURE A8.1.8   Financial Account Flows (%GDP), Nepal
Source: *International Financial Statistics.*

REFERENCES

Acharya, Shankar. 2010. 'Overvalued Rupee Worsens External Deficits', unpublished manuscript.

Ahmed, M., S. Islam, M. Quashem, and N. Ahmed. 2005. 'Health Microinsurance—A Comparative Study of Three Examples in Bangladesh', Good and Bad Practices Case Study No. 13. Available at www. microfinancegateway.org, accessed on 4 April 2010.

Ahya, Chetan. 2010. 'Capital Inflows', Morgan Stanley Global Economic Forum. Available at www.morganstaley.com, accessed on 21 May 2010.

Almekindes, Geert, Svitlana Maslova, and Zino Abenoja. 2009. 'Remittances in Bangladesh and the Philippines: Determinants and Outlook', in *Bangladesh: Selected Issues*. Washington, DC: IMF (28 December). Available at www. imf.org, accessed on 15 January 2010.

Arora, Dayanand and Francis Rathinam. 2010. 'The Recent Surge in Capital Inflows and Policy Options for India', *ICRIER Macro Perspectives and Updates* (16 June), ICRIER, New Delhi.

Asian Development Bank. 2010. 'Managing Capital Flows', in *Asian Economic Outlook* (chapter 4). Manila: ADB (May).

Bangladesh Bank. 2010. *Monetary Policy Statement*. Dhaka: Bangladesh Bank (January).

Committee on Financial Sector Reforms. 2008. *A Hundred Small Steps: Report of the Committee on Financial Sector Reforms*. New Delhi: Committee on Financial Sector Reforms.

Dey, Kumar. 2010. 'Private Banks' Leverage Ratio Rises to 10.8%, PSBs' Lingers at 5.39%', *Financial Express*, 30 June.

Dornbusch, Rudiger. 1976. 'Expectations and Exchange Rate Dynamics', *Journal of Political Economy*, 84: 1161–76.

Eichengreen, Barry. 2000. 'Taming Capital Flows', *World Development*, 28: 1105–16.

———. 2008. 'The Real Exchange Rate and Economic Growth', Commission on Growth and Development Working Paper No. 4. World Bank, Washington, DC.

———. 2009a. 'Financial Cooperation to Protect Against Climate Change in South Asia', unpublished manuscript, University of California, Berkeley (March).

———. 2009b. 'Integrating Financial Markets in South Asia', unpublished manuscript, University of California, Berkeley (November).

——— 2010. 'Managing Openness: Lessons from the Crisis for Emerging Markets', prepared for the World Bank Conference on Managing Openness, 10 May, World Bank, Washington, DC.

Eichengreen, Barry and Michael Mussa. 1998. 'Capital Account Liberalization: Theoretical and Practical Aspects', Occasional Paper No. 65. IMF, Washington, DC.

Expert Committee. 2010. *Harnessing the India Post Network for Financial Inclusion.* New Delhi: Departments of Post, Financial Affairs, and Economic Affairs and Invest India Economic Foundation.

Gehrig, Thomas. 2000. 'Cities and the Geography of Financial Centers', in Jean-Marie Hurriot and Jacques-Francois Thisse (eds), *Economics of Cities: Theoretical Perspectives.* Cambridge: Cambridge University Press, pp. 415–46.

Gopalan, Sasidaran and Ramkishen Rajan. 2010. 'External Financing in South Asia: The Remittances Option', ARTNeT Policy Brief No. 23 (January), Asia-Pacific Research and Training Network on Trade, Bangkok.

High Level Expert Committee on Corporate Bonds and Securitization. 2005. *Report of the High Level Expert Committee on Corporate Bonds and Securitization.* New Delhi: Ministry of Finance.

High Powered Expert Committee. 2007. *Mumbai—An International Financial Center.* New Delhi: Ministry of Finance.

International Monetary Fund. 2005. 'Two Current Issues Facing Developing Countries: Workers' Remittances and Economic Development', *World Economic Outlook*, Fall: 69–107.

―――. 2008. 'India: 2007 Article IV Consultation', IMF Country Report No. 08/51. Available at www.imf.org, accessed on 4 April 2011.

―――. 2010a. 'Global Liquidity Expansion: Effects on Receiving Economies and Policy Response Options', in *Global Financial Stability Report* (chapter 4). Washington, DC: IMF (April).

―――. 2010b. 'India: 2009 Article IV Consultation: Staff Report; Staff Statement; Public Information Notice'. Available at www.imf.org, accessed on 4 April 2011.

Kumar, Rajiv and Pankaj Vashisht. 2009. 'The Global Economic Crisis: Impact on India and Policy Responses', ADB Institute Working Paper No. 164 (November). Tokyo: Asian Development Bank Institute.

Ma, Guonan and Eli Remolona. 2006. 'Learning by Doing in Market Reform: Lessons from a Regional Bond Fund', unpublished manuscript, BIS.

Milesi-Ferretti, Gian Maria, and Assaf Razin. 2000. 'Current Account Reversals and Currency Crises: Empirical Regularities', in Paul Krugman (ed.), *Currency Crises.* Chicago: University of Chicago Press, pp. 285–326.

Mohan, Rakesh and Muneesh Kapur. 2009. 'Managing the Impossible Trinity: Volatile Capital Flows and Indian Monetary Policy', Working Paper No. 401, Stanford Center for International Development (November), Stanford, California.

Nomura Securities. 2009. *Multi-Strategy Asia* (various issues). Tokyo: Nomura.

Ostry, Jonathan, Atish Ghosh, Karl Habermeier, Marcos Chamon, Mahvash Qureshi, and Dennis Reinhart. 2010. 'Capital Inflows: The Role of Controls', IMF Staff Position Note SPN/10/04 (19 February), IMF, Washington, DC.

Patnaik, Ila. 2010. 'Capital Controls and Unhedged Currency Exposure among Indian Firms', unpublished manuscript, National Institute of Public Finance and Policy (June), New Delhi.

Qayyam, Abdul. 2008. 'Does Monetary Policy Play an Effective Role in Controlling Inflation in Pakistan', MPRA Paper No. 13080, unpublished manuscript, University of Munich.

Ratha, Dilip, Sanket Mohapatra, and Ani Silwal. (2009). 'Migration and Remittance Trends 2009', *Migration and Development Brief 11*, World Bank, Washington, DC (November).

Reserve Bank of India. 2007. *Annual Policy Statement for the Year 2007/8*. Mumbai: RBI (April).

Rodrik, Dani. 2006. 'The Social Cost of Foreign Exchange Reserves', *International Economic Journal*, 20: 253–66.

————. 2008. 'The Real Exchange Rate and Economic Growth', *Brookings Papers on Economic Activity*, 2: 365–412.

Shah, Mehul, Rajesh Abraham, and Yassir Pitalwalla. 2008. 'No Problems Ahead for Indian Investment Banks', *Financial Chronicle* (23 September). Available at http://www.mydigitalfc.com, accessed on 4 April 2011.

Shin, Hyun. 2010. 'A Necessary Automatic Stabilizer', *The Economist* (5 June). Available at www.economist.com, accessed on 4 June 2010.

Singer, David Andrew. 2010. 'Migrant Remittances and Exchange Rate Regimes in the Developing World', *American Political Science Review*, 104 (2): 307–23.

Singh, Bhupal. 2010. 'Monetary Policy Behavior in India: Evidence from Taylor-Type Policy Frameworks', RBI Staff Study 2/2010 (April), RBI, Mumbai.

Skees, Jerry R. 2006. 'Risk Management Challenges in Rural Financial Markets: Blending Risk Management Innovations with Rural Finance', unpublished manuscript, University of Kentucky.

Subbarao, Duvvuri. 2010. 'Volatility of Capital Flows: Some Perspectives', Comments to the High Level Conference organized by the IMF and Swiss National Bank, Zurich (11 May).

9

Managing Efficient Urbanization

Rakesh Mohan*

URBANIZATION: A RECENT PHENOMENON

Widespread all-pervading urbanization is a truly 20th century phenomenon although cities have always existed. Cities, such as Memphis, Babylon, Thebes, Athens, Sparta, Mohen-jo-daro, and Anuradhapura existed even in antiquity. However, there is little evidence of widespread urbanization in the early years of civilization. South Asia was perhaps as urbanized as any other civilization then. But at the turn of the current century, South Asia as a whole was among the least urbanized regions in the world. What is remarkable now is that along with accelerated economic and urban growth, by 2030 we can expect that this region will be home to at least five cities that will have more than 20 million people: Mumbai, Delhi, Kolkata, Karachi, and Dhaka. The complexity of urban management in the region will be no less than in the most advanced countries of the world.

In 1800, only 2 per cent of the world's population was urbanized. By 1900, out of a total world population of close to 1.5 to 1.7 billion, only 15 per cent, or about 250 million people, lived in urban areas, a number lower than the total urban population of India alone today. By 1950 the proportion of urban to total global population had increased to around 30 per cent, with Europe, North America, and Oceania having the highest levels of urbanization. By 2000, 2.8 billion people, equalling approximately 47 per cent of the world's population, lived in urban areas. So the pace of urbanization witnessed in the 20th century

* I am grateful to Amod Jain for very able research assistance.

was truly unprecedented, and it is a wonder that the world has coped as well as it has. We are now at a turning point in human history: the number of people living in cities has only recently started exceeding that of those in the countryside.

The last 50–60 years have been truly remarkable in terms of the number of people who have been successfully absorbed in cities in a time period that is incredibly short by historical standards. While the world's urban population grew by approximately 500 million between 1900 and 1950, it grew by 2.1 billion in the next 50 years and is expected to grow by a similar magnitude in the first 30 years of this century. The speed of urbanization in Latin America in the second half of the 20th century was spectacular, vaulting from just over 40 per cent to 75 per cent by the end of this period, which was also a period of rapid population growth and demographic transition. As may be seen from Table 9.1, the focus of change is now in Asia with the urban population expected to double between 2000 and 2030. Such rapid urbanization is indeed unprecedented and it has changed human geography beyond recognition.

The whole South Asian region experienced relatively slow economic growth for almost 30 years from the late 1940s to the late 1970s. Since then there has been gradual acceleration in growth, with East Asian-type growth beginning to manifest itself across the region over the past decade. As this acceleration took place it might have been expected that, as has been observed elsewhere at this stage of development (for example in Latin America and East Asia), the pace of urbanization would also pick up speed. However, even by 2010 the overall urbanization level was estimated to be only about 30 per cent across the region. India, at about 27 per cent level of urbanization in 2001, when the last census was taken, was lower than almost all projections. While economic growth was accelerating, urbanization actually slowed down in India during the 1980s and 1990s. The level of urbanization is lower in all South Asian countries relative to the global cross-country trend line with respect to per capita levels.

Although South Asia has been somewhat late in coming to the urbanization party, this is changing and this region will also now witness epoch-making change over the next 20 to 30 years. Total urban population in the region will double from an estimated 500 million in 2010 to over a billion in 2040 (Table 9.2). The current projections suggest that the urbanization level over the region will be around 50 per cent by 2040, with doubling of the absolute level of urban population over the period.

TABLE 9.1 Urban Population Growth across the Globe

Country	1900		1950		2000		2030	
	Urban Population (million)	Per cent of Total Population (%)	Urban Population (million)	Per cent of Total Population (%)	Urban Population (million)	Per cent of Total Population (%)	Urban Population (million)	Per cent of Total Population (%)
Africa	–	–	33	14.5	295	35.9	759	50.0
Asia	–	–	237	16.8	1,373	37.1	2,669	54.1
Latin America & Caribbean	–	–	69	41.4	394	75.3	603	84.6
Oceania	–	–	8	62.0	22	70.4	31	72.6
Europe	–	–	281	51.2	520	71.4	550	77.8
North America	–	–	110	63.9	250	79.1	351	86.7
Global Total	~250	~15	737	29.1	2,854	46.6	4,965	59.7

Source: United Nations (2007).

TABLE 9.2 Urban Population in South Asia

Country	1950 Urban Population (million)	1950 Per cent of Total Population (%)	2010 Urban Population (million)	2010 Per cent of Total Population (%)	2040 Urban Population (million)	2040 Per cent of Total Population (%)	Last 60 Years Additional Urban Population (million)	Next 30 Years Additional Urban Population (million)
India	62	17.3	367	30.1	764	47.8	305	397
Pakistan	7	17.5	64	37	153	56.9	57	89
Bangladesh	2	4.3	47	28.1	116	48.7	45	69
Nepal	0.2	2.7	5	18.2	18	38.2	5	13
Sri Lanka	1	15.3	2.9	15.1	5.4	27.2	2	2.5
Total	72	15.8	486	30.3	1,056	48.6	414	571

Source: United Nations (2007).

In the process, the complexion of development objectives and processes will have to undergo significant change in the region as a whole.

We could, therefore, be entering a new era of change in terms of both absolute numbers and pace. But will this actually happen? Will acceleration in urbanization actually take place along with economic growth? In order to design policy processes that nurture healthy urbanization, it is first necessary to understand why deceleration of urban growth took place earlier.

WHY HAS URBANIZATION BEEN SLOW IN SOUTH ASIA?

The deceleration of urban growth at this stage of development in a growing economy is a cause for disquiet. Some of the crucial differences in the growth of urban populations in the region vis-à-vis the other parts of the world could be due to the following:

Inadequate increase in rural productivity: Deceleration in rural productivity growth could, ironically, contribute to slow urban growth. It is possible that because of slow growth in agricultural productivity in most regions in South Asia, it has not been possible to release agricultural labour from rural areas. It is clear, for example, that public investment in agriculture fell as a proportion of gross domestic product (GDP) in India throughout the 1990s. Along with the plateauing of productivity growth in main cereal products, there was also inadequate diversification away from cereals to other higher-productivity agricultural activities which would result in higher overall agricultural growth. With income growth, as diets in the region get diversified away from the traditional cereal-based ones, we may now expect a corresponding supply response in agriculture. Such a shift will accelerate with faster urban growth. So overall agricultural productivity growth should accelerate with the emergence of higher-productivity agricultural activities in the coming years. In this process, we can expect rural demand for labour to fall, thereby releasing labour which will then increasingly seek urban employment.

Inappropriate technology choice in industry: Inappropriate technology choice or product composition in the process of industrialization could also lead to lower absorption of labour in urban areas. It is possible that earlier this may have been caused by a faulty customs tariff structure providing greater protection to capital-using industries (Kelkar and Kumar 1990). Tariff reforms that have taken place across the region over the past two decades have largely corrected this bias. Labour-intensive manufactured export sectors, such as ready-made garments and textiles have gained market shares (from the dismantling of the Multi-Fiber Agreement) and attracted buyers at both low (Bangladesh) and high (Sri Lanka) ends, as have other sectors, such as leather, gems and jewellery, carpets, and frozen foods. The gains from this have, however, been muted in India because other problems remain.

Labour legislation and small-scale industry reservations: In India, the growth in industrial employment was not commensurate with that in industrial output and value added in the 1980s and 1990s. The possible reasons for this could be the tightening of labour legislation accompanied by expansion of small-scale industry reservations in the late 1970s. As argued in Mohan (2002) these policy rigidities could have had a major role in the slowdown of growth in manufacturing output as well as in employment. Other developing countries, particularly in Asia, have exhibited much higher industrial employment growth at similar stages of development. Success of the clothing industry in Bangladesh and the consequent rapid increase in employment there illustrate the constraints that wrong policies have placed on labour-using industrialization in India. With small-scale industry reservation having been largely abolished, it is possible that this bias may now be gradually reversed. Rigidities in labour legislation may, however, still inhibit new investment in labour-using industries. What is needed is greater flexibility in labour use while ensuring social security provisions that mitigate labour hardships. As labour gets released from rural areas at a faster rate in the coming years, it is essential that along with the services sector, new manufacturing activities are able to absorb this released labour.

Location restrictions on industries: There have been other policies as well that have inhibited the location of industrial units, both large and small, in urban areas since the early 1970s. Industries were not permitted to locate within any urban area until the industrial policy reform of 1991, when this restriction was lifted except in million plus cities. The original idea was to encourage dispersal of industrial activity. But, in effect, industries were denied the economic benefits of urban agglomeration and thus rendered more inefficient. It is also possible that industries became more capital intensive as a result, since skilled labour is generally more difficult to get outside existing urban areas. Industrial employment growth suffered overall, and in urban areas in particular.

Central cities have often been observed to be 'incubators' for entrepreneurship. Firms typically minimize localization costs by locating nearer their suppliers and markets. Locations within cities are also usually better served with essential infrastructure. As firms grow and their technology changes, requiring greater space they move out to areas where more space is available. In India, however, the function of cities as entrepreneurial incubators has been inhibited by its perverse industrial location policies, thereby imposing additional costs on its emerging industrial firms and slowing down both industrialization and urbanization. The prejudice against location of industries in cities in India continues. For example, court judgements related to improvement of the urban environment have decreed the wholesale shifting of industries from some cities.

There is hence no reason to discourage the location of manufacturing industry within cities as long as pollution norms are observed.

Urban infrastructure investment: Investment in urban infrastructure in areas, such as water and sanitation facilities, affordable urban transport, and urban land development has been much lower than needed (McKinsey and Company 2010; EGCIP 1996). Although there has been some improvement, the provision of overall basic urban amenities in South Asian cities remains among the worst in the world. The poor availability of potable water, accessible sanitation, solid waste disposal, affordable transportation, and the like all contribute to a very low quality of life for the vast majority of urban residents in South Asia (Table 9.3). It is possible therefore that the real costs of locating in urban areas could be perceived to be high by prospective migrants, thereby slowing down urbanization. McKinsey and Company (2010) has estimated that Indian cities will need capital investment of about US$ 1.2 trillion over the next 20 years. It is notable that of this total requirement, full provision of water, sewerage, solid waste disposal, and storm water drainage can be made with only one-sixth of the total estimated requirement. The adequate provision of these amenities can do much for the quality of life in South Asian cities.

Rigidities in urban land policy: The promulgation of the Urban Land Ceiling Act in India in the mid-1970s introduced great rigidity in the urban land market. Change in land use became very difficult unless it was undertaken by government agencies. Thus, the supply of developed urban land got greatly reduced, leading to large increases in urban land values. The result has been the proliferation of illegal or semi-legal habitations and increase in the cost of housing and hence of urban life. Almost all the states have now repealed the Urban Land Ceiling Act so, in principle, it should become much easier to undertake land consolidation for urban

TABLE 9.3 Water and Sanitation Penetration Statistics for South Asia, 2000–6

Country	2000				2006			
	Urban Population with Access to Improved Water (%)	Urban Population not Provided (million)	Urban Population with Access to Improved Sanitation (%)	Urban Population not Provided (million)	Urban Population with Access to Improved Water (%)	Urban Population not Provided (million)	Urban Population with Access to Improved Sanitation (%)	Urban Population not Provided (million)
India	94	16.9	49	143.5	96	12.9	52	154.4
Pakistan	95	2.3	85	6.9	95	2.8	90	5.6
Bangladesh	86	4.7	51	16.3	85	6.1	48	21.2
Nepal	95	0.2	42	1.9	94	0.3	45	2.5
Sri Lanka	96	0.1	88	0.4	95	0.2	89	0.3

Source: World Bank (2010).

development purposes, for building multiple unit housing, for setting up factories, and for service activities, such as large retail formats. The existence of rent control laws since the 1940s and 1950s had in any case inhibited the supply of urban housing.

It is perhaps coincidental that a number of these policy distortions were introduced in mid- to late 1970s, thereby slowing down subsequent urbanization in the 1980s and 1990s. The net result is that employment growth has fallen in both urban and rural areas.

Land availability is a prerequisite for urbanization and sustained economic growth. In the urban environment competing uses vie for constrained land resources, making it the most important input. Focusing on this aspect, a study (McKinsey Report 2001) identified inefficient urban real estate markets as perhaps the single most important constraint on India's ability to sustain the increase in growth experienced in the years since the country's liberalization programme began in the early 1990s. Thus, urban land market reform is essential for efficient urban growth.

There has been continuing concern over 'unwarranted' increases in urban land values. The control of urban land values has been regarded as a major objective of urban policy. Delhi is the best example of a policy of large-scale acquisition of land. In this approach, the idea was that all the land on the yet undeveloped periphery of the growing city would be notified at an early stage and acquired by a public authority at the prevailing agricultural prices, thereby removing any possible speculative land prices in peri-urban areas. The benefits of this method were also thought to include: (i) that any increase in land value would accrue to the public agency which would use it for public purposes: essentially monetizing the value of land assets; (ii) the same public authority could better plan for the future growth of the city since it had control over the peripheral lands; and (iii) the public agency could also then plan for the poor.

The experience of public acquisition of land has, however, been poor. Public authorities are able to obtain the land at very low prices, leading to very wasteful, uneconomic, and inefficient methods of utilization of the land. Moreover, there are no market signals on when to bring the land into the market. The tendency in such a system is to hoard land in order to generate resources for urban investment by the public authority. Monetization of land assets is now advocated as a major source of funds for urban infrastructure investment by the private sector (for example, McKinsey and Company 2010). The experience with public agencies using such methodology has not been a happy one. Giving land grants to the private sector as part of infrastructure concessioning has then to be done very carefully in order to avoid excessive increases in urban land prices and monopoly rights to private sector concessionaires.

Building byelaws more directly controlled by the local bodies themselves in most locations have a significant impact on the form of the city, thereby having a comprehensive impact on its economy. The reform of floor area ratio (FAR), a primary part of building regulations, should be part of a general reform of many urban policies. The benefits of FAR reform would occur only if the increase in FAR in central business districts and other commercial areas results in a massive redevelopment of existing structures offering modern floor space equipped with a level of infrastructure and mechanical equipment compatible with a modern wired economy. For this to happen, an accompanying package of urban reforms should aim at:

1. reducing real estate transactions costs,
2. better managing public urban space, such as streets and sidewalks,
3. auditing institutional landholdings in urban areas, putting back on the market grossly underused land, and
4. increasing the share of the fiscal revenue of cities directly linked to the prosperity of its real estate industry.

The formulation of urban land policy needs to be informed by knowledge of the dynamics of urban growth and recognition of the limits of the efficacy of public policy. The basic problem of urban land policy is the supply of serviced land in adequate quantity, at the right locations, the right time, and the right price. These four considerations are closely interlinked.

CHANGING CONTOURS OF URBANIZATION IN SOUTH ASIA

How then do we look at South Asia's evolving urban future over the next 20–30 years? How will it be different from the experience of the last half century? The first key difference is that with increasing globalization and ever higher levels of income that the region as a whole can now expect, the residents of South Asian cities will be much more demanding relative to their predecessors in terms of the quality of urban services that they deem to be their right and the urban amenities of living that are now seen as normal. Hence, it is likely that urban investment will be different in terms of its composition and intensity.

Second, with increasing globalization and reduction in trade protection, each South Asian city will have to be more competitive on a global scale than has been the case in the past. In the larger countries there will be inevitable tension between the claims of coastal urban areas that possess natural comparative advantages and the vast hinterland that will need greater infrastructure investment for attaining competitiveness. Hence, policymakers probably need to give explicit attention to the ingredients of competitiveness, the corresponding public investment that will be appropriate in this regard, and the modes of financing that will need to be mobilized.

Third, whether South Asian urbanization in the coming decades will be able to mimic the East Asian experience which was based disproportionately on city-based rapid manufacturing growth in labour-intensive industries remains an open question. This generated adequate demand for labour thereby relieving rural areas of excess labour and hence enabling growth in both rural and urban productivity. With the changes in technology that have taken place over the past decade or two, it is an open question whether labour-intensive industry will now be able to survive and grow in the manner and experience of the East Asian countries. Moreover, with the possible slowing down of demand growth in developed countries in the years to come, new entrants in the area of labour-intensive manufacturing may not be able to benefit from the demand pull that was exercised by the United States and Europe over the past couple of decades. This could, however, be substituted by similar demand growth within Asia. Will South Asia be able to compete with China, Vietnam, and other South East Asian countries? These are the issues that need to be addressed to devise policy that still enables South Asian cities to absorb the kind of rural–urban migration that is projected to take place over the next two or three decades.

This issue is of great importance to India since the share of manufacturing in its economy is somewhat lower than could be expected at its current level of economic development (Mohan 2002). If India is not able to change its economic and urban-specific policies to encourage labour-using manufacturing in and around urban concentrations, and if the global economic imperative is that such patterns of industrialization are no longer feasible, how will its cities grow and absorb the large rural population that needs to get off the farm so that both rural and urban productivity can grow faster? Thus, we can expect the pattern of South Asian industrialization and urbanization to be different from that of East and South East Asian countries.

However, for successful and sustainable urbanization the share of manufacturing will still need to increase, but with somewhat different characteristics (Yusuf and Nabeshima 2006). The manufacturing process has itself changed significantly so that many activities that were earlier concentrated in one location in one plant are now often outsourced to many different locations within an urban concentration and even across borders. For such a pattern to succeed it needs efficient connectivity within an economic region and to the coast for cross-border transportation. Often product design is now increasingly information technology dependent and typically locationally divorced from the core manufacturing plant. Moreover, product development and design are now increasingly being outsourced on a global basis. The availability of competent engineering skills at a lower cost in India is contributing significantly to the relocation of product development and design from developed countries to India (Marsh 2006 a, 2006b, 2006c). Other South Asian countries need to step up their capacity building in this area at both professional and technician levels. In India, whereas professional engineering education has been expanding at a fast pace in the face of increased demand, vocational education needs greater attention if the current unskilled labour in rural areas is to be efficiently absorbed in urban areas.

With the quality of manufactured goods improving all the time, it is becoming clear that the demand for low-skilled labour is unlikely to accelerate. Hence, a core component of economic and urban policy would have to be enhancing the skills of the labour force at all levels. The provision of vocational training has been difficult in most countries since successful training needs to be market determined, but the private sector often finds it difficult to design an appropriate revenue model and public provision is typically not market sensitive. The need is for public-private partnership, which is not easy to design. Successful urbanization in the future will be crucially dependent on the availability of labour with appropriate skills.

Thus, for South Asian cities to grow in a healthy fashion in the next 20–30 years, it is becoming increasingly clear that the key will indeed lie in the continuous enhancement of human resources. In the globalizing world, creativity and entrepreneurial dynamism will be the essence of successful cities (Yusuf and Nabeshima 2006). All the East Asian cities, such as Bangkok, Beijing, Singapore, China, Seoul, and Tokyo exhibit high levels of educational attainment, and have impressively endowed educational and research institutions. In fact, it is noteworthy that some of these cities, such as Hong Kong and Singapore, which did not traditionally have higher education institutions that were particularly noted for quality, have in the last two decades consciously invested intensively in higher education institutions in terms of both quantity and quality. Each of these major Asian cities now houses large numbers of universities. Illustratively, Tokyo has 113 universities and Beijing 59, although there is a great deal of variation in the quality of these universities (Yusuf and Nabeshima 2006). Similarly, in India, it is the southern region where a large number of private colleges and universities have emerged to cater to the increasing demand for technical personnel from industry. Thus, apart from the traditional needs for physical urban infrastructure investment for successful urbanization, similar attention now has to be given to soft infrastructure that is related to the creation, production, and retention of knowledge, along with facilities that enable continuous skill enhancement.

Increased global competition is also leading firms to look for continuous reduction in core manufacturing costs in whatever ways are practical. Local outsourcing of components and processes is one of the common practices that has been found to be useful in this regard. The requirements of inventory control and management necessitate such outsourced manufacturing activities to be located in close proximity to mother plants. Starting with Japanese growth in the Tokkaido region, rapid urban growth in East and South East Asia has been characterized by a concentrated pattern of urbanization around coastal areas. The 'just-in-time (jit)' pattern of inventory control was enabled by this kind of concentrated urban growth along with corresponding infrastructure investment. Thus, successful industrialization in this manner in South Asia would increasingly require greater concentration of these activities than has been experienced in the past and infrastructure investment planned accordingly, particularly with regard to transportation in such areas.

The South Asian countries have carried out major trade reforms over the past couple of decades so their economies are now largely open on the current account. Similar opening has been carried out in welcoming foreign investment and technology. Openness to the outside world, however, does not just mean increase in trade in goods and services. It also means greater openness to ideas and new practices. This has been found to be of great benefit even in the most developed of countries. In a conference on 'Urban Dynamics in New York City' organized by the Federal Reserve Bank of New York, Kenneth Jackson attributed the great success of New

York City to its openness to new waves of immigrants over time: 'The constant infusion of new energy and ideas into the metropolis over the years enabled New York to meet economic and technological challenges that destroyed the prospects of competing cities' (Jackson 2005). It is quite remarkable that most of the successful East and South East Asian cities have remained very open to the presence of foreign citizens with high levels of education and skills. There are said to be almost 100,000 foreign citizens in Beijing alone (Yusuf and Nabeshima 2006). Such a high presence of foreigners contributes greatly to the economic vitality so needed by growing cities, as it provides new competition to residents, while facilitating the flow of new ideas in both directions. South Asian cities do not exhibit such characteristics yet and the presence of higher-educated foreign citizens is still very small in these cities. In fact, a large number of universities and other technical institutions in the developed world have also started realizing that it would be increasingly efficient for them to relocate some of their activities to Asian cities rather than drawing Asian personnel to their parent campuses. Thus, enhancement of human capital at different levels will involve different strategies and increasingly greater openness to cross-border flows of institutions and personnel. India is already witnessing the beginning of a major reform process in higher education that is likely to lead to much greater openness in its higher education institutions. Similar actions will have to be taken in the other South Asian countries.

In sum, in thinking about prospective urban growth in South Asia we need to understand the emerging contours of economic development better as they are likely to impact the future pattern of urbanization in the region. We will need to pay as much attention to the 'soft' aspects of urbanization as to the bricks and mortar type of physical investment. Indeed the latter will have to be guided by the expected pattern of economic development in the presence of globalization and the consequent need for both human resource and physical development.

CITY MANAGEMENT

With this kind of urban future there has to be a new focus on city management. Our traditional approach to city management arose during an era of slow urban growth. Urban local bodies have traditionally been weak in all respects: quality of leadership and of management. Moreover, their financial base is generally precarious. As a consequence, most cities do not have the financial or managerial wherewithal to undertake, finance, or manage the kind of infrastructure investments that a modern growing city needs. What has generally been done in South Asian cities is for the national and/or state governments to step in to make such investments through entities such as urban development authorities. This process weakens the municipal governments further as power shifts to these authorities. The staffing of such authorities at the top level is generally from the transferable civil services who have little stake in the city itself. Thus, there is a great degree of fragmentation in city government and in the planning and delivery of urban services. No one then has a holistic view of the city and where it is likely to go. The damage that such an approach could do was not too serious in a low-growth scenario, but will be totally inadequate in the new environment of high growth.

So mega-city management is a new emerging area that needs consistent focus of policymakers. Cities are now larger and more complex than they have ever been. They often have very large budgets and, depending on the context, these budgets are sometimes bigger than the budgets of many countries and many provincial or state governments. As an example, the New York City budget is larger than that of all the states in the United States except two. Fewer than 15 countries have larger budgets. The Greater Mumbai Municipal Corporation budget is larger than that of nine Indian states. Thus, management of mega cities is as complex as that of most countries. Yet the attention given to such management can only be described as one of benign neglect. Thus, there has to be a new focus on city management in South Asia. National governments are too distracted to bother about city-level issues, even if they are mega cities, and even if they are the country's major engines of growth.

The huge challenge facing South Asian cities would need new ways of planning and managing. The patterns of urbanization and cities' direct relationship to global economic processes have made cities very important considerations in locating businesses. In this scenario, in many cases local city-level planning and management innovations are more important that national policies. The effort should also be to decentralize management to the lowest effective level where decisions can be made quickly so as to reduce the decision-making burden on higher functionaries in the government. Increased competition in service delivery through benchmarking standards and new methods of attracting the private sector to assist in the delivery of services should be approached on a much wider scale.

Whereas there is no received wisdom on best practices for the management of metropolitan areas, there is increasing agreement on empowering some kind of metropolitan-level government to oversee overall city management. Since local traditions and practices vary greatly there can be no one-size-fits-all approach. One approach could be to retain the various municipal bodies that exist but integrate them through a 'mayor-in-council' approach as practised, for example, in cities such as London or Kolkata. Another could be to just have one city government at the metropolitan level.

For city managers to be effective, the burden on local governments must be reduced and they must be strengthened. This can be done by limiting the financial role of city governments to the provision of public goods and services. Whereas the metropolitan-level government should assume overall responsibility for city governance and coordination in terms of both planning and provision of services, the actual delivery should be decentralized as far as possible. All services that can be paid for can be delegated to corporatized public or private sector providers, as appropriate, but who would be accountable to the metropolitan government. As far as possible, it is essential to introduce competition to induce efficiency in these corporatized entities. The corporatization of such service providers would forge direct links between the financing of urban infrastructure and the returns that they generate through user charges, thereby inducing accountability. Services for which user charges can be levied, such as water supply and sewerage, electricity, solid waste disposal, and transportation, can all be provided by autonomous public- or private-sector companies. Other public services, such as roads, street lighting, and the like have, however, to be supplied by the local government itself and financed from tax revenues. Such division of work would enable the metropolitan government to concentrate on its governance functions while delivery is done by specialized organizations. The metropolitan government would be responsible to the people and would need to ensure adequate citizens' participation in the planning and design of urban services. Although specialized service providers do exist in some South Asian cities, a discussion on empowered strong metropolitan governments has not even started.

The metropolitan government would eschew detailed master planning at the city level in favour of strategic city planning. The basic approach in urban planning has been the preparation of city land-use plans which are prepared once in a decade or two in each city. Such plans delineated the city based on factors such as planned differentiation in land use (residential, commercial, and industrial), road pattern, transportation links, and so on. These factors were then, in principle, predicated on the expected or planned density of use. These traditional city land-use plans, which typically incorporate statutory directives in a static framework, are not the right methodology to address the changing contours of a developing city (Mohan 1994). So their directives have generally been followed more in the breach. Constant change is now the norm, not an exception. Land-value patterns, land usage, population densities, employment densities, and transportation patterns, all change rapidly in the presence of fast city growth. So flexibility has to be built into urban planning and corresponding city management. Much greater attention has to be given to the needs of residents as they arise and the imperatives of changing economic scenarios. Moreover, with the emergence of large cities in the region, explicit attention has to be given to the problems intrinsic to such large urban systems. In addition to the five cities in the region which are expected to have more than a 20 million population, there will be a large increase in the number of million plus cities. By 2030, India is likely to have at around 70 such cities and Pakistan and Bangladesh another 15 to 20 between them.

One of the most important challenges facing local governments presently is the low prestige of working for or being associated with the local government. The prestige of mayors and legislators has to be increased so that the elected or appointed city managers are those with leadership qualities that inspire trust from both citizens and staff. Similarly, local government staff is typically at the lowest rank in public service in terms of salary structure and competence. This must change so that professionalism is inculcated in city management. Being the most neglected tier of government, no individual thinks of it as providing key management challenges. There is, therefore, a strong case for significantly enhancing the prestige of city managers and upgrading the skills of local government staff, especially recognizing their key role in providing services. The difficulty of the task facing city management in developing countries is the difference in revenues raised by them relative to those in developed countries. Thus, city managers and staff in South Asian cities have to be that much more efficient and innovative in order to make their cities function.

The national civil services of South Asian countries attract some of the most talented educated youth. There is tremendous competition for entry to these services. Staff for municipal corporations of, say, million plus cities could be recruited from the same pool, or from a similar nationally conducted competitive examination. It would, however, be a mistake to form a national cadre of such recruits since that would detract from their intrinsic loyalty to and interest in their cities of service. It should be feasible to recruit local citizens or others interested in the reference city to each municipal corporation, but from the same national competitive examination. Such competitive entry would enhance the prestige of working for local bodies. Urban planning, financing, management, and transportation are areas of city management that need expertise, and students who have specialized in such disciplines could form the pool of applicants for such examinations and entry into city management.

FINANCIAL DEVELOPMENT FOR URBANIZATION

South Asian cities have a tremendous backlog in basic urban services like the availability of clean water. As urban growth accelerates over the next two or three decades, new urban investment will have to provide for both the existing backlog and for the new emerging demands. Thus, as argued earlier, city management and delivery systems would need to be redesigned to meet this large demand. This fact, accompanied with the demand for improvements in the quality of services delivered, would need a new way of thinking for managing the provision of urban infrastructure services. The challenges over the next few years would be immense, especially if urban infrastructure has to support economic development and not emerge as the key bottleneck in India's economic ambitions for growth. If urban population growth is to be accelerated, it will need even greater acceleration in urban infrastructure investment.

City growth can be constrained by the lack of adequate investment supporting economic development in the country, state, sub-region, or city, be it in agriculture, extractive industries, manufacturing industries, or the tertiary sector. Adequate provision of infrastructure services removes constraints on the growth of these sectors. It is important to time investments in urban services and shelter to coincide with investments that result in accelerated city growth. Therefore, urban policies and programmes should essentially focus on increasing investment in urban infrastructure services. With the rapid urbanization that is now expected in ensuing decades in South Asia, it would be desirable to decentralize the instruments of infrastructure provision so that the agencies providing such services are able to finance themselves and can respond flexibly to the changing demands of a growing city. The mechanism of self-financing is important because it serves as a self-correcting procedure whereby higher-priority projects are implemented first and realistic planning becomes a necessity. Self-financing by an agency does not necessarily imply commercial financing. It can include subventions from higher-level governments; commercial, government, and soft loans; and servicing of these loans through affordable user charges. It does, however, mean greater agency autonomy than in a system in which infrastructure programmes are part of a central planning mechanism that is sought to be fully funded from above or through some form of credit allocation. What is important is that such autonomous agencies, such as various public utilities, develop the ability to respond to the emerging demands of people in growing cities.

Given the limited financial and managerial capacity of such government managed utilities in South Asia, it will be prudent to allow private initiatives to flourish whenever possible. This is not so much a matter of ideology as of necessity. Urban land development is a case in point. Urban development authorities, state housing boards, and urban local bodies have typically had a monopoly on land assembly and development in Indian cities since the late 1960s and early 1970s. They have usually not had the financial, planning, or managerial wherewithal to actually develop urban land as rapidly as it should have been, thus giving rise to unconscionable land price increases. It would be much better if private land developers are given a greater opportunity to perform this function, albeit within prudent norms, and in a competitive framework. But this has to be done carefully. Any monopoly elements in the private development of urban land would be even worse than public-sector monopolies.

Provision of public transport is also woefully inadequate in most South Asian cities, particularly at the second and third levels. Here too it will be much better if private investment in public transport is allowed to flourish in such a way that high service levels are achieved at low economic and financial costs. This is indeed possible through extensive use of private initiatives within a public regulatory framework. The availability of efficient public transport is essential, both for citizens' welfare and city efficiency. The scarcity of public resources has typically inhibited the provision of such transport availability in India, and thus this constraint should be loosened through the use of private resources for investment and service delivery.

The financing of urban infrastructure investment that will be needed over the next 20–30 years in South Asia will need much more focused attention. The task is essentially threefold. First, local governments have to be made creditworthy. Second, urban infrastructure projects must be made commercially viable. If these two requirements are met in the context of a developed capital market, the financial resources that are needed will get generated automatically. However, bond markets in South

Asian countries are not yet well developed and will still take quite some time to be large enough to provide for such resource needs. Hence, third, there is critical need for attention to the development of institutional mechanisms that efficiently intermediate financial resources for urban investment needs, while financial and capital markets are developed.

In the past, during the rapid urbanization phases of some countries in Europe, North America, and Latin America, available domestic savings were inadequate for financing the massive urban investment needs that arose during those periods. Thus, large cross-border flows were necessary to bring to bear external savings for urban infrastructure investment purposes in these countries and regions. The situation in South Asia is somewhat different at present. The available external resources are not being absorbed adequately and domestic savings have been rising. Yet huge resource gaps exist in investment in urban infrastructure since city governments are often not creditworthy and urban infrastructure projects are not perceived to be commercially viable. Thus, if these two generic problems are solved, the surpluses now being observed in these countries will get absorbed. Potentially, there could indeed be need for the use of higher magnitudes of external resources.

The strengthening of city management outlined earlier is therefore a must. As this strengthening takes place it will enable the organic connection of city governments with capital markets, both local and international. The key reform needed to make city governments creditworthy on a permanent basis is a revamp of the property tax systems that will make property taxes more buoyant. As cities of all sizes grow and densify, not only will the number of properties grow indefinitely in every city, but so should the average property value. Hence, a well-administered property tax system should yield buoyant property tax revenues on a continuous basis. For property tax to become more buoyant, urban property markets have to be liberalized: regulations, such as rent control and the any remaining urban land ceiling controls need to be scrapped or substantially modified. Subventions from higher levels of governments will have to continue, but these need to be made less discretionary and more predictable. More and more services need to be decentralized to the private sector if possible, or to corporatized public service providers, or through public-private partnerships. As these reforms take root, it will be possible for strengthened urban municipal administrations to become creditworthy and hence be enabled to raise resources for urban infrastructure investment and maintenance.

Urban infrastructure projects are typically messy, complex, and difficult to implement. Thus, project management skills in Asian cities need to be enhanced. For such projects to be seen as commercially viable there is a need to find all kinds of credit-enhancement mechanisms that can then effectively connect lenders and investors with urban infrastructure entities. Since urban infrastructure projects often have positive externalities that, by definition, cannot be captured by the project entities, there is a good case for governments to engage in different kinds of credit enhancement. Some possible measures are as follow.

1. *Availability of 'free' equity for project agencies:* Depending on the level of positive externalities, a project agency that is not otherwise commercially viable can become viable if, in principle, the government provides some share of equity that is not to be recompensed. The remaining equity can then receive appropriate market returns, as can the debt, while the project as a whole may have lower-than-market financial returns through high economic rates of returns. A similar role could be played by the provision of 'free' or subsidized debt.

2. *Guarantee mechanisms:* Different kinds of risks can be mitigated by different kinds of guarantee mechanisms. Such guarantee mechanisms can be commercially priced, or otherwise, depending on the source of risk.

3. *Appraisal agencies:* The existence of information asymmetries gives rise to reluctance by investors and lenders to invest in urban projects. The government can help in funding professional institutions specialized in such appraisal techniques, which can then build professional credibility and provide project appraisals that are respected, and therefore address information asymmetries effectively.

4. *Programmes for staff professionalization:* National governments and international institutions can invest in directed programmes to upgrade professional staff in local governments and project entities. This can then lead to more efficient governments as well as project executors and maintenance agencies, thereby promoting creditworthiness.

Many such examples can be given for the credit enhancement of local governments and urban project entities. All such measures would help in linking both domestic and international capital markets to the financing requirements of cities.

The United States developed the market for municipal bonds for financing urban governments—both for general revenue financing as well as for specific projects. Germany developed 'Pfandbriefs' that are issued by mortgage banks to finance lending for both housing and for municipal and state government lending. In both the cases, market development needed different levels of government and regulatory intervention. Such markets will need to be created for the financing of cities in Asia, and we will need to continue the search for new institutions and mechanisms that are relevant for each country in Asia.

The experience of rapid and massive urbanization that occurred in the 20th century was historically unprecedented. It first spread from Europe to North America, and then later to Latin America in the second half of the century. It is now the turn of Asia, and particularly of large countries like China, India, Indonesia, Pakistan, and Bangladesh, to undergo the kind of pace of urbanization that Latin America did in the last half century. This will pose new challenges in terms of city management and urban infrastructure investment that will need to be made in the relatively short time span of the next 30 years.

Whereas there is a great degree of lamentation regarding the ravages and ills that the urbanization process has brought in its wake, the world has coped relatively well with the huge magnitude of increase in urban population that has taken place in the last 50 years. Urban income levels have increased, urban services have continued to expand, and poverty has fallen. This experience should provide us with a great degree of confidence that the rapidly urbanizing Asian countries will indeed be able to cope in the next 30 years and beyond. The greater sophistication of financial markets and of various technologies that make it easier to make urban infrastructure investments, to charge for them, and to maintain them should actually make it easier to cope with the urbanization that is expected.

For these positive results to take place in South Asia, we need to strengthen all aspects of city management actively. This will need action at all levels: federal, state, and local. City management needs to be professionalized, city governments need to be made creditworthy, and urban infrastructure projects need to be made commercially viable.

Strengthening city management will enable a connection with capital markets, both national and international. To enable lenders and investors to invest in urban infrastructure it will be necessary to develop financial instruments for enhancing credit. Borrowing will then get facilitated by the public and private sectors alike. In this approach, we need to be strategic and develop long-term capital markets for investment in municipal infrastructure, as have been developed in different ways in Germany and the United States. The objective would be to move from a top–down to bottom–up marketization approach and develop new institutional forms and mechanisms. The practice of prudent macroeconomic and trade policies will be essential for maintaining continuous access to international capital markets.

REFERENCES

Expert Group on the Commercialisation of Infrastructure Projects (EGCIP). 1996. *The India Infrastructure Report: Policy Imperatives for Growth and Welfare.* New Delhi: National Council of Applied Economic Research.

Jackson, Kenneth T. 2005. 'The Promised City: Openness and Immigration in the Making of a World Metropolis', *FRBNY Economic Policy Review,* December, pp. 81–8.

Kelkar, Vijay and Rajiv Kumar. 1990. 'Industrial Growth in the Eighties: Emerging Policy Issues', *Economic and Political Weekly,* 23 January, 25: 209–22.

Marsh, Peter. 2006a. 'A New Manufacturing Mantra', *Financial Times,* 16 May.

———. 2006b. 'Feast of a Moveable Work Force', *Financial Times,* 17 May.

———. 2006c. 'India's Fight to Slay the Dragon', *Financial Times,*18 May.

McKinsey & Company. 2001. 'India—From Emerging to Surging', *McKinsey Quarterly,* December. Available at http://www.mckinsey.com.

———. 2010. *India's Urban Awakening: Building Inclusive Cities, Sustaining Economic Growth,* Report, McKinsey Global Institute.

Mohan, Rakesh. 2002. 'Small Scale Industry Policy in India: A Critical Evaluation', in Anne O. Krueger (ed.), *Economy Policy Reforms in the Indian Economy.* Chicago: University of Chicago Press, pp. 212–302.

———. 1994. *Understanding the Developing Metropolis: Lessons from the City Study of Bogota and Cali.* New York: Oxford University Press.

United Nations. 2007. *World Urbanization Prospects.* New York: United Nations.

World Bank. 2010. *World Development Indicators.* Available at http://data.worldbank.org/, accessed on 17August 2010.

Yusuf, Shahid and Kaoru Nabeshima. 2006. *Post Industrial Cities in East Asia.* Palo Alto: Stanford University Press.

10

Avoiding Informality Traps

Ravi Kanbur

There seems to be a consensus in the development economics and development policy discourse that 'informality' is 'bad'—for economic growth, equity, and poverty reduction. A variety of reasons are given as to why informality is bad. This relates, of course, to the different ways in which informality is conceptualized and operationalized, as well as to the precise definition of 'bad'. Differing conceptualizations, and differing objective functions, lead to various diagnoses of why informality is a trap, and thence to various policy prescriptions. Thus, we can end up with a situation where extension of labour regulations is put forward by some as a way of reducing informality, while the precise opposite, deregulation of labour markets, is proposed by others to achieve the same end.

These debates have intensified in recent years with evidence and arguments which state that during this period of globalization-driven growth, the extent of informality has not declined significantly, and has perhaps even increased in some countries. This has questioned a presumed 'natural' tendency for informality to decline with economic growth. Again, for some it is the economic strictures of heightened competition in an era of globalization that have led to informalization despite economic growth, or indeed as a natural concomitant of growth. But for others it is the prevalence of certain types of state interventions in labour and other markets that has prevented the growth spurt made possible by globalization from being translated into a decline in informality.

This chapter hopes to clarify the precise sense in which informality is bad—a trap for development and growth—and to highlight policies that could help escape the trap. A key component of the argument is achieving clarity on what exactly is meant by informality by different participants in the analytical and policy debates, and to show how these different perspectives lead naturally to their policy prescriptions. Based on this clarification, and the anchor of a well-specified objective function for development policy, we can then discuss and delineate policies for avoiding the informality trap.

The next section of this chapter sets about clarifying the notion of informality and looks at recent trends. The section that follows takes up the issue of the precise sense in which informality is a trap at individual and economy-wide levels. The final section follows on from this to propose a policy framework for avoiding informality traps; it also provides a conclusion.

WHAT EXACTLY IS INFORMALITY?

Ever since the notion of informality was introduced to the literature by Keith Hart (1973), it has played a central role in the development discourse. There are many reasons for this. The notion has been elastic enough to accommodate a range of interpretations with sufficient commonality to allow interpreters to feel that they are discussing the same phenomenon. Hart himself used informality to denote economic activity that was outside the reach of state regulations, either because the regulations did not apply or because they were not enforced. But in subsequent literature, informality was also seen in light of an earlier discourse on 'dualistic development' (Lewis 1954), characterizing the economy as divided into a 'modern' and a 'traditional' sector. Informality has been linked to poverty and to economic activity with low productivity and low-income-generation prospects. And, most recently, it has been expanded to generally capture all employment in which there is no employer-provided social protection. Cutting across these related but different uses of the term informality are the concepts and operationalizations used by official statistics, which frame policy debates by producing figures on the levels and trends in informality.

It is useful to start with official definitions of informality as an entry point into measurement and concepts. The Indian National Commission on Employment in the Unorganized Sector (NCEUS 2009: 3) captured recent trends in the debate defining informality as:

Informal sector: All unincorporated private enterprises owned by individuals or households engaged in the sale and production of goods and services operated on a proprietary or partnership basis and with less than ten total workers.

Informal worker/employment: Those working in the [informal] sector or households, excluding regular workers with social security benefits provided by the employers and [including] the workers in the formal sector without any employment and social security benefits provided by the employers.

Informal economy: The informal sector and its workers plus the informal workers in the formal sector constitute the informal economy.

The NCEUS statement crystallizes a broadening in the concept of informality in terms of official statistical sources. The traditional definition, still prevalent, is based on the characteristics of units of economic activity. This is how the International Conference of Labour Statisticians (ICLS 2003: 48) puts it:

Conceptualizing the informal sector as a subsector of the SNA institutional sector 'households', the Fifteenth ICLS defined *informal sector enterprises* on the basis of the following criteria:

- They are private unincorporated enterprises … i.e. enterprises owned by individuals or households that are not constituted as separate legal entities independently of their owners, and for which no complete accounts are available that would permit a financial separation of the production activities of the enterprise from the other activities of its owner(s).
- All or at least some of the goods or services produced are meant for sale or barter.
- Their size in terms of employment is below a certain threshold to be determined according to national circumstances, and/or they are not registered under specific forms of national legislation (such as factories' or commercial acts, tax or social security laws, professional groups' regulatory acts, or similar acts, laws or regulations established by national legislative bodies as distinct from local regulations for issuing trade licences or business permits), and/or their employees (if any) are not registered.
- They are engaged in non-agricultural activities, including secondary non-agricultural activities of enterprises in the agricultural sector.

This definition captures several strands in the conceptualization of informality. The Lewis (1954) modern/traditional dichotomy is present in the incorporated/unincorporated distinction ('no complete accounts available'). The Hart (1973) perspective is further present in the criterion that a range of laws and regulations does not apply to these enterprises. The size criterion, present in many, if not most, official definitions (including that of NCEUS), is important because as we shall see, smallness of size is often associated in the literature with low productivity and growth potential. Finally, note that agriculture is excluded in this definition, although some authors include it as a part of the informal sector.

With this base, Chen (2006: 76) points to a recent drive to widen the circumstances relative to which informality is defined: 'Extend the focus to include not only enterprises that are not legally regulated but also *employment relationships* that are not legally regulated or protected. In brief, the new definition of the "informal economy" focuses on the nature of employment in addition to the characteristics of enterprises.'

The NCEUS (2009) definition captures this broadening, as does the recent OECD publication, *Is Informal Normal?* (Jutting and de Laiglesia 2009:19): 'Informal employment refers to jobs or activities in the production and sales of legal goods and services which are not regulated or protected by the state.'

Of course, this broadening then has to be operationalized and the NCEUS (2009) definition is one such attempt for India. The essence of the operationalization, however, is to add to employment in the traditionally defined informal sector the employment in the formal sector which is not protected by the state (the latter itself being operationalized by the NCEUS as cases where there is no employer-provided social security benefits). Employment in the informal sector, therefore, is smaller than that in the informal economy. However, national statistics are not as yet fully geared to producing estimates of employment in the broader informal economy. As Charmes (2009: 9) notes, 'the use of proxies is still necessary for understanding trends in informal employment'. Self-employment is one such proxy (Charmes 2009: 30): 'Self-employment is the complement to wage employment (employees) in total employment and comprises own-account workers, employers, contributing family workers and members of producers' cooperatives .... The growth of self-employment ... can be interpreted as an indicator of the growing importance of less codified labour relations and therefore of informalisation.'

Other authors rely on household surveys and questions asked of workers about their work conditions to identify the extent and nature of informality (for example, NCEUS 2009 and Unni 2005). Do these alternative definitions and conceptualizations matter in terms of the broad picture on the extent of informality? The answer is that for South Asia the sheer magnitude of informality is so high that while the alternative conceptualizations matter a lot for the discourse on what to do about informality, they are not so important for the broad numerical characterizations of informality at the national level. Thus, for example, in a recent review on informality in South Asia, Chen and Doane (2008: 7) conclude as follows:

According to recent national labour force surveys, informal employment comprised a significant share of non-agricultural employment in all countries: accounting for 62 per cent of non-agricultural employment in Bangladesh, 72 per cent in India, 74 per cent in Nepal and Pakistan, and 45 per cent in Sri Lanka ....Since a relatively large share of total employment is in agriculture and employment in agriculture is largely informal, the share of informal employment in total employment is higher still accounting for 79 per cent of total employment in Bangladesh, 92 per cent in India, over 80 per cent in Nepal, and 66 per cent in Sri Lanka.

In a forthcoming World Bank study (2011: Figure 2.6), the following estimates are given of the share of informal employment (per cent) in non-agricultural employment and in total employment respectively: Afghanistan (79, 92), Bangladesh (74, 87), Bhutan (51, 88), India (72, 88), Maldives (21, 40), Nepal (82, 95), Pakistan (78, 88), and Sri Lanka (58, 71). Notice the broad agreement between these figures and those cited by Chen and Doane (2008: 7). Notice also (apart from the island state of Maldives) the sheer size of the informal economy in all of these countries.

On trends, however, some differences emerge between different estimates. Charmes (2009) finds that the share of informal employment in total non-agricultural employment increased from 76.2 per cent in 1985–9 to 73.7 per cent in 1990–4, and 83.4 per cent in 1995–9. But the World Bank (2011) study reaches different conclusions for India for a later dataset.

Even in countries where informality is on the decline, there remains the question (in India, for example) of whether the decline is fast enough relative to the rapid rate of growth of the economy as a whole.

The informal sector and the informal economy remain overwhelmingly large in South Asia. They are also heterogeneous. To begin with, there is the issue of agriculture versus non-agriculture. Assessments of the evolution of informality at the national level cannot be divorced from a general discussion of the transition of an economy from an agricultural base towards manufacturing and services. Even within non-agriculture there is a spread between self-employed entrepreneurs, own-account workers, unpaid family workers, and causal labour (Chen 2006). And there is heterogeneity across sectors (Chen and Doane 2008: 9):

In India ... 33 per cent of all male informal workers are engaged in trade, 23 per cent in manufacturing, 16 per cent in construction, 21 per cent in other services (mainly in transport and storage), and 7 per cent in other sectors .... In Pakistan, the sector in which the largest percentage of all informal workers is engaged is …. trade (34 per cent) followed by manufacturing and personal services (both around 20 per cent).

This heterogeneity should warn us against a uniform policy towards the informal sector, and this will be taken up in later sections.

Another type of heterogeneity is emphasized by this author in an earlier work (Kanbur 2009) as particularly relevant for how policy debates are framed. In that work I follow throughout, and specify in greater detail, conceptualizations where formality and informality are seen as pertaining to state regulations and laws. Those economic activities which come under the purview of a given set of rules and laws, and do not evade them, are conceptualized as 'formal' (A). But it should be noted that there are then two distinct categories of 'informal': activities that are covered but are evading these regulations illegally (B), and activities that are not covered by the set of state rules and laws being discussed. And even within the second of these there are two further categories—those that have adjusted their activity to avoid the regulations by falling outside their purview (C), and those that would always have been outside (D). These four categories of economic activity—A, B, C, and D—turn out to be central in framing opposing policy positions. Thus, those who see labour and other regulations as being the 'cause' of informality focus on category C. Those who support direct interventions to help the informal economy focus on category D. Very few discuss category C explicitly, although evasion of laws is sometimes part of the discourse of those who support and oppose labour regulations. Of course, getting empirical estimates of these different types of informality is not easy, it is almost non-existent in the literature, even though they are crucial in policy positions taken up by different groups in the informality discourse.

WHY IS INFORMALITY BAD?

There are different senses in which informality can be seen as being 'bad'. The most obvious is that it is correlated with low incomes and with poverty status. For India, the NCEUS (2007: 24) estimated that: 'Workers in the unorganised sector had a much higher incidence of poverty (20.5 per cent) than their counterparts in the organised sector (11.3 per cent), almost double. This is an indicator of inadequate income levels and the extent of vulnerability of workers in the unorganised sector.'

Surveying global estimates, a recent OECD study concludes (Jutting and de Laglesia 2009: 18): 'Informal jobs are often precarious, have low productivity and are of low general quality … Moreover, certain groups, such as the young or women, seem to be over represented within this category of jobs.' The central issue for policy, however, is that of causality. Is informality a mere correlate of poverty and low development, an indicator that captures broader processes, or is the informality itself the cause of poverty and a break on development? The literature touches on both these aspects.

Linking to the early literature on growth and development, for example in the Lewis (1954) model of development, a decline in the relative weight of the traditional sector was seen as a natural concomitant and an indicator of growth and development. In the Lewis (1954) model, a traditional sector supplies labour to the modern sector at a wage given by subsistence. As the modern sector expands through capital accumulation, labour transfers to this modern sector; the transfer is necessary for, and a correlate of, economic growth. Lewis (1954) saw the agriculture sector and the urban petty trade and casual labour sector as being the suppliers of labour to the modern capitalist sector (which in his formulation included manufacturing and plantation agriculture). Now, in this set-up of 'unlimited supplies of labour' there would be no improvement in the standard of living of the workers as economic growth took place, but the size of the informal economy would diminish over time until the 'Lewis turning point' was reached and wages started rising in the traditional sector as well. In this perspective, therefore, informality is bad because it is a signal of an insufficiently low level and pace of development and of the time still needed before incomes in that sector start rising. But notice also that in this perspective, 'informality'—a traditional sector which supplies labour to the modern sector at a given wage—contributes to accumulation and hence growth by keeping wages down.

In contrast to Lewis's 'classical' model of the economy, once the Lewis turning point is reached we are in a post-Lewis 'neoclassical world' in which two sectors (manufacturing and agriculture, say) compete for labour. But if in one of these sectors (manufacturing) the labour market is not perfectly competitive, wages are kept above their marginal product through labour power or state intervention. This induces migration in the hope of a 'good' job, but not all migrants can get these jobs, and this creates a pool of labour which is neither in agriculture nor in manufacturing but waiting for a chance to get into the good jobs sector. This labour engages in a number of activities that are low-productivity and low-income, this low income being balanced by the prospect of a high-income job. Lewis (1954: 2) already had this sort of activity in mind when he talked about the workers on the docks, the young men who rush forward asking to carry your bag as you appear, the jobbing gardener, and the like. These occupations usually have a multiple of the number they need, each of them earning very small sums from occasional employment … retail trading is also exactly of this type; it is enormously expanded in overpopulated economies; each trader makes only a few sales; markets are crowded with stalls.

This type of employment matches well the informal sector and informal work discussed in the previous section. However, in the line of argument developed by Harris and Todaro (1970) and others, the 'cause' of this informality is very clearly the above-market clearing wage in the (what we might now call) formal sector. If the high 'minimum wage' or labour regulations more generally did not exist, then the informal sector would not exist either. Here the informality is bad not only because those in informal activity have a low income, but because labour allocation is inefficient.

Generalizing beyond labour regulations to regulation of enterprises, the argument goes that as a result, the (non-agricultural) informal sector also has enterprises that are avoiding or evading the regulations that define formal activity. That these enterprises are smaller than those in the formal sector follows from the structure of the regulations and their evasion—regulations might apply only to enterprises above a certain size, or enforcement of regulations might be particularly difficult for small enterprises. Either way, it is then argued that enterprise size in the informal sector is sub-optimally small, foregoing economies of scale and dynamic prospects of investment and growth. This argument has been made powerfully for Latin America by Levy (2007). For South Asia, the thrust of the 'missing middle' discourse is essentially that regulation of enterprises has led to a bimodal distribution of enterprise size, with enterprises having to be either very large to overcome the costs of regulations, or very small to avoid them. For India this argument has been made forcefully by Mazumdar and Sarkar (2008).

This low productivity of small enterprises translates into low wages for their workers and low incomes for their owners, linking the productivity and growth perspective to a perspective driven by poverty.

This argument would seem to be cut and dried—the regulations that define the formal sector also, in effect, create the informal sector of small-scale enterprises with low productivity and low incomes. The informal sector is 'bad' in this sense, but escaping the trap depends on the regulations being lifted. However, not all small-scale enterprises are small because they are avoiding or evading regulations. In terms of categories

A, B, C, and D mentioned in the previous section, there is still category D—activities that are not touched by regulations and would remain small with low productivity and low incomes even if the regulations that bind the formal sector were removed.

To give an illustrative example, suppose the regulations state that an enterprise has to register and then pay various worker benefits if its size exceeds nine workers. Now consider an enterprise that would have had 15 workers without the regulations. This enterprise has three options. It could continue to have an enterprise size greater than nine and comply with all relevant regulations (but presumably be of size less than 15 because of the costs of the regulations), in which case it would be formal (A). It could continue to have an enterprise size greater than nine but evade the regulations (but presumably at an enterprise size much less than 15 because smaller size aids evasion). This would be informal category B. Or it could adjust its size just below nine so that the regulations do not apply to it (category C). But what of enterprises whose 'natural size', that is, even without regulations, is below nine (category D)? Enterprises in category D would be classified as informal; they would be small and for that reason have lower productivity and low incomes, but removal of regulations would not be the way of releasing the informal trap.

Before proceeding further one caveat should be noted. While informality is certainly strongly correlated with low incomes and poverty, it is not all bad news. There is heterogeneity within the informal economy, and above-poverty incomes can also be found in this sector. For India, NCEUS (2007: 50) documents this and comments further as follows:

The Commission considers it important to also emphasize the fact that the category of self employed, unlike that of casual workers, is not necessarily and uniformly poor. As we shall see later in this Chapter, there are those with some significant physical and/or human capital and also those with very little capital. Independent professionals such as doctors, architects, lawyers, accountants, small workshop owners, urban shop owners, etc. may be self employed but with incomes that are several times higher than a street vendor, rickshaw puller or a handloom weaver. Our focus and concern here is on the latter groups, who lack the critical minimum by way of either physical or human capital or both.

This perspective is also confirmed at the global level by the International Labour Organization (ILO 2002: 31), which recognizes

the links between working informally and being poor are not always simple. On the one hand, not all jobs in the informal economy yield paltry incomes.

The background studies prepared for this report indicate that many in the informal economy, especially the self employed, in fact earn more than unskilled or low-skilled workers in the formal economy. There is much innovation and many dynamic growth-oriented segments in the informal economy, some of which require considerable knowledge and skills. One of these is the fast-growing information and communications technology (ICT) sector in the large cities of India.

This heterogeneity, at the very least, cautions against a uniform policy stance. It also suggests that it may not be informality in and of itself that is the sole cause of poverty; it has to be seen in conjunction with other factors and policy has to address these other factors as well.

Finally, a related issue at the micro-level is whether there is in fact mobility out of informality and poverty, or whether there is persistence over the working life of an individual, and perhaps across generations. Fields (1975, 2005) introduced the idea of the informal sector as one where workers can be seen as waiting to move from 'bad jobs' to 'good jobs' and that within the informal sector there could be a lower tier and upper tier of bad and less bad jobs. In Latin America there is now growing evidence of significant mobility between the formal and informal sectors. In Mexico, for example, 19.7 per cent of the workers in the informal sector in 2002 were in the formal sector in 2005, while 18.2 per cent of the workers in the formal sector ended up in the informal sector three years later (Gagnon 2009: Box 5.2).

We do not, unfortunately, have the same extent of information on mobility by labour-market status for South Asia, mainly because of the paucity of panel datasets. For mobility by poverty status, based on household survey panels, Mckay and Baulch (2004: Table 1) present estimates for the probability that a household with consumption below the national poverty line would still be poor in five years' time. The range of estimates is 25–35 per cent for India, Pakistan, and Bangladesh. This means, of course, that the probability of moving out of poverty is in the range 65–75 per cent. Bhide and Mehta (2010: 18, 20) review the results on rural poverty dynamics in India and conclude:

The fact that a fairly significant proportion of the poor continue to remain poor over long periods of time, significant proportion exit from poverty, and many non-poor enter into poverty highlight [*sic*] the need to understand the factors that influence this dynamics .... In summary, factors that are related to the *persistence of poverty* are the scheduled tribe status, larger household size, increase in household size, larger number of dependent children and increase in number of dependent children.

Escape from poverty is enabled by literacy, ownership of a house, increase in cultivated area and income from livestock. In addition, infrastructure and a large urban population in the neighbourhood were other factors that helped exit from poverty.

To the extent that poverty and informality are correlated, this suggests both that there is mobility and that the escape from poverty is dependent on a range of factors going beyond informality itself.

To summarize, there are several perspectives in the literature on the question of why informality is bad—macro versus micro and correlation versus causation. At the macro-level, in a dual economy framework the size of the informal sector is seen as an indicator of the level of per capita income and development since growth in the modern sector relies upon and then depletes labour in the traditional sector. At the same time, dynamism and growth potential is seen to be negatively affected by the smallness of size of enterprises in the informal sector at the micro-level. There is also the issue of the extent to which regulations and laws affecting the labour market protect those in the informal sector and the extent to which they instead stand in the way of transmitting the beneficial effects of economic growth to the poor in the informal sector and of escape from the informal sector to the 'better jobs' in the formal sector. With this background, we now move to a discussion of policy options for avoiding 'informality traps'.

HOW CAN INFORMALITY TRAPS BE AVOIDED?

Informality—defined as a larger share of the economy accounted for by activities outside the net of a well-defined set of state laws and regulations (categories B, C, and D as discussed earlier)—is very high in South Asia compared to the global average. Moreover, it has not declined by nearly as much as might have been predicted by the growth rates in the region. Particularly in the last two decades, growth rates have been at historical highs, and yet the size of the informal sector has not declined by very much. Indeed, by some accounts it may actually have increased.

Before discussing policy responses to these trends, let us consider possible explanations for them in terms of the framework developed in the second section. A useful way of approaching this question is to ask how each of the three categories of informal activity—B, C, and D—might have behaved over the past two decades.

Category B is economic activity that is covered by regulations but the regulations are being evaded— illegality in other words. The size of this category is determined by the strength of enforcement. It has been argued that in the face of growing global competition, authorities are increasingly 'turning a blind eye' to evasion of regulations, such as on registration and worker benefits if the enterprise is larger than 10 workers. Although difficult to isolate directly in official statistics for obvious reasons, indirect evidence on minimum wage violations and anecdotal back-up suggest that this feature has indeed increased over the last two decades (ILO 2002: 52–3):

The labour inspection services in many developing and transition countries are not adequately staffed or equipped to effectively enforce standards in the informal economy, especially in terms of covering the myriads of micro- and small-enterprises or the growing numbers of homeworkers ... The system of labour courts and industrial tribunals, especially in developing countries, may be very weak, may lack resources and is all too frequently corrupt. Strengthening the labour administration and justice systems and promoting good governance would go a long way to achieving decent work and enabling informal workers to move into the formal economy.

Category C is economic activity that has adjusted itself to fall outside the purview of regulations and thus avoid them. As noted earlier, an example would be an enterprise that would have hired 15 workers but chooses to hire nine workers to avoid registration and the obligations and costs that would then follow. Another example would be an enterprise that would have been vertically integrated, with many functions from cleaning to accounts carried out by enterprise employees. These functions are now outsourced to enterprises that have less than 10 workers.

Category C is the one around which most of the debate on regulations has focused. The fact that firms adjust their operations to avoid regulations has been seen as evidence of the inappropriateness of the regulations. To many, the large size of the 'informal sector' is nothing other than a testament to the private and social costs of the web of regulations that it is trying to avoid by (legally) getting out of the way. To others, the increase in informalization through this category is a reflection of the evolution of technology. Breaking up of production processes into smaller components is now possible in a way that it was not three decades ago—the rise of 'cluster-based' production in China is but one example of this (Long and Zhang 2009). In this view the increased informalization is explained by changing technology in the face of current regulation structures appropriate for the cost and benefit structures of activity integration of three decades ago. More generally, the point being made is that part of the explanation of category B informality is the evolution of the regulation structure itself relative to that of technology.

Note also that categories B and C are not entirely independent of each other. A more lax enforcement structure will increase the share of category C, but for that reason will decrease the share of category B—there is now less reason to adjust economic activity to get out of the way of regulations, since the regulations themselves are being enforced less intensively.

Finally, let us come to category D—those activities which are outside the scope of current regulations. If this category has grown in relative size then it could be either because of the retreat of some types of regulations or because of increasing difficulties of activities to evolve in a way that brings them into the regulatory net—specifically difficulties of activities growing to a size sufficient to warrant their registration (taking into account the costs and benefits of regulation).

With this background, and building on the discussion in the last two sections, there are two lines of argument which point us to the reasons for and the interventions needed to avoid informality traps. The first focuses on the efficiency and growth costs of high levels of informality, while the second highlights the distributional consequences. Both would like greater formality, but may differ on the methods for achieving this.

Taking the efficiency angle first, it is possible to further classify the arguments into two broad themes. The first pays great attention to the size of an enterprise. It argues that enterprise size in the informal sector in developing countries is too small to reap the gains from efficiency, and the costs imposed by regulations on the formal sector encourage the adoption of smaller enterprise size than would otherwise be the case by those that come under the purview of regulations. This can happen in one of two ways. When registration is required at a certain enterprise size, the enterprise can decide not to grow beyond that level even though it has the potential to do so. Or it can grow beyond that size but evade regulations—the argument now is that the size will still be lower than the firm would otherwise wish it to be, because evasion is easier for smaller enterprises. To this are added other costs of illegality, all of which hamper growth and efficiency.

The second theme in the efficiency strand of concern over rising informality is that by remaining informal an economic activity loses access to contractual and other benefits that accrue through state legal and service structures. There are several elements to this argument. For example, registration of an enterprise can bring benefits through recognition in courts. Thus, although the firm may face some costs of registration, such as having to pay employment benefits, it gets benefits as well. This is, of course, in principle—it all depends on how well the enforcement of courts and contracts works. But this line of argument takes us to category D, those who are completely outside the net of regulations and laws. If a subset of these laws, for example those pertaining to property rights, could be extended to this category then, it is argued by Hernando de Soto (2000) and others that the productive potential of even quite small home-based enterprises in urban slums could be enhanced by allowing them to use their property as collateral.

Notice, however, that while the first theme seems to suggest a narrowing of the purview of the state, for example registration and worker benefits being required at a much larger size of enterprise to encourage increase of enterprise size, the second suggests (albeit in a different domain) a broadening of the purview of the state, for example providing legal protection of the courts in the heart of urban slums.

Let us now turn to more distribution-based concerns about the trend of growing informality. First of all, notice that there is some convergence between the efficiency and distribution-based views for category D of informality—those activities that are completely outside the purview of the state. For some state interventions, for example integration into the legal system if it could be done well, there might be agreement that this could be efficiency enhancing and distribution improving, since this category will generally contain among the poorest of society.

But consider now the distributional concern on increasing informality that flows from the fact that, by and large, workers in the informal sector do not have social security benefits. This is either because enterprises are not legally required to provide these benefits (categories C and D), or because they are required to but are not providing them (category B). If the response to this is to extend the scope of state regulations by, for example, decreasing the size of enterprise at which registration and the payment of benefits becomes mandatory, then this could lead to a further decline in enterprise size and thus loss in productivity feared by the efficiency strand of concern over growing informality. However, if the response is to provide social security benefits through more general means, not tied to place of work or enterprise, then the efficiency concern may be mitigated (Levy 2007).

Based on this discussion, it should be clear that there is no single overarching policy intervention that can address the growth and poverty consequences of the high and stubbornly stable levels of informality in South Asia. If the objectives of policy combine efficiency and distribution, then a number of interventions could enhance both.

1. Improved enforcement of regulations (to reduce the size of category B).
2. A review of regulations, particularly the enterprise size cut-off, in light of new technology and competition which changes the old cost benefit of optimal enterprise size (to reduce the size of category C).
3. An expansion of state services, both hard and soft infrastructure (the latter including property rights and contract enforcement), to enhance the productivity of those outside state structures (to reduce poverty in category D and to aid its mobility into formality).

Let us discuss each of these in turn, and the possible trade-offs that policymakers may face.

To many, the widespread violation of labour and enterprise regulations that is seen in South Asia and elsewhere in developing countries is itself an indication of the inappropriateness of the regulations. Whatever the resolution of the debates on the regulations themselves, there is little point in passing laws and regulations without, at the same time, focusing on their enforcement, including in this inspections and monitoring as well as court proceedings. There is a strong case for strengthening labour inspectorates as well as enterprise inspectorates more generally to ensure that laws and regulations are complied with.

The sharpest debates in the literature concern the role that regulations themselves play in creating informality by inducing the adoption of production structures that avoid them. Such avoidance will always be present—the real questions are to do with how easy it is, how socially costly it is, and how regulations need to be adjusted to the costs and benefits of avoidance (and evasion). The 'missing middle' literature on South Asia suggests strongly that regulations conditioned on enterprise size of say 10 workers lead to enterprises that are below this size to avoid the regulations or well above this size to recoup the costs of regulations. This would lead to a recommendation to raise the enterprise size at which regulations bite, which would help induce more enterprises to become formal. At the same time, changes in technology and the pressures of competition may be leading to greater viability of smaller-scale enterprises, which would suggest a tightening of the enterprise size at which regulations bite. There is no clear answer to this question, which needs more empirical research to establish the trade-offs.

The distinction between category C ('informality by choice') and category D ('naturally informal') is a key one in policy debates in South

Asia and globally (see, for example, Chen 2006 and Maloney 2004). If category C was dominant, then the focus would be on regulations governing enterprises and their enforcement. If, on the other hand, category D was dominant, then the focus would be on how to help those who are outside the current swathe of state regulations. Unfortunately, there is no detailed empirical work that gives us a handle on the relative size of 'informality by choice' and 'naturally informal' in South Asia. However, given the huge size of the informal economy, it is likely that category D is of substantial significance.

Direct assistance to the 'naturally informal' sector must therefore play an important part in any policy framework to address informality as a cause of low productivity and poverty. Chen and Doane (2008: 35–6) propose an array of policies under the headings of 'Regulation, Protection, and Promotion'. Specific policies include: 'regulation (and taxation) of informal enterprises', 'legal protection of informal workers and enterprises, including commercial rights for informal businesses, labour rights for informal wage workers, property rights for all informal workers', 'social protection for all informal workers through targeted schemes, universal schemes, some mix thereof', 'raising productivity of informal enterprises', and 'increasing employability of informal workers'.

This emphasizes again that no single solution will do—a range of interventions is needed. It is this broad perspective that leads Jutting and de Laiglesia (2009) to propose a three-pronged strategy for addressing informality:

Informal employment comprises different phenomena that require distinct policy approaches

1. For the world's working poor, working informally is often the only way to participate in the labour market. Policies should consequently try to unlock these people from their low-productivity activities .... Specific recommendations include active labour market policies such as training and skill development programmes, that reopen the doors to formality.
2. If informal employment is a deliberate choice to avoid taxes or administrative burdens ... [c]ountries should aim to introduce formal structures that can offer the same or (higher) levels of flexibility and efficiency that informal channels occasionally may provide .... [This report also] advises countries to spend more resources on labour inspections....
3. In many countries, finally, informal employment is mainly a consequence of insufficient job creation in the formal economy. [This report] thus also recognises the need for a general push for more employment opportunities within the formal sector.

CONCLUSION

The central thrust of this chapter is to emphasize the heterogeneity of the informality discourse. While informality has a core commonality of concern in analysis and policy, there are diverse conceptualizations, empirical measurements, causal channels, and theories of informality and policy concerns. For policy, the single most important conclusion is that there is no 'magic bullet' to address the concerns that arise with informality, and that a range of interventions needs to be examined and implemented.

The conceptualization of informality ranges from the 'traditional' sector of Lewis (1954), seen in contra-distinction to a 'modern' or 'capitalist' sector to 'activities outside the reach of the state regulation' of Hart (1973), and 'lack of employer provided protection and benefits' of the ICLS (International Conference of Labour Statisticians 2003). In between, and overlapping, are conceptualizations and empirical implementations that touch on the organization structure of enterprise, the size of enterprise, and poverty and vulnerability of workers.[1] Alternative conceptualizations and measures do not make a big difference to the size of the informal sector, which is very large in South Asia, or to the conclusion that it has not declined commensurate with the growth rates of countries in the region. Where the differing perspectives do make a difference, however, is in policy prescriptions—with some measures receiving greater emphasis than others depending on the core conceptualization in play.

The literature as a whole, however, suggests that a range of policy interventions will be necessary to address the issue of informality. Higher growth, but growth whose sectoral pattern is more labour absorbing is the first and most general policy conclusion. With the given level and structure of growth, extending the coverage of state protection to workers currently uncovered is the second recommendation. At the same time, reviewing current interventions to improve their flexibility and application is also needed. Direct measures to increase the productivity and incomes of enterprises in the informal sector, which include targeted measures of training and enterprise support as well as general measures of bringing legal and other state infrastructure support to these enterprises, are another recommendation. Finally, better enforcement of regulations that do exist and assessing enforcement possibilities before regulations are passed are also recommendations that emerge from the literature.

[1] For a full review, see Guha-Khasnobis et al. (2006).

Informality has not disappeared in South Asia and is unlikely to do so in the coming two decades. Policymakers need to recognize that it is a complex phenomenon and that it is an integral part of the economy and of society. Addressing informality to reduce poverty and spur development requires a better understanding of the phenomenon, the readiness to eschew simplistic single solutions, and the willingness to adopt a wide range of country-specific tailor-made policies and interventions.

REFERENCES

Bhide, Shashank and Aasha Kapur Mehta. 2010. 'Poverty and Poverty Dynamics in India: Estimates, Determinants and Policy Responses'. Available at http://www.chronicpoverty.org/uploads/publication-files/mehta-bhide.pdf, accessed on 3 November 2010.

Charmes, Jacques. 2009. 'Concepts, Measurements and Trends', in Johannes P. Jutting and Juan R. de Laiglesia (eds), *Is Informal Normal? Towards More and Better Jobs in Developing Countries.* Paris: OECD.

Chen, Martha. 2006. 'Rethinking the Informal Economy: Linkages with the Formal Sector and the Formal Regulatory Environment', in Basudeb Guha-Khasnobis, Ravi Kanbur, and Elinor Ostrom (eds), *Linking the Formal and Informal Economy: Concepts and Policies.* Oxford: Oxford University Press, pp. 75–92.

Chen, Martha and Donna Doane. 2008. 'Informality in South Asia: A Review'. Available at http://www.wiego.org/publications/SIDA-regional-reviews/South-Asia-Review-Chen-2008.pdf, accessed on 28 October 2010.

de Soto, Hernando. 2000. *The Mystery of Capital: Why Capitalism Triumphs in the West and Fails Everywhere Else.* New York: Basic Books.

Fields, Gary. 1975. 'Rural–Urban Migration, Urban Unemployment and Underemployment, and Job-search Activity in LDCs', *Journal of Development Economics,* 2 (2): 165–87.

———. 2005. 'A Guide to Multisector Labor Market Models', World Bank Social Protection Discussion Paper Series, No. 0505, World Bank, Washington, DC.

Gagnon, Jason. 2009. 'Moving Out of Bad Jobs: More Mobility, More Opportunity', in Johannes P. Jutting and Juan R. de Laiglesia (eds), *Is Informal Normal? Towards More and Better Jobs in Developing Countries.* Paris: OECD.

Guha-Khasnobis, Basudeb, Ravi Kanbur, and Elinor Ostrom (eds). 2006. *Linking the Formal and Informal Economy: Concepts and Policies.* Oxford: Oxford University Press.

Harris, J. and M. Todaro. 1970. 'Migration, Unemployment and Development: A Two-Sector Analysis', *American Economic Review,* 60 (1): 126–42.

Hart, Keith. 1973. 'Informal Income Opportunities and Urban Employment in Ghana', *Journal of Modern African Studies,* 11 (1): 61–89.

ICLS. 2003. *Seventeenth International Conference of Labour Statisticians: Main Report.* Available at http://www.ilo.org/public/english/bureau/stat/download/17thicls/r1gen.pdf, accessed on 28 October 2010.

ILO. 2002. *Decent Work in the Informal Economy.* Geneva: International Labour Office. Available at http://www.ilo.org/public/english/standards/relm/ilc/ilc90/pdf/rep-vi.pdf, accessed on 3 November 2010.

Jutting, Johannes P. and Juan R. de Laiglesia (eds). 2009. *Is Informal Normal? Towards More and Better Jobs in Developing Countries.* Paris: OECD.

Kanbur, Ravi. 2009. 'Conceptualizing Informality: Regulation and Enforcement', *Indian Journal of Labour Economics*, 52 (1): 33–42.

Levy, Santiago. 2007. *Good Intentions, Bad Outcomes: Social Policy, Informality and Economic Growth in Mexico.* Washington, DC: Brookings Institution.

Lewis, W. Arthur. 1954. 'Economic Development with Unlimited Supplied of Labour', *Manchester School of Economic and Social Studies*, 22: 139–91.

Long, Cheryl and Xiaobo Zhang. 2009. 'Cluster Based Industrialization in China: Financing and Performance', International Food Policy Research Institute, Working Paper No. 00937. Available at http://www.ifpri.org/sites/default/files/publications/ifpridp00937.pdf, accessed on 3 November 2010.

Maloney, William. 2004. 'Informality Revisited', *World Development*, 32 (7): 1159–78.

Mazumdar, Dipak and Sandip Sarkar. 2008. *Globalization, Labor Markets and Inequality in India.* New York: Routledge. Available at http://www.idrc.ca/openebooks/373-7/, accessed on 3 November 2010.

McKay, Andrew and Bob Baulch. 2004. 'How Many Chronically Poor People Are There in the World? Some Preliminary Estimates', Working Paper No. 45, Chronic Poverty Research Centre, University of Manchester. Available at http://www.chronicpoverty.org/uploads/publication-files/WP45-McKay-Baulch.pdf, accessed on 3 November 2010.

NCEUS. 2007. *Report on Conditions of Work and Promotion of Livelihoods in the Unorganised Sector.* Available at http://nceuis.nic.in/Condition-of-workers-sep-2007.pdf, accessed on 3 November 2010.

———. 2009. *The Challenge of Employment in India, An Informal Economy Perspective, Volume I: Main Report.* Available at http://nceuis.nic.in/The-Challenge-of-Employment-in-India.pdf, accessed on 20 October 2010.

Unni, Jeemol. 2005. 'Wages and Incomes in Formal and Informal Sectors in India', *Indian Journal of Labour Economics*, 48 (2): 311–17.

World Bank. 2011 (Forthcoming). *South Asia Employment Report.*

11

Managing Conflict

Lakshmi Iyer*

South Asia experienced one of the fastest rates of economic growth in the first decade of the new millennium and several factors suggest that the region is poised to continue on a path of high growth. These factors include the demographic dividend, the rising middle class, a thriving entrepreneurial culture, and policies to encourage economic openness and provide a better environment for private businesses. For these favourable factors to be fully utilized, ensuring political and policy stability in the region is essential. This will be a major challenge for South Asia going forward, given that the region has experienced a high degree of internal conflict over the past decade.

Internal conflict refers to violence carried out by a relatively organized group of non-state actors and directed specifically with the intent of destabilizing the state. In 2009, South Asia experienced the second-highest rate of fatalities from armed conflict across the world, and more than a million people are estimated to have been displaced as a result of internal conflict. Such conflicts pose a significant challenge to political stability and the ability of the state to implement policies. Of the different types of institutions that have been identified as important to development—market-creating institutions, market-regulating institutions, and market-substituting institutions—the type that has received relatively little attention is that of conflict-management or

* I would like to thank Pranab Bardhan and Ejaz Ghani for helpful comments.

market-legitimizing institutions.[1] What are the factors that predispose regions to a higher risk of conflict? What policies can governments adopt to bring an end to such a conflict and prevent its recurrence in the future? This chapter examines the evolution of conflict over the past decade in South Asia, with a view to providing answers to these questions.

The first part of the chapter documents recent trends in armed conflict in the countries in South Asia. My focus is on internal conflict, that is violent acts carried out by relatively organized groups of non-state actors and directed specifically against the state. South Asian countries vary considerably in the nature, extent, intensity, and evolution of conflict. While the civil wars in Sri Lanka and Nepal have ended, the conflicts in Afghanistan and Pakistan have not. Some conflicts have an explicit ethnic dimension, while others do not. Some conflicts are nationwide, while others are limited to certain parts of the country.

I empirically examine the spatial incidence of conflict and find that economically lagging areas have experienced higher levels of conflict. This is true both across South Asian countries (for example Afghanistan and Nepal are among the poorest countries) and when comparing across regions of the same country (district-level analysis for India and Nepal). Insurgent-favourable geography, such as the presence of forests, is also associated with higher levels of conflict, probably because such geography makes it difficult for government forces to counter insurgencies. These results suggest that poverty-reduction strategies might yield not just economic benefits but a political one as well.

I also examine the degree of persistence of conflict in South Asia. Cross-country studies show that prior experience of conflict is a significant predictor of future conflict: 40 per cent of post-conflict countries experience a resurgence in conflict within a decade of the end of civil war. The data also show that economic growth significantly reduces the

---

[1] See Knack (2003) or Rodrik (2002) for a broad discussion of growth-facilitating institutions. Many studies have focused on market-creating institutions, such as property rights, the rule of law, and the legal system (Acemoglu et al. 2001; Knack and Keefer 1995; La Porta et al. 1998), or on market-regulating institutions, such as financial development (Beck et al. 2000, 2008). The literature in macroeconomics and political economy has devoted considerable attention to the conduct of fiscal and monetary policy, including such institutional features as central bank independence or the impact of constitutions and electoral rules on fiscal policy (Arnone et al. 2008; Persson and Tabellini 2004). A large body of literature examines the role of 'market-substituting' institutions, such as the government provision of health and educational facilities (Banerjee et al. 2008; World Bank 2004).

probability of resurgence (Collier et al. 2008). My analysis of South Asia shows only a limited degree of persistence of conflict over time. In particular, I show that the economically leading regions of India and Pakistan had the highest levels of conflict in the 1980s and the 1990s, while it is the economically lagging regions which experienced the biggest increases in conflict after 2000. This suggests that a history of conflict can be overcome and again that economic growth has the potential to yield a significant political dividend as well.

The second part of the chapter focuses on issues of managing conflict. South Asian countries have employed a wide variety of strategies to counter internal conflict. I briefly review the use of police and armed forces, political negotiations, and economic compensation in the region. There does not appear to be a specific magic bullet in dealing with conflict, suggesting that a holistic approach using all of these strategies is likely to be the best way to bring conflicts to an end.

Conflict-affected areas face special challenges in generating a sustainable economic growth path. Private firms are often reluctant to operate in these areas due to concerns over security, inadequate or destroyed infrastructure, and low levels of human capital. The role of the public sector and of international agencies is therefore particularly important. However, implementation of public policies and programmes is hampered by the presence of large numbers of displaced people, low administrative capacity, and financial constraints. I discuss some innovative ways for countries to overcome these challenges. Failure to achieve economic growth and large-scale job creation runs the risk of reigniting conflict, to the long-term detriment of South Asia's growth prospects.

THE EVOLUTION OF INTERNAL CONFLICT IN SOUTH ASIA

Focus on Internal Conflict

In this chapter, I focus on internal conflict directed against the state. Examples of this are civil war, separatist movements, and terrorist activities with the destabilization of the state machinery as a primary objective. These kinds of conflict are carried out by a relatively organized group of non-state actors and directed specifically against the apparatus of the state, or with the intent of destabilizing the state. This is the definition of internal conflict by the PRIO-UCDP conflict database and is similar to the typical definition of 'terrorism' adopted in most incident-level data sets dealing with internal conflict.[2] I, therefore, refer to conflict and terrorism interchangeably in this chapter.

Note that this definition excludes two types of conflict. First, inter-state conflict, such as wars between two countries or the long-standing dispute between India and Pakistan over Kashmir.[3] Globally, this kind of conflict has declined over the past half century. Indeed, internal conflicts have resulted in three times as many deaths as external conflicts, or inter-state wars, since World War II (Fearon and Laitin 2003).

Second, it also excludes person-to-person violence, such as clashes between rival ethnic or social groups, localized land conflicts, religious riots, homicides, domestic violence, common violence, or other crimes. There are two reasons for this: first, these types of conflict are not directed against the state, and therefore pose somewhat less of a threat to political stability than conflicts explicitly aimed at destabilizing the state. Of course, these types of conflict can still have significant human and economic costs. Second, these have been on the decline in recent years, at least in India. The murder rate in India declined from 4.6 per 100,000 population in 1991 to 2.8 in 2007; the number of riots declined from 12.4 per 100,000 population in 1991 to 5.7 in 2007; and the number of fatalities in communal incidents declined from 134 in 2004 to 125 in 2009.[4] In contrast, as I show later in the chapter, the prevalence of internal conflict/terrorism has shown a sharp rise in many South Asian countries over the past decade. Person-to-person conflict is likely to be a weaker threat to continued progress in the region, compared to organized internal conflict directed against the state.

High Levels of Internal Conflict in South Asia

South Asia has experienced very high levels of internal conflict over the past decade. In 2009, direct casualties from armed conflict surpassed 58,000 worldwide; over one-third of these were in South Asia (IISS 2010). Most countries in South Asia are currently immersed in—or are just emerging from—conflicts of varying nature and scope, ranging from the recently ended civil wars in Sri Lanka and Nepal to escalating insurgency

---

[2] See Appendix A11.1 for definitions employed by the different datasets used in this chapter.

[3] The conflict in Kashmir is driven partly by internal rebellion against the Indian state. However, it is difficult to separate out this component from the overall conflict environment, which includes the inter-state dimension.

[4] Data from the National Crime Records Bureau of India and annual reports of the Ministry of Home Affairs, India.

in Afghanistan and Pakistan and low-level localized insurgency in India. South Asian countries, on average, have experienced armed conflict for half of the time since 2000 (Figure 11.1). This is the highest incidence of conflict among all the major regions in the world.

Even after adjusting for the large population size of South Asia, we find that the region experienced the second highest level of deaths due to armed conflict in the world (Figure 11.2). Four out of the region's eight countries—Afghanistan, Pakistan, India, and Sri Lanka—were among the top 10 most violent countries worldwide in 2008 (NCTC 2009).

Conflicts in South Asia are far from homogenous, varying considerably in terms of scope, duration, intensity, and evolution. The civil wars in

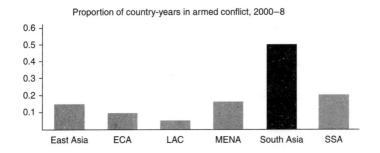

FIGURE 11.1   High Levels of Conflict in South Asia in the Past Decade

Source: UCDP/PRIO (2009).

Note: Armed conflict here refers to internal armed conflicts, with a minimum of 25 battle-related deaths per year, between the government of a state and one or more internal opposition group(s). ECA: Europe and Central Asia, LAC: Latin America and the Caribbean, MENA: Middle-East and North Africa, SSA: Sub-Saharan Africa.

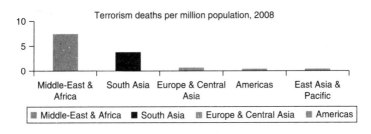

FIGURE 11.2   High Number of Conflict Deaths in South Asia

Source: Number of deaths in terrorist incidents from NCTC (National Counterterrorism Center 2009: 19); population data from *World Development Indicators* and *CIA Factbook*.

Nepal and Sri Lanka have officially ended, but several conflicts are still ongoing, including civil wars in Afghanistan and Pakistan, the long-running separatist movements in India's north-eastern region, and the escalating violent activities of left-leaning ('Maoist') groups in the eastern and central parts of India. These conflicts have inflicted a significant human cost on the region's population. More than 100,000 lives are estimated to have been lost, and more than a million people have been displaced (Table 11.1).

Conflicts in South Asia also vary in their evolution: the intensity of armed conflict has been on the rise in some South Asian countries, while in others violence has decreased. Between 2001 and 2007, the number of casualties due to conflict increased significantly in Afghanistan and Pakistan following the fall of the Taliban, and in India, where left-wing extremism showed a marked rise after the merger of the two main extremist groups in 2004 (Figure 11.3). On the other hand, in Bangladesh, Nepal, and Sri Lanka the number of casualties due to armed conflict has decreased significantly (in Sri Lanka, we expect a significant decline in casualties in 2010 after the military victory by government forces over the Liberation Tigers of Tamil Eelam [LTTE] in 2009).

Conflicts in South Asia differ substantially in other dimensions as well: some conflicts are motivated by ethnic or class disparities, while others are driven by demands for regional autonomy. These differences are important in designing strategies both for ending conflict as well as in designing appropriate policies in the aftermath of conflict. In the next section, I conduct an empirical analysis of the spatial incidence of conflict in South Asia and compare it to the global picture.

Analysing the Spatial Incidence of Conflict in South Asia

A considerable literature in economics and political science has examined the determinants of internal conflict across time and space. Several studies based on cross-country evidence show that poor countries are at greater risk of civil war (Collier and Hoeffler 2004; Fearon and Laitin 2003). Any observed relationship with poverty can be interpreted in several different ways. It might be easier for rebels to recruit people to their cause in poorer areas because their opportunity cost of conflict is relatively low. This 'opportunity cost' hypothesis means that the relationship between poverty and conflict will be different for an ethnically based or separatist conflict because recruitment will be made on the basis of ethnicity or regional affiliation rather than the lowest cost of recruitment (Collier and Hoeffler 2004). Another interpretation is that poorer regions have

TABLE 11.1   Variation in Duration and Intensity of Recent Internal
Armed Conflicts

Country	Region	Approximate Start and End Dates	Estimated Number of Fatalities (2000–9)	Outstanding Number of IDPs
Afghanistan	Nationwide	1978–	51,580	>235,000
Bangladesh	Nationwide	2005–7	93	n.k.
India	Assam	1990–	3,838	257,000
India	Manipur	1982–2008	2,712	180,000
India	Nagaland	1992–2007	710	62,000
India	Tripura	1978–2006	1,708	n.k.
India	CPI (Maoist) in several states	1980–	5,290	60,000
Nepal	Nationwide	1996–2006	13,592	60,000
Pakistan	Balochistan	2004–	1,294	80,000
Pakistan	NWFP/K-P and FATA*	2002–	20,261	900,000
Sri Lanka	Northern and Eastern provinces	1980–2009	51,815	320,000

Source: Approximate start and end dates from UCDP/PRIO Armed Conflict Dataset Version 4 (2009), available at http://www.prio.no/CSCW/Datasets/Armed-Conflict/UCDP-PRIO/Armed-Conflicts-Version-X-2009/, accessed in March 2010. Armed conflict here refers to internal armed conflicts, with a minimum of 25 battle-related deaths per year, between the government of a state and one or more internal opposition group(s). Number of fatalities and displaced from Armed Conflict Database compiled by the International Institute for Strategic Studies (based on Internal Displacement Monitoring Centre), available at http://www.iiss.org/publications/armed-conflict-database/, accessed on 29 September 2010.
Note: n.k.= not known; * North West Frontier Province (renamed Khyber Pakhtunkhwa in 2010); FATA stands for Federally Administered Tribal Areas.

poorer state capacity, and hence the government is not able to deal with the rebels effectively (Fearon and Laitin 2003). The positive association of greater poverty with greater conflict risk is demonstrated in Figure 11.4, based on a cross-country sample. We find that richer countries are much less likely to experience internal conflict. It is also interesting to note that most South Asian countries lie above the regression line, that is their

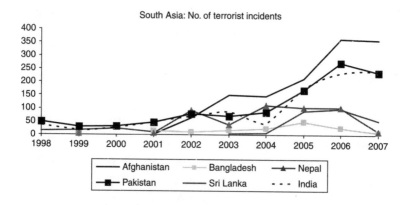

FIGURE 11.3   Trends in Conflict for South Asian Countries

Source: MIPT (see Table A11.1.1 for details).

Note: 2007 figures have been annualized.

conflict risk is considerably greater than that predicted by their average per capita gross domestic product (GDP). As we will see, this is because conflict in these countries is concentrated in the poorer regions, where GDP per capita is considerably less than the country average.

Do such correlations imply causation? After all, conflict itself might result in greater poverty. Time-series studies of conflict find that poor economic circumstances are more likely to result in conflict: Miguel et al.

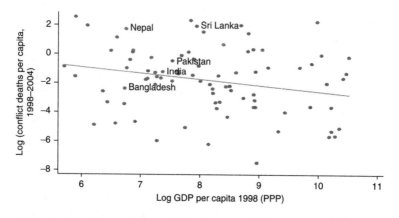

FIGURE 11.4   Conflict Intensity and GDP per Capita across Countries

Source: Conflict data from GTD2 (see Table A11.1.1 for details); GDP and population data from *World Development Indicators*.

(2004) find that civil war is more likely to begin in African countries in years following poor rainfall, Hidalgo et al. (2010) find that poor rainfall is associated with an increased incidence of land invasions in Brazil, and Dube and Vargas (2009) document a robust association between reduced coffee prices and the incidence of terrorism in Columbia. Do and Iyer (2010) find similar results in an analysis of conflict intensity across the districts of Nepal where poverty rates were measured before the conflict began.

Poverty has been cited as a driving force behind the Naxalite conflict in India. For instance, the Indian Prime Minister Manmohan Singh stated, 'A large proportion of the recruits to extremist groups come from deprived or marginalized backgrounds or from regions which somehow seem disaffected by the vibrant growth in many other parts of the country' (Singh 2007).

The cross-country literature on civil wars has documented several other factors that appear to be important. For instance, Fearon and Laitin (2003) show that geographical conditions that favour insurgency, such as the presence of forest cover, are significantly associated with the incidence of conflict. Montalvo and Reynal-Querol (2005) find that ethnic polarization is a major driver of civil wars across countries, after controlling for factors such as poverty and insurgent-favourable geography. In fact, separatist or ethnic conflicts are often driven by the perception of a specific region or group being discriminated against by the state. Such perceptions, of course, may be factually based on specific policies. This directly ties into the question of what kinds of state institutions are needed to reduce the possibility of conflict.

I now briefly examine whether the spatial incidence of conflict in South Asia is consistent with documented cross-country patterns. First, I look at its relationship with poverty or economic backwardness. Figure 11.5 shows the relationship between poverty rates and conflict intensity across regions in South Asia, where poverty is measured by the headcount ratio.[5] We see that, similar to the cross-country results, regions with higher poverty rates have experienced higher levels of conflict. There are two caveats in interpreting this figure. The first is that the poverty rates are the most recent numbers for each country, dating from around 2004–5, after the rise in conflict began. Therefore, these

[5] The headcount ratio measures the percentage of population in a given area whose consumption is below the poverty line for that region. Here the headcount ratio has been calculated with respect to national poverty lines for the different countries.

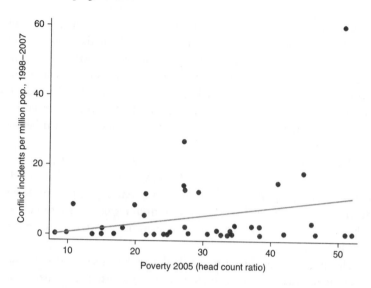

FIGURE 11.5   Conflict Intensity and Poverty Rates across Regions of
South Asia

Source: Conflict data from MIPT (see Table A11.1.1 for details). Poverty rates from
country-specific household surveys.

poverty figures may reflect the effect of conflict in that region as well and
thus cannot be used to make a causal statement. Further, the existence of
conflict complicates the collection of detailed data. In particular, poverty
figures are not available for the Northern and Eastern provinces of Sri
Lanka, which had the highest levels of conflict in the whole of South Asia.
I will go on to perform more sensitive analyses using poverty rates from
earlier periods and at a more disaggregated level for India and Nepal.

What about the other determinants of conflict identified in the cross-
country literature? We see a strong relationship between conflict intensity
and higher forest cover, suggesting that insurgent-favourable geography
is likely to play a role in explaining the spatial incidence of conflict
(Figure 11.6). This is consistent with numerous accounts of Naxalites
using forest cover to hide effectively from law enforcement forces. Data
from Sri Lanka and Nepal show a similar relationship (not shown). An
alternative hypothesis is that the presence of forests is often associated
with the presence of mineral and timber resources, and conflict is often
the result of multiple groups vying to control these resources. In such
cases, it is also possible that higher economic growth results in greater

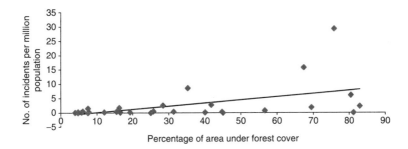

FIGURE 11.6   Forest Cover and Conflict Intensity across States of India
Source: MIPT (see Table A11.1.1 for details).

demand for such resources and thereby exacerbates conflict in these areas. In the cross-country context, a positive relationship has been documented between the onset of civil war and the prevalence of natural resource exports (Collier and Hoeffler 2004; Fearon and Laitin 2003).

In addition to economic and geographic circumstances, social divisions are often cited as a driver of conflict. For instance, the separatist movement in Sri Lanka began with demands for greater autonomy by ethnic Tamils. Similarly, the Maoist rebels in Nepal often claim to be fighting on behalf of the marginalized sections of society, such as members of the lower castes. India's north-eastern states, which are the scene of long-running separatist movements, are socially and ethnically different from a majority of the states in the country.

While these figures are suggestive, they do not give us an idea of the relative importance of the different factors discussed. I now perform a multiple regression analysis to estimate the effect of all these factors jointly. I use the following specification:

$$Conflict_j = a + X_j'b + e_j \qquad (11.1)$$

where $Conflict_j$ is either the number of conflict incidents or conflict-related deaths (normalized by population) in region j; X_j is a vector of economic, demographic, and geographic characteristics; and e_j is an error term. The key variables considered are poverty rates, measured in 2002 or earlier (to avoid reverse causality to some extent), geographic variables, and measures of social diversity. We show regressions at the region level for the whole of South Asia, as well as for more disaggregated data which compare the incidence of conflict across the districts of Nepal and India.

We find no statistically significant relationship between conflict intensity and poverty variables in the regional analysis (Table 11.2, Column 1), though we do find a strong association with social exclusion, measured as the fraction of socially disadvantaged sections of society. These sections of society are usually economically disadvantaged as well: the Scheduled Castes and Scheduled Tribes in India have higher levels of poverty, as do areas dominated by lower castes in Nepal. The relationship with insurgent-favourable geography, as measured by the extent of forest cover, is positive. Multiple regression analysis at the level of the region is hampered by the small number of observations. I overcome some of the data limitations of the regional analysis by performing an in-depth analysis for two countries where district-level data on both conflict intensity as well as the explanatory variables are available: India and Nepal.[6]

The district-level regressions show that poorer districts have significantly greater incidence of conflict in both India and Nepal (Table 11.2, Columns 2–4). The magnitude of the coefficient on poverty is quite large: an increase in poverty by 10 percentage points is associated with a 0.14 standard deviation increase in conflict intensity, or 0.26 incidents of conflict per district (see Table 11.2, Column 2). This is quite high compared with the mean level of 0.77 incidents per district. In terms of conflict fatalities, a 10 percentage point increase in poverty is associated with a 0.11 standard deviation increase in conflict-related deaths or 0.39 more deaths for an average district (compared with the mean level of 0.60 deaths per district). For Nepal, the impact of poverty is much higher: a 10 percentage point increase in district poverty is associated with 23–5 additional conflict-related deaths. The presence of mountains and forest cover is also a significant predictor of conflict intensity in Nepal (see Table 11.2, Column 4). The presence of disadvantaged minorities is not significantly associated with conflict intensity in either of these countries. This finding for the detailed district-level data suggests that the earlier high correlation at the region level was driven primarily by data from Sri Lanka, where the conflict had an explicitly ethnic character.[7]

---

[6] District-level regressions for Sri Lanka are unlikely to yield useful conclusions both because of small sample size (a total of 25 districts) and the non-availability of data on several key variables for the most conflict-affected areas. District-level data on most variables for Pakistan are not available.

[7] See Sambanis (2001) for a cross-country comparison of ethnic and non-ethnic civil wars.

TABLE 11.2   Multiple Regression Analysis for Conflict Intensity across Regions and Districts

Countries	Incidents per Million Population		Fatalities per Million Population	
	India, Nepal, Sri Lanka	India	India	Nepal
Level of analysis	Regions	Districts	Districts	Districts
	(1)	(2)	(3)	(4)
Poverty rate (%)	−0.263	1.593***	2.251***	1.028***
	(0.197)	(0.414)	(0.802)	(0.312)
Altitude		−0.059**	−0.038	0.063***
		(0.028)	(0.049)	(0.023)
% forested	0.095	0.004	0.003	1.134***
	(0.124)	(0.004)	(0.006)	(0.324)
Fraction disadvantaged minorities	0.604**	0.346	0.212	−0.196
	(0.284)	(0.371)	(0.559)	(0.372)
Observations	32	340	340	70
R-squared	0.57	0.09	0.05	0.36

Source: MIPT and INSEC (see Table A11.1.1 for details). Region-level figures on fraction of disadvantaged minorities computed by author using data from the 2001 censuses of India, Sri Lanka, and Nepal. Per cent forested area computed by author using data from Statistical Abstracts of relevant countries. Poverty numbers are computed by the World Bank staff from individual country data sources. District-level figures on fraction of disadvantaged groups computed by author using data from the 2001 Census of India, and the 2001 Census of Nepal. District-level poverty data for India come from Topalova (2005) and for Nepal from Do and Iyer (2010).

Note: Poverty rate is the poverty rate in 2002 or earlier. This is measured in 1999 for India, 2001 for Pakistan, 2000 for Bangladesh, 2002 for Sri Lanka, and 1996 for Nepal. Fraction disadvantaged minorities is computed as the fraction of Scheduled Castes and Scheduled Tribes for India, non-Sinhalese for Sri Lanka, and population not belonging to the high castes in Nepal. Robust standard errors in parentheses. *** represents significance at 1 per cent, ** represents significance at 5 per cent. Results for Indian districts are robust to using a Tobit specification in place of a linear model.

Overall, my analysis has found that the higher conflict is associated with higher levels of poverty over South Asia, and particularly for India and Nepal. However, such a relationship with poverty is not uniform. In particular, the ethnic conflict in Sri Lanka appears to be driven primarily by the extent of social diversity. The contextual nature of conflict is thus an important input into any analysis of the causes. Favourable geography also appears to play an important role by lowering the costs of insurgency.

How persistent is conflict? I compare trends in conflict over the last decade across regions of South Asia which experienced some conflict in 1998 and those which did not. For the most part, very similar trends for both types of places can be seen, that is, a prior history of conflict is not necessarily a predictor of a future outbreak in that region (Figure 11.7a). In terms of fatalities due to conflict, we see a greater degree of persistence

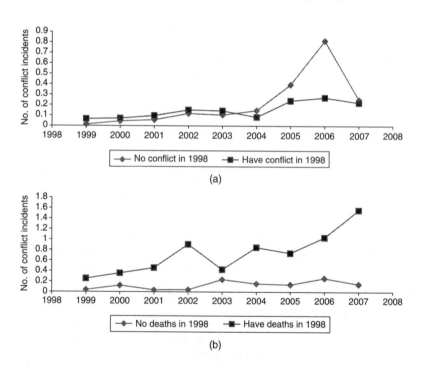

(a)

(b)

FIGURE 11.7   Persistence of Conflict in South Asia, 1998–2007
(a) Trends in Conflict Incidents (per 100,000 pop.)
(b) Trends in Conflict Fatalities (per 100,000 pop.)

Source: MIPT (see Table A11.1.1 for details).

in South Asia, that is places which had some fatalities in 1998 continue to have higher fatalities over the next few years (Figure 11.7b). This suggests that pre-existing conflicts are becoming more intense in terms of fatalities over time. These patterns remain very similar if we examine variations only across the states of India, though the data is more noisy.

Data from earlier decades also suggest that it is possible to overcome a history of conflict. Over the period 1983–97, the economically leading regions of India and Pakistan witnessed more incidents of terrorist violence than the lagging regions (see Figures 11.8a and 11.8b), in contrast to the finding of economically lagging regions having greater conflict in the period after 1998 (Table 11.2). This finding also suggests that the nature of conflicts in South Asia may have changed in the new millennium, and that economic growth or poverty alleviation has an important role to play in conflict prevention.

The analysis of conflict trends in South Asia highlights two important facts. First, there is a strong association between conflict incidence and poverty. Economically lagging regions in South Asia have experienced far greater incidence of internal conflict over the past decade, compared to economically leading regions. This is very similar to findings from the cross-country literature and suggests that economic growth is likely to

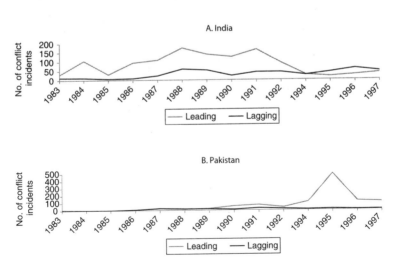

FIGURE 11.8   Conflict Trends in Leading and Lagging Regions of
South Asia, 1983–97

Source: GTD1 (see Table A11.1.1 for details).

yield benefits in terms of political stability as well, thereby making further economic growth possible. A major policy implication is that economic growth needs to be widespread; in particular, it must not be confined to already developed regions. Second, an analysis of long-term conflict trends shows that many of the current conflicts are not long-running ones. In India and Pakistan, it was the leading regions that experienced greater levels of conflict in prior decades. This strongly suggests that it is possible to reduce conflict through appropriate policy measures. The next section discusses different strategies to manage conflict.

MANAGING CONFLICT

Strategies to End Conflict

A wide variety of strategies have been employed by South Asian countries to bring an end to conflict within their borders. These are now briefly summarized.

The Security Approach: The most common approach for dealing with insurgencies, terrorism, or internal violence is using the usual police forces to establish law and order in the affected areas. The police forces in South Asian countries, however, tend to be understaffed and underequipped. South Asian countries have adopted many strategies to augment the effectiveness of police forces to deal with internal conflict: devoting more resources to existing police forces, raising local militias, and calling in the armed forces. For instance, India deployed 33 battalions of Central Paramilitary Forces to conflict-affected states and sanctioned the recruitment of an additional 32 battalions of reserve forces. Other initiatives have been specifically targeted towards the Maoist insurgency, such as establishing the Counter Terrorism and Jungle Warfare College in 2005 to provide specialized training in counter-terrorism and jungle warfare or establishing dedicated counter-terrorism forces, such as the Greyhounds in the state of Andhra Pradesh (Sahni 2007). The record of using local militias to combat insurgency has been mixed.

A key factor in dealing with terrorist groups is the gathering of intelligence to prevent or investigate violent incidents. South Asian countries are making efforts to improve both intelligence-gathering and intelligence-sharing mechanisms within their countries. For instance, India has started setting up a comprehensive database on organized crime and the criminals involved, the Organized Crime Intelligence System, which includes terrorist activities.

The Military Approach: In extreme cases, when police forces turn out to be insufficient, the armed forces are called in to deal with insurgency. Cases of military action in South Asia include Nepal, Sri Lanka, and Pakistan. The record of such military initiatives is somewhat mixed: while the Sri Lankan army won a decisive victory over the LTTE forces in 2009, the Nepal army was not able to put an end to the Maoist insurgency in that country.

A recent study of terrorist groups around the world finds that the military strategy is not the most successful. Of the 268 terrorist groups that ended between 1968 and 2006, 40 per cent were penetrated and eliminated by police and intelligent agencies; 43 per cent reached peaceful political accommodation with their governments; 10 per cent achieved victory; and only 7 per cent were eliminated by military action (Jones and Libicki 2008).

The Political Approach: A different approach to dealing with insurgencies is to conduct negotiations and sign peace agreements with the insurgents. This needs two (seemingly obvious) conditions to be effective. First, the government must do this in a coordinated way and have the intention of fulfilling at least some of the insurgents' demands. The second condition for effective talks is for the insurgent group to be seriously interested in joining the political mainstream. In South Asia, the Indian government has pursued successful negotiations with Bodo groups in Assam (granting them limited autonomy) and has on-going peace agreements with some insurgent groups in Nagaland and Tripura. In Sri Lanka, some Tamil militant organizations, like the Eelam People's Revolutionary Liberation Front (EPRLF), had been brought successfully into the political mainstream, but negotiations with the LTTE resulted only in a short-lived ceasefire from 2002 to 2005.

Regional Cooperation in Conflict Management: Many of the internal conflicts in South Asia have cross-border dimensions. The LTTE and the Taliban are examples of such entities. In such a context, regional cross-border cooperation is an essential part of any counter-insurgency strategy. Considerable potential exists for regional cooperation in reducing conflict, but this has been an underutilized strategy in combating terrorism in the region.

The Economic Approach: Complementary to the security-based solution is an economic solution, whereby the government tries to spur economic development in the conflict-affected areas with a view to undercutting support for the insurgency. This is consistent with the empirical evidence that economic backwardness is a significant predictor of conflict. The Government of India has designated all the north-eastern states 'Special Category' states for purposes of funding: all these states received more than Rs 1,000 per capita from the Planning Commission in 2003–4, compared to the nationwide average of Rs 438.[8]

An alternative strategy is to deliver the services that the insurgents blame the government for not providing. For instance, the Government of Andhra Pradesh distributed more than 300,000 acres of land to poor people in 2005 and has since followed it up with two further phases of land distribution. A related step is the enactment of new legislations that seek to recognize forest rights and vest the occupation of forest land with members of the Scheduled Tribes and other traditional forest dwellers whose rights had not previously been recorded. Given the previously observed correlation between the extent of forest cover and the intensity of conflict (see Figure 11.7), this might be a positive step towards reducing support for Naxalite movements.

Are direct economic incentives effective in reducing conflict? Cross-country analysis shows that post-conflict economic growth significantly reduces the risk of resurgence of conflict; a per capita GDP growth rate of 10 per cent per year reduces the risk of conflict from 42 per cent to 27 per cent in the post-conflict decade (Collier et al. 2008: 469). Looking across the states of India over the period 1998–2005, we do not find strong effects of economic growth in reducing conflict risk (Figure 11.9). Perhaps this is because we are measuring economic growth over a relatively short period of time (seven years) and sustained growth over longer periods of time could have a bigger impact on reducing conflict.

What about the effects of increased social spending by governments, which might be expected to have some growth effects and also increase the legitimacy of the government? The evidence on the effectiveness of social spending is mixed. District-level data from Iraq find that provision of greater services by the government results in a decline in insurgency (Berman et al. 2009a), but funds geared towards reducing unemployment do not appear to have any impact (Berman et al. 2009b). Looking across the Indian states we do not find a strong correlation between increases in social spending and decreases in conflict (Figure 11.10). Some states like Maharashtra and Kerala show the biggest increases in social spending

---

[8] Report of the Twelfth Finance Commission, Government of India, and Fiscal Profiles of States compiled by Finance Commission, Ministry of Statistics and Programme Implementation, Government of India.

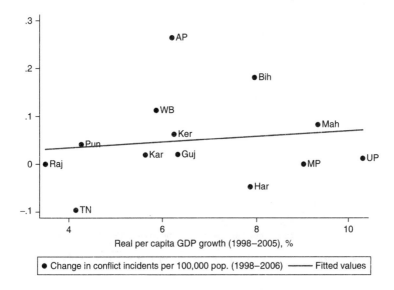

FIGURE 11.9   Economic Growth and Increases in Conflict

Per capita GDP growth 1998–2005 and change in conflict incidents per 100,000 pop. across Indian states, 1998–2005

Source: Conflict data from MIPT (see Table A11.1.1 for details); population data from Census 2001; state GDP data from Reserve Bank of India. Graph excludes the state of Orissa, which is an outlier.

and very little change in conflict intensity; others like Bihar and Andhra Pradesh show a large rise in conflict intensity despite a moderate increase in social spending; yet others like Madhya Pradesh show very little change in either of these variables, that is no rise in conflict despite very low increases in social spending. Note that these relationships are statistically insignificant. We see very similar relationships if we use specific categories of social services expenditures, such as education or health.

Policy Challenges in Conflict Zones

A very important question is the choice of economic policies in conflict-affected regions. This is important both in preventing an escalation of conflict as well as in post-conflict reconstruction. Given the strong relationship between poverty and conflict in both cross-country and within-country studies, it seems likely that achieving economic progress might also have a political pay-off by avoiding conflict. Several constraints exist in the implementation of successful growth-inducing strategies in areas affected by conflict.

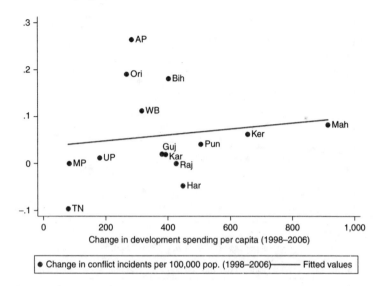

FIGURE 11.10   Social Spending and Conflict

Change in per capita expenditure on social services and change in conflict incidents per
100,000 pop. across Indian states, 1998–2006

Source: Conflict incidents data from MIPT (see Table A11.1.1 for details); state budgets for expenditure on social services; Census 2001 for population figures. Expenditure data are not adjusted for inflation.

Private-sector investments in conflict zones are likely to be low due to widespread security concerns, poor or destroyed infrastructure, and low levels of human capital. Even when a particular conflict officially ends, security concerns might still be prevalent. For instance, Nepal witnessed 514 deaths attributed to groups other than the Maoists and the government in 2007 after the peace agreement had been signed, an increase over the 327 such deaths in 2006 (INSEC 2008; in 2006, the Maoists and government together killed more than 600 people).

Conflict typically results in heavy damages to physical infrastructure, leading to shortfalls in service provision or difficulties in connecting communities to markets. For instance, 70 per cent of school buildings were destroyed or damaged during the civil war in Bosnia and 30–40 per cent of the hospitals in Liberia were destroyed during that country's civil war. In Sri Lanka, only 11.4 per cent of the population in the Northern province, and 19.6 per cent in the Eastern province had access to piped water.

Such lack of private investment is also reflected in the nature of employment in conflict-affected areas. A significantly higher proportion of the workforce is employed in agricultural activities, and therefore not likely to be very productive (Table 11.3). This is not surprising in light of the difficulties in connecting to markets and the investment risks present in undertaking higher-value activities, such as manufacturing. A greater proportion of the working-age population was employed in

TABLE 11.3   Employment Characteristics in High and Low Conflict Areas

	Low Conflict Areas	High Conflict Aareas
% of workers employed in agriculture		
Afghanistan(2008)	51.5	70.6
India (2000)	58.3	61.6
India (2005)	53.3	57.7
Nepal (1996)	77.9	87.2
Nepal (2004)	72.9	84.8
% of workers in wage and salaried jobs		
Afghanistan (2008)	27.9	14.6
India (2000)	46.4	44.8
India (2005)	43.1	40.2
Nepal (1996)	25.4	16.4
Nepal (2004)	25.3	10.9

Source: World Bank staff calculations based on household surveys from individual countries for the years indicated. Household surveys used are: Afghanistan National Risk and Vulnerability Assessment 2007–8; India National Sample Surveys 1999–2000 and 2004–5; Nepal Living Standards Surveys 1996 and 2004.

Note: For Afghanistan, high-conflict areas are provinces where total deaths per 1,000 population was greater than 0.1 in 2008. Conflict data are based on NCTC (2009). The following provinces were classified as high-conflict: Wardak, Ghazni, Paktika, Paktya, Khost, Kunarha, Takhar, Baghlan, Farah, Nimroz, Helmand, Kandahar, Zabul, Urozgan, and Panjsher. For India, high-conflict areas are defined as those states which had no conflict fatalities in 2000, but experienced some fatalities by 2005. Conflict fatality data are derived from the MIPT (see Table A11.1.1 for details). The following states are classified as high-conflict areas: Bihar, Chhattisgarh, Jharkhand, Karnataka, Maharashtra, Meghalaya, Nagaland, Orissa, Uttar Pradesh, and West Bengal. For Nepal, high-conflict areas are districts where the number of fatalities per 1,000 population between 1996 and 2006 was greater than the median. Conflict data are from INSEC.

conflict areas in Afghanistan and Nepal, but they were significantly more likely to be employed in informal jobs, that is jobs which do not pay regular wages or salaries (many of these are unpaid jobs). While some of these differences were likely to be present even before the onset of the conflict, the results from India and Nepal show that these differences actually increase after the onset of conflict. Finally, we should note that some studies indicate that labour force participation of women increases in conflict zones (Menon and Rodgers 2010). These differences in the nature of employment and the nature of the workforce need to be kept in mind when formulating appropriate policies for post-conflict regions.

The successful implementation of public policy faces considerable challenges in areas where conflict is either on-going or has ended recently. Given the constraints to private sector participation, the role of the public sector is particularly important. Governments in conflict-affected areas typically have to deal with inadequate funding, low levels of administrative capacity, a lack of legitimacy for the central government in many areas, and the fact that large numbers of people have migrated during the conflict, making it difficult to target public policy initiatives. In addition, it is desirable that economic policies be geared not just at maximizing growth but also at addressing the factors that led to the conflict. This means that policy choices may need to be structured to reduce real or perceived inequities (Stewart et al. 2007), or that the focus should be to prioritize short-term job creation first and address longer-term efficiency considerations later (USAID 2009).

Among the earliest programmes to be implemented in conflict-affected areas are disarmament, demobilization, and rehabilitation (DDR) programmes. In South Asia, DDR programmes have been implemented in Afghanistan and Nepal. In Nepal, nearly 20,000 members of the People's Liberation Army have been demobilized and confined to designated cantonment areas at a cost of nearly $50 million. In Afghanistan, 63,000 fighters have been demobilized since 2003 at a cost of $140.9 million. The high cost of DDR programmes is often a constraint to their successful completion (Carames and Sanz 2009).

Public works programmes (cash-for-work or workfare) can be a good way of providing employment in conflict zones, rebuilding destroyed infrastructure, and encouraging displaced people to return. Such programmes are targeted towards the unemployed or underemployed poor, typically using a below-market wage rate to enable self-selection by the target population. In conflict-affected areas, determining an appropriate wage can be problematic in the face of ill-functioning markets.

A minimum amount of security also has to be in place to enable workfare participants to travel to work sites. While such government-funded programmes can be useful in providing a social safety net and jump-starting the local economy, they cannot take the place of broad-based job creation or carry out major capital-intensive infrastructure projects.

In South Asia, a prominent example of such a public works programme is Sri Lanka's Northern Emergency Recovery Project, implemented in the Northern province after the end of conflict in 2009. The wage rate in this programme was set at 15 per cent below the market wage determined by a district price fixing committee, and participants were allowed to work for 10 days to rebuild their destroyed homes as part of the public works programme. Around 275,000 displaced people have returned to their villages after the end of the conflict, partly because of the employment opportunities provided by such public works programmes. These have also been useful in rebuilding infrastructure destroyed during the conflict: 145 wells have been repaired and 1,500 km of road rebuilt.[9]

The constraints posed by limited government capacity and legitimacy can be partly overcome by devolving projects to the local community for management. In Afghanistan, the National Solidarity Programme has provided block grants to community development councils, which select local infrastructure projects and contribute 10 per cent of the project cost. The councils are required to have participation by women. An initial evaluation of this programme found that it has led to greater engagement of women in community life, improved the perception of government figures, and resulted in better access to services (Beath et al. 2010). In Nepal, starting in 2002, communitites were empowered to take over the management of public schools by applying formally to the government and putting together a school management committee consisting of parents and influential local citizens. By 2010, more than 10,000 out of 25,000 public schools had been transferred to community management during a period of nationwide conflict. A World Bank evaluation found that community schools had a lower dropout rate for children of disadvantaged groups, as well as enhanced community participation and parent involvement (Chaudhury and Parajuli 2009).

The constraints posed by inadequate funding can be partly relaxed by turning to international institutions. In addition to funding, international institutions can play a key role in the initial stages of post-conflict reconstruction by providing technical support and, in some cases, greater

---

[9] Government of Sri Lanka (2010).

legitimacy for public policies. Chauvet et al. (2010) find that aid projects implemented in post-conflict situations are more likely to be successful in the immediate post-conflict period and that the probability of success improves with better supervision.

Conflict-affected countries can also attract private-sector funding in several ways. Many of these countries often have a large diaspora living outside the country, who might be willing to purchase bonds with slightly lower yields than typical international investors. Countries such as India and Israel have used innovative financing mechanisms like diaspora bonds to attract capital from abroad (Ketkar and Ratha 2009). Several conflict-affected countries have followed a strategy of removing regulatory barriers and adopting anti-corruption policies in order to attract foreign investors. For instance, Liberia established a one-stop shop to advise potential entrepreneurs, reduced the number of days needed to establish a business from 68 in 2008 to 20 in 2010, and the number of days needed to get a construction permit from 398 in 2008 to 77 in 2010.[10] Net inflows of foreign direct investment increased from \$21 million in 2005 to \$144 million in 2008.

KEY MESSAGES

This chapter has reviewed trends in internal conflict in South Asia and the policy challenges posed by the presence of such conflict. South Asia was found to have experienced a very high degree of internal conflict in the first decade of the new millennium. While some of these conflicts have ended, others are still ongoing as of November 2010. In the places where conflict has recently ended, the right policies need to be in place to prevent a future resurgence of such conflicts. Managing conflict is a key public policy issue for ensuring future stability and growth in South Asia. A holistic approach, combining military, political, economic, and regional strategies, is needed to manage conflict over the next decade.

A second major finding of the analysis is that internal conflict in South Asia is significantly higher in economically lagging regions, suggesting that economic growth and poverty reduction should be key policy priorities.

However, generating economic growth in conflict-affected areas is particularly difficult. These areas suffer from poor infrastructure, low levels of human capital, and a preponderance of low-value-added jobs.

---

[10] After debuting at number 170 in the World Bank's Doing Business rankings in 2007, Liberia moved up to 149th rank in 2010.

Private investments are deterred by security risks, infrastructure deficits, and regulatory uncertainty. Public policy in these regions is hampered by the presence of large numbers of displaced people, low administrative capacity, and financial constraints.

Countries can use innovative mechanisms to overcome these policy challenges. These strategies include leveraging the roles of international institutions and community leaders, as well as implementing regulatory changes to attract private-sector investment.

APPENDIX A11.1

TABLE A11.1.1 Details of Conflict Databases Used

Data Set	Full Name	Years Covered	Definition of Conflict Employed
PRIO-UCDP	PRIO-UCDP Armed Conflict Database	1946–2008	A contested incompatibility that concerns government and/or territory where the use of armed force between two parties, of which at least one is the government of a state, results in at least 25 battle-related deaths.
MIPT	RAND-MIPT Terrorism Incident Database (1998–present)	1998–2007	Violence calculated to create an atmosphere of fear and alarm to coerce others into actions they would not otherwise undertake, or refrain from actions they desired to take. Acts of terrorism are generally directed against civilian targets.
IISS	IISS Armed Conflict Database	1997–2009	None specified.
GTD2	Global Terrorism Database 2	1998–2004	Incidents of intentional violence perpetrated by sub-national non-state actors, satisfying two of the following three criteria: aimed at attaining a specific political, economic, religious, or social goal; evidence of an intention to coerce, intimidate, or convey some message to a larger audience than the immediate victims; the action is outside the context of legitimate warfare activities.

GTD1	Global Terrorism Database 1	1983–97 (except 1993)	The threatened or actual use of illegal force and violence by a non-state actor to attain a political, economic, religious, or social goal through fear, coercion, or intimidation.
INSEC (Nepal)	Informal Sector Service Center, Kathmandu	1996–2006	None specified.

Notes: PRIO/UCDP Armed Conflict Dataset version 4-2009; http://www.prio.no/CSCW/Datasets/Armed-Conflict/UCDP-PRIO/Armed-Conflicts-Version-X-2009/, accessed in March 2010.

MIPT data was collected by the National Memorial Institute for the Prevention of Terrorism (MIPT), in collaboration with the National Counter Terrorism Center (NCTC). Data for India is from 1998 to April 2007; data for other South Asian countries is from 1998 to 2007, but excludes July–September 2007.

IISS data obtained from http://www.iiss.org/publications/armed-conflict-database/, accessed on 29 September 2010.

GTD1: LaFree, Gary, and Laura Dugan. GLOBAL TERRORISM DATABASE 1.1, 1970–97 [Computer file]. ICPSR22541-v1. College Park, MD: University of Maryland [producer], 2006. Ann Arbor, MI: Inter-university Consortium for Political and Social Research [distributor], 2008-05-30. Based on data originally compiled by the Pinkerton Global Information Service.

GTD 2: LaFree, Gary, and Laura Dugan. GLOBAL TERRORISM DATABASE II, 1998–2004 [Computer file]. ICPSR22600-v1. College Park, MD: University of Maryland [producer], 2007. Ann Arbor, MI: Inter-university Consortium for Political and Social Research [distributor], 2008-06-18. http://www.start.umd.edu/data/gtd/, accessed in May 2008.

INSEC (Nepal): data obtained from printed annual issues of Human Rights Yearbook, published by the Informal Sector Service Center, Kathmandu, Nepal.

REFERENCES

Acemoglu, Daron, Simon Johnson, and James A. Robinson. 2001. 'The Colonial Origins of Comparative Development: An Empirical Investigation', *American Economic Review*, 91 (5): 1369–1401.

Arnone, Marco, Bernard J. Laurens, Jean-Francois Segalotto, and Martin Sommer. 2008. 'Central Bank Autonomy: Lessons from Global Trends', IMF Staff Papers, International Monetary Fund, Washington, DC.

Banerjee, Abhijit, Lakshmi Iyer, and Rohini Somanathan. 2008. 'Public Action for Public Goods: Theory and Evidence', in T. Paul Schultz and John Strauss (eds), *Handbook of Development Economics* (Volume 4). Amsterdam and Oxford: Elsevier Science and Technology Books.

Beath, A., C. Fotini, R. Enikolopov, and S. Kabuli. 2010. 'Randomized Impact Evaluation of Phase-II of Afghanistan's National Solidarity Programme (NSP): Estimates of Interim Program Impact from First Follow-up Survey'. Available at http://www.nsp-ie.org/reports/BCEK-Interim_Estimates_of_Program_Impact_2010_07_25.pdf, accessed on 20 August 2010.

Beck, Thorsten, Ross Levine, and Norman Loayza. 2000. 'Finance and the Sources of Growth', *Journal of Financial Economics,* 58 (1–2): 261–300.

Beck, Thorsten, Asli Demirguc-Kunt, Luc Laeven, and Ross Levine. 2008. 'Finance, Firm Size and Growth', *Journal of Money, Credit and Banking,* 40 (7): 1379–1405.

Berman, Eli, Jacob H. Shapiro, and Joseph H. Felter. 2009a. 'Can Hearts and Minds Be Bought? The Economics of Counterinsurgency in Iraq', NBER Working Paper 14606, National Bureau of Economic Research, Cambridge, MA.

———. 2009b. 'Do Working Men Rebel? Insurgency and Unemployment in Iraq and the Philippines', NBER Working Paper 15547, National Bureau of Economic Research, Cambridge, MA.

Carames, A. and E. Sanz. 2009. 'Analysis of Disarmament, Demobilization and Reintegration (DDR) Programmes in the World during 2008', Bellaterra: School for a Culture of Peace. Available at http://escolapau.uab.es/img/programas/desarme/ddr/ddr2009i.pdf, accessed on 7 July 2010.

Chaudhury, N. and D. Parajuli. 2009. 'Pilot Evaluation: Nepal Community School Support Project'. Available at http://siteresources.worldbank.org/SOUTHASIAEXT/Resources/223546-1192413140459/4281804-1215548823865/NepalCSSP.pdf, accessed on 26 September 2010.

Chauvet L., P. Collier, and M. Duponchel. 2010. 'What Explains Aid Project Success in Post-Conflict Situations?,' Policy Research Working Paper 5418, World Bank, Washington, DC.

Collier, Paul and Anke Hoeffler. 2004. 'Greed and Grievance in Civil War', *Oxford Economic Papers,* 56: 563–95.

Collier, Paul, Anke Hoeffler, and Mans Soderbom. 2008. 'Post-Conflict Risks', *Journal of Peace Research,* 45 (4): 461–78.

Do, Quy-Toan and Lakshmi Iyer. 2010. 'Geography, Poverty and Conflict in Nepal', *Journal of Peace Research*, 47 (6): 735–48.

Dube, Oeindrila and Juan F. Vargas. 2009. 'Commodity Price Shocks and Civil Conflict: Evidence from Colombia', Working Paper, New York University. Available at http://politics.as.nyu.edu/docs/IO/13746/Commodity_shocks_civil_conflict.pdf, accessed in January 2010.

Fearon, James and David Laitin. 2003. 'Ethnicity, Insurgency, and Civil War', *American Political Science Review*, 97: 75–90.

Government of Sri Lanka. 2010. *Operational Guidelines for ENReP Cash for Work Program*. Colombo: Government of Sri Lanka.

Hidalgo, F. Daniel, Suresh Naidu, Simeon Nichter, and Neal Richardson. 2010. 'Occupational Choices: Economic Determinants of Land Invasions', *Review of Economics and Statistics*, 92 (3): 505–23.

IISS (International Institute for Strategic Studies). 2010. *Armed Conflict Database*. Available at http://www.iiss.org/publications/armed-conflict-database/, accessed on 29 September 2010.

INSEC (Informal Sector Service Center). 2008. *Human Rights Yearbook 2008*. Kathmandu: Informal Sector Service Center.

Jones, Seth G. and Martin C. Libicki. 2008. *How Terrorist Groups End: Lessons for Countering al Qa'ida*. Santa Monica, CA: RAND Corporation.

Ketkar, Suhas and Dilip Ratha. 2009. 'New Paths to Funding', *Finance and Development*, 46 (2). Available at http://www.imf.org/external/pubs/ft/fandd/2009/06/ketkar.htm, accessed in August 2010.

Knack, Stephen. 2003. *Democracy, Governance and Growth*. Ann Arbor: University of Michigan Press.

Knack, Stephen and Philip Keefer. 1995. 'Institutions and Economic Performance: Cross-Country Tests Using Alternative Measures', *Economics and Politics*, 7: 207–27.

La Porta, Rafael, Florencio Lopez de Silanes, Andrei Shleifer, and Robert Vishny. 1998. 'Law and Finance', *Journal of Political Economy*, 106 (6): 1113–55.

Menon, Nidhiya and Yana Rodgers. 2010. 'War and Women's Work: Evidence from the Conflict in Nepal', Working Paper, Brandeis University.

Miguel, Edward, Shanker Satyanath, and Ernest Sergenti. 2004. 'Economic Shocks and Civil Conflict: An Instrumental Variables Approach', *Journal of Political Economy*, 112 (4): 725–53.

Montalvo, Jose G. and Marta Reynal-Querol. 2005. 'Ethnic Polarization, Potential Conflict and Civil Wars', *American Economic Review*, 95 (3): 796–816.

National Crime Records Bureau (various issues). *Crime in India*. New Delhi: National Crime Records Bureau.

NCTC (National Counter Terrorism Center). 2009. *2008 Report on Terrorism*. Washington, DC: NCTC.

Persson, Torsten and Guido Tabellini. 2004. 'Constitutional Rules and Fiscal Policy Outcomes', *American Economic Review*, 94 (1): 25–45.

Rodrik, Dani. 2002. 'Trade Policy Reform as Institutional Reform', in B. Hoekman, A. Mattoo, and P. English (eds), *Development, Trade, and the WTO: A Handbook.* Washington, DC: World Bank, pp. 3–10.

Sahni, Ajai. 2007. 'Andhra Pradesh: The State Advances, the Maoists Retreat', *South Asia Intelligence Review*, 6 (10). Available at http://satp.org/satporgtp/sair/Archives/6_10.htm, accessed on 7 August 2008.

Sambanis, Nicholas. 2001. 'Do Ethnic and Nonethnic Civil Wars Have the Same Causes?', *Journal of Conflict Resolution*, 45 (3): 259–82.

Singh, Manmohan. 2007. 'Speech at the Chief Minister's Conference on Internal Security', 20 December. Available at http://www.satp.org/satprogtp/countries/india/document/papers/20071220pmspeech.htm, accessed on 14 March 2008.

Stewart, Frances, Graham Brown, and Arnim Langer. 2007. 'Inequalities, Conflict and Economic Recovery', Background Paper for the Post-Conflict Economic Recovery (PCER) Project, Bureau for Conflict Prevention. New York: United Nations Development Programme.

Topalova, Petia. 2005. 'Trade Liberalization, Poverty and Inequality: Evidence from Indian Districts', NBER Working Paper 11614, National Bureau of Economic Research, Cambridge, MA.

UCDP/PRIO (Uppsala Conflict Data Program and International Peace Research Institute, Oslo). 2009. 'Armed Conflicts Dataset Version 4'. Available at www.prio.no/CSCW/Datasets/Armed-Conflict/UCDP-PRIO/, accessed in January 2010.

USAID (US Agency for International Development). 2009. 'A Guide to Economic Growth in Post-Conflict Countries'. Available at http://pdf.usaid.gov/pdf_docs/PNADO408.pdf, accessed in January 2010.

World Bank. 2004. *World Development Report 2004: Making Services Work for Poor People.* Washington, DC: World Bank.

Contributors

DAVID E. BLOOM is Clarence James Gamble Professor of Economics and Demography, Harvard School of Public Health.

DAVID CANNING is Professor of Economics and International Health, Department of Global Health and Population, Harvard University, Boston.

BARRY EICHENGREEN is George C. Pardee and Helen N. Pardee Professor of Economics and Political Science, University of California, Berkeley.

EJAZ GHANI is Economic Adviser, South Asia Poverty Reduction and Economic Management, The World Bank, Washington, DC.

WEISHI GRACE GU is a PhD student in the Department of Economics, Cornell University, Ithaca, NY.

LAKSHMI IYER is Associate Professor of Business Administration, Harvard Business School, Boston.

RAVI KANBUR is T.H. Lee Professor of World Affairs, International Professor of Applied Economics and Management, and Professor of Economics, Cornell University, Ithaca, NY.

WILLIAM R. KERR is Associate Professor of Business Administration, HBS Entrepreneurial Management Unit, Harvard Business School, Boston.

HOMI KHARAS is Senior Fellow and Deputy Director, Global Economy and Development, Brookings Institution, Washington, DC.

RAKESH MOHAN is Professor in the Practice of International Economics and Finance, School of Management and Senior Fellow, Jackson Institute of Global Affairs, Yale University.

STEPHEN O'CONNELL is Chancellor's Fellow in the Economics PhD Programme at The Graduate Center, City University of New York.

ÇAĞLAR ÖZDEN is Senior Economist, Development Research Group (DECTI), The World Bank, Washington, DC.

ARVIND PANAGARIYA is Jagdish Bhagwati Professor of Indian Political Economy and Professor of Economics, Columbia University, NY.

CHRISTOPHER ROBERT PARSONS is PhD student at the University of Nottingham.

ESWAR PRASAD is the Nandlal P. Tolani Senior Professor of Trade Policy, Cornell University, Ithaca, NY, and Senior Fellow, Brookings Institution, Washington, DC.

LARRY ROSENBERG is Research Associate, Department of Global Health and Population, Harvard School of Public Health.